Global Queer Politics

Series Editors
Jordi Díez
University of Guelph
Guelph, Canada

Sonia Corrêa
Brazilian Interdisciplinary Association for AIDS (ABIA)
Rio de Janeiro, Brazil

David Paternotte
Université Libre de Bruxelles
Brussels, Belgium

Matthew Waites
University of Glasgow
Glasgow, United Kingdom

The Global Queer Politics book series is a new outlet for research on political and social processes that contest dominant heteronormative orders in both legal and policy frames and cultural formations. It presents studies encompassing all aspects of queer politics, understood in the expansive terms of much activism as addressing the politics of sexual orientation, gender identity and expression and intersex status, as well as non-heteronormative sexualities and genders more widely – including emerging identities such as asexual, pansexual, or non-binary. As struggles over violence, human rights and inequalities have become more prominent in world politics, this series provides a forum to challenge retrenchments of inequalities, and new forms of contestation, criminalization and persecution, situated in wider geopolitics. Particularly welcome are works attentive to multiple inequalities, such as related to class and caste, race and ethnicity, nationalism, religion, disability and age, imperialism and colonialism. Global, regional, transnational, comparative and national studies are welcome, but that speak to international processes. Books in the Global Queer Politics series will initially be published in hardback and ebook formats, and are made available in paperback after two years. Ebook package subscriptions for libraries in less developed countries are in accessible scaled rates relative to the size and location of institutions, enabling free access to library patrons. Additionally these package subscriptions make it possible for library patrons to purchase personal paperback editions of each book when it is released, through the MyCopy scheme. The Global Queer Politics book series welcomes:

all academic disciplines and approaches that can contribute to the study of politics, including, but not limited to, international relations, political theory, sociology, socio-legal studies, contemporary history, social policy, development, public policy; cultural studies, media studies and gender and sexuality studies.

methodologies which may include comparative works and case studies with relevant transnational dimensions, and analyses of global processes; and research from authors who have activist, governmental and international experience, as well as work that can contribute to the global debate over LGBTIQ rights with perspectives from the Global South.

More information about this series at
http://www.palgrave.com/series/15246

Bronwyn Winter
Maxime Forest
Réjane Sénac
Editors

Global Perspectives on Same-Sex Marriage

A Neo-Institutional Approach

Editors
Bronwyn Winter
European Studies
The University of Sydney
Sydney, New South Wales, Australia

Réjane Sénac
Sciences Po - CNRS
Center for Political Research
CEVIPOF
Paris, France

Maxime Forest
Sciences Po - OFCE
Center for Political Research
CEVIPOF
Paris, France

Global Queer Politics
ISBN 978-3-319-87388-6   ISBN 978-3-319-62764-9   (eBook)
https://doi.org/10.1007/978-3-319-62764-9

© The Editor(s) (if applicable) and The Author(s) 2018, Corrected publication 2018
Softcover reprint of the hardcover 1st edition 2017
This work is subject to copyright. All rights are solely and exclusively licensed by the Publisher, whether the whole or part of the material is concerned, specifically the rights of translation, reprinting, reuse of illustrations, recitation, broadcasting, reproduction on microfilms or in any other physical way, and transmission or information storage and retrieval, electronic adaptation, computer software, or by similar or dissimilar methodology now known or hereafter developed.
The use of general descriptive names, registered names, trademarks, service marks, etc. in this publication does not imply, even in the absence of a specific statement, that such names are exempt from the relevant protective laws and regulations and therefore free for general use.
The publisher, the authors and the editors are safe to assume that the advice and information in this book are believed to be true and accurate at the date of publication. Neither the publisher nor the authors or the editors give a warranty, express or implied, with respect to the material contained herein or for any errors or omissions that may have been made. The publisher remains neutral with regard to jurisdictional claims in published maps and institutional affiliations.

Cover illustration: Photo taken by Rose Pappakalardo; models are Veronica Wensing and Krishna Sadhana

Printed on acid-free paper

This Palgrave Macmillan imprint is published by Springer Nature
The registered company is Springer International Publishing AG
The registered company address is: Gewerbestrasse 11, 6330 Cham, Switzerland

The original version of this book was revised.
An erratum to this chapter can be found at
https://doi.org/10.1007/978-3-319-62764-9_12

Foreword

Same-sex marriage has become a major twenty-first century social and political cause, central to debates over equality, citizenship and the democratic rights and the representation of minorities. This book, which brings together key international authors in the field, analyses same-sex marriage in countries ranging from Europe and North America, to Africa, Asia, Latin America and Australia. The diversity of countries covered provides new understandings of the politics of same-sex marriage, the factors that contribute to it being achieved and the factors that prevent it. Furthermore, this collection highlights the extent to which same-sex marriage has become a global issue, not only in those countries with positive outcomes but also in those countries where opponents have succeeded in mobilizing against it, sometimes on the international as well as national stage.

However, interest in this book should go far beyond those readers who study Lesbian, Gay, Bisexual, Transgender, Intersex and Queer/Questioning (LGBTIQ) issues. The contributors repeatedly demonstrate that analysing same-sex marriage provides a fascinating, alternative lens on how political systems work. Consequently, this book makes new contributions to both the literature on domestic politics in specific countries and to the existing comparative politics literature. It makes particularly significant contributions to academic writing on neo-institutionalism—an approach that analyses political institutions in their broader context, including their historical and discursive one. Readers will therefore gain a deeper understanding of the ways in which particular institutions, including parliamentary, federal and judicial institutions, work in specific countries and the similarities and differences between such institutions in countries that are being compared. Consequently, this is a collection that should be of just as much interest to students of federalism as to students of human rights law. However, contributors do not confine themselves to neo-institutional analyses but also draw on other useful tools and approaches, ranging from social movement studies to party analysis and discursive studies of international norm diffusion.

Same-sex marriage provides such a crucial lens because, as key contributors explain, sexuality tends to lie at the heart of how traditional citizenship regimes have been constructed. It is a key element underlying political and social relationships. Traditional citizenship regimes were frequently heteronormative, designed around heterosexual family relations. Consequently, as this book reminds us, analysing same-sex marriage throws new light not only on how dominant forms of citizenship rights and entitlements were constituted but also on the construction of both majority and minority identities. That construction includes the protections to which minority groups are entitled, the discrimination they may face and the barriers they can encounter in struggling for key rights. Analysing same-sex marriage therefore throws significant light on the opportunities for, and processes by which, social change is instituted in specific countries. It can assist in understanding the differing conceptions of equality and social inclusion to which particular societies adhere, and their influence on the role played by both social movements and more traditional political actors.

In addition, examining the issue of same-sex marriage, and the resistance to it, reminds us of the ongoing importance of the relationship between religion and the state, even in many countries which ostensibly pride themselves on being secular, as well as in countries where religion and/or religious courts play a major role. Similarly, the diversity of countries covered in this collection highlights the fact that Western liberal democratic divisions between public and private and between civil society and the state are merely one form of political and social organization in the world today.

While same-sex issues should never be reduced to issues of gender, as various contributors explain, they do intersect closely with constructions of gender as well as sexuality. Examining issues of same-sex marriage can therefore identify changing gender regimes. It also identifies the price that can be paid by those who do not perform their gender in the ways that society expects, both in terms of the gender of the person to whom they are attracted and their own performances of masculinity and femininity.

However, this book highlights the diversity of personal and political identities related to issues of gender and sexuality that exist in different countries and cultures and that influence the outcome of struggles. Yet, as several analyses in this book reveal, the globalization of LGBTIQ identities, and of the same-sex marriage movement, is in turn impacting back on those identities. At the same time, a global polarization over LGBTIQ issues is being used to mobilize both inclusive and exclusive forms of national identity. Same-sex marriage is at the heart of those struggles.

Same-sex marriage is not unproblematic though, as several contributors who refer to queer critiques of the normalizing nature of marriage relations make clear. Indeed, marriage is in decline in some of the countries studied. Nonetheless, given that the traditional relationship between the state and homosexuality in many countries has historically been a repressive one, this collection also illustrates fundamental changes in the relationship between homosexuality and the state. Once again, analysing same-sex marriage can provide a particularly useful lens for examining the role of path dependency, as both forms of policy continuity and discontinuity, and the factors influencing them, are identified. Moving beyond issues of decriminalization to issues of mainstream recognition and even endorsement can be seen as part of a broader, more equitable and inclusive, change in the understanding of the relationship between citizens and the state in those countries that have instituted same-sex marriage. However, the extent of countries covered in the collection will also remind readers of the diversity of experiences that same-sex attracted people have encountered, and continue to encounter, throughout the world, including in countries where homosexuality is still criminalized.

In short, this collection throws light on multiple issues that lie at the heart of contemporary politics and contemporary societies internationally. It is both an important new contribution to the literature on same-sex marriage and a major contribution to our broader understanding of politics and society.

University of Adelaide, Adelaide, SA, Australia   Carol Johnson

Series Editors Preface

Same-sex marriage has undoubtedly become a central political issue. As Jeffrey Weeks put it a few years ago, it should be regarded as a "key issue in the LGBT world, and a hot political issue more widely in Western democracies" (Weeks 2011, 168). This reveals a surprising change, given the long-standing critique of marriage as an institution in feminist circles and early lesbian and gay movements. The new embrace of marriage within LGBTQI[1] communities unveils more profound transformations, which confirm why marriage debates are so crucial.

First, the institution of marriage itself has altered in many constituencies, and—although it can hardly be seen as egalitarian—it is no longer the oppressive and highly gendered institution it used to be. Second, homosexuality is more widely accepted in certain parts of the world and, under certain conditions, gays and lesbians are regarded as respectable enough to access the institution of marriage. Finally, LGBTQI movements have dramatically transformed in recent decades, largely abandoning their subversive critique of society in favor of a collaboration with political institutions.

These transformations have created a fertile soil for a claim like same-sex marriage to emerge and to be heard. Furthermore, unlike what is assumed in Jeffrey Weeks' quote, these debates are no longer restricted to Western States. Same-sex marriage has for instance been adopted in places as different as Taiwan, Malta, Chiapas and Germany in mid-2017, and this right is available to citizens living in four continents, with Western Europe, North America and Latin America clearly leading. The global nature of this debate becomes even clearer when we take into account the various forms of opposition to LGBT rights. These often include the prevention of same-sex marriage among their main objectives.

This book is a major contribution to the understanding of same-sex marriage struggles around the globe, and an important addition to our book series. Using the various tools offered by contemporary neo-institutionalist approaches, it focuses on the reasons why same-sex marriage is allowed—or not—in specific national settings. While initiating interdisciplinary discussions, it shows political science at its best, highlighting the central role played by institutions in equality struggles. By focusing on a wide set of countries covering the whole world apart from Russia and the Middle East, this book does not only shed light on the institutional dynamics of marriage in states such as Canada, the UK or the USA, but covers a truly global spectrum of countries, with a strong focus on both Latin America (Argentina, Brazil, Chile, Mexico) and South-East Asia (China, Indonesia, Singapore, Taiwan). Furthermore, each chapter is comparative in itself, which is another strength of this collection.

Interestingly, most authors tend to regard same-sex marriage as a domestic issue, which is then compared across borders. They give more space to global and transnational dynamics in their analysis when they examine why marriage did not happen and discuss various forms or resistances and oppositions, building upon the literature on the globalization of LGBTQI rights, in particular Kelly Kollman's (a series board member) groundbreaking work on same-sex marriage and norm diffusion. In conclusion, this book undoubtedly furthers the literature on same-sex marriage, and crucially charts global trends in contemporary queer politics. It also shows that much remains to be explored, providing an opportunity for additional contributions.

Guelph, Canada	Jordi Díez
Rio de Janeiro, Brazil	Sonia Corrêa
Brussels, Belgium	David Paternotte
Glasgow, UK	Matthew Waites

Notes

1. Lesbian, Gay, Bisexual, Trans*, Queer, Intersex.

Reference

Weeks, J. 2011. *The Languages of Sexuality*. London: Routledge.

Acknowledgements

First, the editors would like to thank Manon Tremblay for bringing the editorial team together for this book. Second, we thank all the wonderful authors who have worked so diligently—sometimes under time pressure or under difficult personal circumstances—to apply their diverse knowledges and skills to make this book a truly comparative and international work. Third, we are grateful to Carol Johnson for her endorsement of the fruit of our collective labour, expressed in her most elegant and comprehensive Foreword. We also owe special thanks to contributor Jordi Díez, who first suggested that the book would fit well within Palgrave's Global Queer Politics series, of which he is an editor.

The series editorial and production team at Palgrave Macmillan have been most enthusiastic about this project and helped make the publication process a smooth journey. We are particularly grateful to series editor David Paternotte for his careful reading of our manuscript, and to John Stegner—and before him, Chris Robinson—and his team at Palgrave who have facilitated every step of the production of this book.

A special mention must be made of PRESAGE, the Gender Studies Program at Sciences Po Paris, which has provided great support for this book, not only through the time contribution of Réjane Sénac and Maxime Forest, but most particularly by covering the indexing costs. Finally, we are indebted to Ruya Legheri, who has worked efficiently and within very tight time frames to produce that essential item for any scholarly work: a comprehensive index.

CONTENTS

1 Introduction　　　　　　　　　　　　　　　　　　　　　　1
　Bronwyn Winter, Maxime Forest, and Réjane Sénac

2 Institutionalizing Same-Sex Marriage in Argentina
　and Mexico: The Role of Federalism　　　　　　　　　19
　Jordi Díez

3 A Tale of Two Congresses: Sex, Institutions,
　and Evangelicals in Brazil and Chile　　　　　　　　　39
　Tyler Valiquette and Daniel Waring

4 Historical Institutionalism and Same-Sex Marriage:
　A Comparative Analysis of the USA and Canada　　　61
　Miriam Smith

5 Understanding Same-Sex Marriage Debates in Malawi
　and South Africa　　　　　　　　　　　　　　　　　　81
　Ashley Currier and Julie Moreau

6   Same-Sex Marriage in France and Spain: Comparing
    Resistance in a Centralized Secular Republic
    and the Dynamics of Change in a "Quasi-Federal"
    Constitutional Monarchy   105
    Réjane Sénac

7   Europeanizing vs. Nationalizing the Issue of Same-Sex
    Marriage in Central Europe: A Comparative Analysis
    of Framing Processes in Croatia, Hungary,
    Slovakia, and Slovenia   127
    Maxime Forest

8   Preserving the Social Fabric: Debating Family,
    Equality and Polity in the UK, the Republic
    of Ireland and Australia   149
    Bronwyn Winter

9   The Globalization of LGBT Identity and Same-Sex
    Marriage as a Catalyst of Neo-institutional Values:
    Singapore and Indonesia in Focus   171
    Hendri Yulius, Shawna Tang, and Baden Offord

10 Pathways to Legalizing Same-Sex Marriage in China
    and Taiwan: Globalization and "Chinese Values"   197
    Elaine Jeffreys and Pan Wang

11 Conclusion   221
    Bronwyn Winter

Erratum to: Global Perspectives on Same-Sex Marriage   E1

Index   229

LIST OF TABLES

Table 7.1. Recognition of LGBTQI rights in CEEC: an overview — 132

CHAPTER 1

Introduction

Bronwyn Winter, Maxime Forest, and Réjane Sénac

Same-sex marriage is now legal in over 20 countries and its legalization is under discussion in several more. The first legalization was voted by the Netherlands in December 2000, and effective from April 1 the following year. The timing of that legalization symbolically associates the entry of lesbian, gay, bisexual, transgender, intersex, and queer/questioning (LGBTIQ) populations into mainstream norms of "family" and "citizenship" in liberal capitalist democracies with the world's entry into the third millennium.

Notwithstanding their commonalities as Western or Western-aligned liberal democracies, the countries where lesbians and gay men can now

---

The editors thank a number of this book's authors for their significant contributions to our discussion of neo-institutionalism and notably discursive institutionalism in this Introduction.

B. Winter (✉)
European Studies, The University of Sydney, Sydney, NSW, Australia

M. Forest
Effective Gender Equality in Research and the Academia,
Framework Project 7, OFCE-Sciences Po, Paris, France

R. Sénac
Centre de recherches politiques de Sciences Po, CNRS - Sciences Po, PRESAGE, Paris, France

© The Author(s) 2018
B. Winter et al. (eds.), *Global Perspectives on Same-Sex Marriage*, Global Queer Politics, https://doi.org/10.1007/978-3-319-62764-9_1

legally tie the marriage knot also present considerable variety, both culturally and politically. They include recent or longstanding democracies, republics and parliamentary monarchies, unitary and federal states, and reflect different positions with respect to religion and the cultural foundations of the nation. Countries opposed to the legalization of same-sex marriage, including those having taken measures in recent years to legally reinforce the heterosexual character of marriage, present a similar diversity. In countries where same-sex marriage has been legal for some time, the level and type of integration into wider politics, society, culture, and economy may also vary substantially. This diversity, in a globalized context where the idea of same-sex marriage has become integral to claims for LGBTIQ equality, citizenship, and indeed human rights, gives rise to the following questions: Which factors contribute to the institutionalization of same-sex marriage or, in those countries where institutionalization remains out of reach, how are legal institutions being used to reinforce the heterosexual character of marriage?

These questions lie at the core of this book. While much of the existing scholarship focuses on how and by whom claims for the recognition of same-sex couples are brought forward, occasionally including how they are articulated within parliamentary politics (Dorf and Tarrow 2014; Tremblay et al. 2011), this book asks questions such as: What do these claims and campaigns do to institutions? How are they embedded into institutionalized conceptions of justice and equality? Through which discursive frames—in the sense developed, for instance, by Mieke Verloo (2007) or Carol Bacchi (1999)—are these claims incorporated into party and policy discourses? What roles are played by policy transfers from one country to another, such as those highlighted by David Dolowitz and David Marsh (1996)? This book also pays attention to the domestic impact of broader supranational or international norms on the articulation of claims in favor of, or in opposition to, same-sex marriage. Through their exploration of these questions, the contributors to this book shed a different light on the institutionalization of same-sex marriage, understood as the set of political, policy, and legal processes by which the institution of marriage is being opened, or closed, to same-sex couples. Simultaneously, they broaden the scope of the analysis to a greater number of intervening variables, thus better accounting for both successful attempts and backlashes.

Scholarship on Same-Sex Marriage

The wave of legalizations, and campaigns for legalization, of same-sex marriage has been accompanied by development of a considerable and growing body of scholarship, including within the context of a globalized articulation of LGBTIQ (human) rights, notably through UN fora (Yogyakarta Principles 2006; Joint Statement before the UN General Assembly 2008; UN Human Rights Council Resolutions 2011, 2014; see also O'Flaherty and Fisher 2008; Lennox and Waites 2013; Baisley 2016; Hellum 2016). This literature discusses historical pathways toward the full enfranchisement of gay and lesbians, notably in the areas of civil and family rights (e.g. Pierceson 2014; Faderman 2016) and the broader issue of sexual citizenship (e.g. Ayoub 2016). More frequently, it addresses the mobilizations and resistances that these claims have triggered, and state responses (Offord 2003; Tremblay et al. 2011; Weiss and Bosia 2013; Dorf and Tarrow 2014). Recently, this focus on the *politics* of LGBTIQ rights, including the recognition of same-sex couples, has expanded to the impact of policy transfers such as those entailed by the enlargement of the European Union (EU) (Slootmaeckers et al. 2016). However, approaches that primarily address the role of social, political, and legal institutions have remained scarce, and with some exceptions (e.g. Rydstrom 2011), largely focused on the Americas (e.g. Mezey 2007, 2009; Smith 2008; Díez 2016; Mello 2016).

Where the focus is exclusively on the state and same-sex marriage, it is often in relationship to social movement lobbying, with the author or authors sometimes taking a specific advocacy standpoint. Other works, on the contrary, canvass debates on same-sex marriage, demonstrating that notwithstanding the globalization of same-sex marriage claims within an equality and human rights framework, lesbian and gay activists are themselves often divided over the question (e.g. Duggan 2002; Bernstein and Taylor 2013). In some cases, such as Spain—where a post-legalization constitutional dispute on same-sex marriage lasted until 2012—post-legalization has been primarily addressed from a juridical perspective (Matía Portilla 2013), while other works consider the sociocultural impacts of same-sex marriage debates and legalization, including how marriage is experienced by gay couples (e.g. Badgett 2009; Verdrager 2014). This last body of work is developing as the first countries to legalize same-sex marriage are now into their second decade since legalization. Badgett (2009), for example, considers the impacts of the Dutch legislation 10 years down the track, and compares it with those US states where marriage has been legal for some years.

Theoretical Framework

The analytical framework we adopt for this book derives from neo-institutionalism, a body of theory that emerged in the 1980s, first as a reaction to behavioralist approaches to politics dominant in the 1960s and 1970s (March and Olsen 1984). We draw on three forms of neo-institutionalism—historical, sociological, and particularly discursive—complemented by other theoretical perspectives drawn from scholarship on social movements, LGBTIQ rights, heterosexuality and social norms, and gender and politics.

Historical institutionalism emphasizes long-term legal and institutional patterns—such as the form of the state, the way social interests and claims are being represented, the role of legal traditions, and, more generally, how political, legal, and policy institutions have emerged over time. In this way, historical institutionalism indicates that polities (including both formal institutions and long-established ways of doing things) are largely path-dependent—that is, dependent on their historical pathways of institutionalization. Elaborating on David Stark's and Laszlo Bruszt's insights (1998) about the dependency of Central and Eastern European Countries (CEECs) on their respective paths of extrication from state socialism, historical-institutionalist approaches have shown that in the field of gender rights and anti-discrimination, the legacies of previous policies or institutional arrangements often provide the raw material and discursive options for constructing new public policy within a given context (Alonso et al. 2012). In comparison, sociological institutionalism pays attention to the ways in which both political players (including political parties and social movements) and policy agents (including senior civil servants and various experts) contribute to how institutions actually work, by acting strategically, shaping opportunity structures, or building alliances.

The most recent field of neo-institutionalist scholarship, discursive institutionalism (DI), is of specific relevance for the study of the institutionalization of the rights of sexual minorities, and thus for this book. Elaborated in the field of Europeanization and policy analysis by Vivien Schmidt (2008, 2010), DI reminds us not only of the importance of deeply embedded norms and discourses, and their impact on policies and institutions, but also of the agency of social and political actors. By taking into account "the substantive content of ideas and the interactive processes by which ideas are conveyed and exchanged through discourse" (Schmidt 2010, 3), DI (also known as the "ideational turn" in neo-institutionalism) has identified specific pathways through which ideas become power resources for political actors, especially in agenda-setting and preference-shaping. Carstensen and Schmidt (2016, 321) define ideational power as "the capacity of actors (whether individual or collective) to influence other actors' normative and cognitive beliefs through the use of ideational elements."

Schmidt (2008) further points out that the "older" neo-institutionalisms—rational choice, historical, and sociological—have largely been able to account for continuity in politics and society but not for *change*. Through their (inter)actions, institutions become at once constraining structures and, through discursive interaction, enablers of change—albeit change that is developed from within those structures. These discursive interventions include the opinion-shaping role of the media, the advocacy role of civil society actors (however organized), the choices made by economic actors, and the political will of governments. To trace how ideas motivate political action, DI scholars thus treat institutions not as "neutral structures of incentives, but as carriers that are changeable over time as actors' ideas and discourse also evolve" (Outshoorn et al. 2015, 12). Drawing on post-structuralist discourse theory, Francisco Panizza and Romina Miorelli (2013, 303) explain that "discourses involve political struggles to inscribe and partially fix the meaning of a term within a certain discursive chain to the exclusion of others." In short, DI has shown that looking more in depth at policy discourses helps to understand the connection between individual agency and broader sociopolitical structures, and to make sense of the political processes through which actors can eventually change them.

DI has been enriched by contributions from feminist and gender scholarship, which foregrounds gender as a core element of institutions and social structures, "and a part of the symbolic realm of meaning-making" (Mackay et al. 2010, 580). It shows how gender is historically and discursively constructed and can present differently in different contexts (Lombardo et al. 2009). The meaning of gender equality, like gender itself, is discursively constructed and contested in policy debates, with subsequent policy (re)framing, for example, in "organising principles that transform fragmentary or incidental information into a structured and meaningful problem, in which a solution is implicitly or explicitly included" (Verloo 2005, 20;

see also Bacchi 1999; Ferree et al. 2002; Kantola 2006; Verloo 2007). DI has found a rich area of implementation in the comparative study of gender and other anti-discrimination policies in the EU, both at the EU and the domestic levels, showing how "Europe"—not only in the sense of a body of EU regulations but also of ways of doing things and a set of legal, financial, and discursive resources—has shaped an infinite variety of discursive usages (Lombardo and Forest 2012). Finally, feminist scholarship has emphasized how the political and legal codification of the relationship between gender and (hetero)sexuality is culturally and discursively constructed. LGBTIQ scholarship has further emphasized the strategic choices made by political actors and social movement activists within specific institutional and discursive contexts (Smith 2008; Bernstein and Naples 2015; Johnson and Tremblay 2016; Díez 2016; Tremblay et al. 2011).

Discussion of paths of institutionalization, sociological dynamics, and discourses means that we can fully take into account the role of external variables, such as globalization, Europeanization (understood as the domestic impact of EU legal norms, institutions, and ways of doing things in EU member states and candidate countries), and policy transfers (Dolowitz and Marsh 1996). More recently, Latin Americanization has emerged as an example of institutional isomorphism, understood as the result of imitation or independent development under similar constraints, in the sense given by DiMaggio and Powell (1983). This book considers whether transnational constants may emerge in pushing governments to decide for or against the legalization of same-sex marriage. For example, what roles does the presence of a human rights charter play in opening marriage to same-sex couples and what are the consequences of its absence? What role do international or regional associations or unions play in debates preceding the institutionalization, or legal prohibition, of same-sex marriage? Rather than top-down processes, policy transfers, institutional isomorphism, or Europeanization appear to be mutually constitutive with domestic dynamics and advocacy coalitions that help steer external variables in their intended direction.

The Role of Legal Incrementalism

A number of contributions to this book canvass the roles of the courts and legal incrementalism, including in relation to policy transfer. Legal incrementalism has been touted by some as a productive pathway toward same-sex marriage—that is, civil partnership legislation and various other forms of legal recognition of same-sex "de facto" relationships can be the incremental "small changes" that pave the way toward legalization of same-sex marriage (Waaldrijk 2001). However, others such as Lee Badgett (2005) and Erez Aloni (2010) have argued that incrementalism as a normative theory that can explain and indeed underpin movement toward same-sex marriage recognition is not transferable from one context (Europe) to another (the United States). Even within Europe, incrementalism seems to have worked better in some contexts than others, and it is arguable that civil partnership recognition has *delayed* the legalization of same-sex marriage in a number of European countries, Germany being a case in point.

Same-sex civil partnerships have been recognized in Germany for as long as same-sex marriage has been legal in the Netherlands—that is, since 2001—but the Christian Democrat coalition government in power since 2005 consistently refused to legalize same-sex marriage until the groundbreaking Bundestag vote of June 29, 2017. Unless the vote is challenged through an action brought to the Constitutional Court (as happened at the time of the civil partnership legalization in 2001), it is probable that Germany will vie with Malta, which has also just voted on the issue at the time of writing, to become the twelfth EU country, and the fourteenth in Europe more generally, to legalize same-sex marriage by the end of 2017 if not before. This relatively tardy legalization could be seen as either the result of a long-term incrementalist strategy to gradually decrease the level of political resistance, resulting in same-sex marriage legalization becoming a mere formality, or alternatively, as being delayed by the civil union legislation, which extended a considerable number of marriage rights to same-sex couples, resulting in same-sex marriage being perceived as unnecessary.

Aloni (2010) has further argued that LGBTIQ activists in a number of contexts have preferred to campaign for civil partnerships, not only as more achievable but also as more politically palatable for the broader LGBTIQ movement, given the strong heteronormative, gendered, and often religious connotations of marriage. At the same time, in the case of Germany, public opinion—bolstered by the British and French legalizations, the Irish referendum, and the rise in popularity of social democrat and former EU parliament leader Martin Schulz (who had committed to legalizing same-sex marriage if elected) in the leadup to the 2017 German federal election—has no doubt forced the issue in Germany. Whatever one's opinion on the role of legal incrementalism in the German case, the combination of developments in other EU countries and the specific political opportunity provided by the 2017 election campaign have clearly both played an important role.

CEECs also provide examples where incrementalism did not work. None of those countries that have legalized some sort of civil partnership since the early 2000s have taken any further step toward institutionalizing gay marriage; moreover, two of them (Croatia and Hungary) recently amended their constitutions to prevent such a development.

All of this said, incrementalism clearly has worked in Western European countries in a way that it has not across the Atlantic. Civil partnership recognition of some form has invariably preceded same-sex marriage, and the timelines from one to the other are remarkably similar across European countries; with the exception of CEECs, same-sex marriage has generally been legalized roughly 10 to 15 years after civil unions.

Overview of Chapters

To address in detail the variegated institutional, legal, cultural, and political landscape covered in this book, which reflects as many paths of institutionalization as there are countries covered, this volume brings together a similarly diverse authorship. Political scientists join forces with sociologists, specialists in women's, gender, and sexuality studies, or cultural or international studies, to fully make sense of the broadest possible range of both endogenous and exogenous variables accounting for the institutionalization of gay marriage. Using diverse combinations of historical, sociological, and discursive neo-institutionalisms, which also reflects the diversity of dynamics covered by their respective case studies, the contributors also bring to this book their own research questions, fieldwork, and an often intimate knowledge of actors and processes at stake, which gives this volume its flesh. Some of this book's authors (e.g. Smith, Forest) have themselves been contributors to the discussion on neo-institutionalism and in particular DI, and further clarify their own positioning in their chapters. In addition to this (inter)disciplinary and geographical reach, the contributors to this book include both senior scholars and early career researchers, those who have covered several cases due to their generic interest in the same-sex issue, and those who entered this discussion through the lens of their fieldwork on one specific country case.

From these multiple perspectives, the book's 13 contributors explore the roles of discourse, institutions, and strategies employed by political and civil society actors in shaping the legal recognition and institutionalization of gay marriage worldwide. They do so comparatively across 21 countries on five continents: 11 where same-sex marriage is now legal—either quite recently, such as France or Ireland, or for over a decade, such as South Africa and Spain—and 10 where it is not legal, either not yet (at the time of writing), such as Australia or Taiwan, or not likely to be in the foreseeable future, such as Malawi or China. We investigate the pathways from claims through policy discourses, to institutional and legal measures—either for or against—focusing in particular on two aspects of the processes contributing to and opposing recognition of same-sex marriage. First, we examine how claims by LGBTIQ movements are being framed politically and brought to parliamentary politics. Second, we discuss the ways in which same-sex marriage becomes institutionalized or faces strong resistance through legal and societal norms and practices.

Each chapter provides a comparison between two, three, or four countries that share a number of features in (geo)political and/or cultural terms, but where the institutionalization of same-sex marriage has taken substantially different paths. These comparisons help us to make sense of the main variables placed under scrutiny, and to offer a significant geographical coverage integrating a broad sample of institutional and party systems, historical contexts with respect to the advocacy of LGBTIQ rights, or policy paradigms. Of particular concern to us here are the tensions between global or regional influences and country-specific path-dependencies, and the sorts of specific framings of the same-sex marriage issue these tensions give rise to.

Collectively, the chapters allow us to identify and discuss a number of apparent paradoxes, such as: Why have some states gone down certain pathways while other comparable states have not? Why, for example, did Québec, a Catholic Francophone enclave in Protestant Canada, join British Columbia and Ontario in leading the road to legalization in a country where gay marriage is now so integrated into society that annual wedding fairs now explicitly focus on the "pink market," while France, considered the bastion of secularism to the point of anticlericalism, took a decade longer, meeting with ferocious and massive opposition by Catholic conservatives? What factors led the very Catholic young democracy of Spain to beat Canada to become the third country to legalize same-sex marriage? Why did Argentina and Ireland, where abortion is still illegal and even divorce was not legal until relatively recently (1987 in Argentina, 1997 in Ireland), both legalize gay marriage, with massive popular support, in 2010 and 2015 respectively? Ireland is also the only country to date to institutionalize same-sex marriage through a referendum, although the case of Slovenia, where a referendum was also held on the issue with precisely the opposite result, shows that neither the promoters nor the outcomes of such initiatives are necessarily the same.

Similarly, why did the United Kingdom legalize same-sex marriage in the very name of conservative family values, while Commonwealth country Australia, which is culturally and politically close to the United Kingdom, move in precisely the opposite direction? How does South Africa confront the disjuncture between its legalization of same-sex marriage in 2006—and indeed the post-Apartheid regime's progressive stance, more generally, on LGBTIQ rights—and ongoing violence against lesbians through the infamous "corrective rapes"? What of post-socialist Eastern European countries: does the image of them being locked into opposition to same-sex marriage correspond to the reality? Or is it more fragmented and differentiated, as have been the paths of passage from state socialism, the politics of gender after socialism, and the impact of EU membership? Croatia, Slovakia, and Hungary constitutionalized heterosexual marriage, while in Slovenia, a civic initiative leading to a referendum organized by the Constitutional Court resulted in a law voted by parliament being rejected by the people, albeit with a very low voter turnout. And in Asia, what has brought Taiwan to be the country most likely to legalize same-sex marriage in the foreseeable future? How does the discursive framing of "Chinese values" come into play in Taiwan and China?

In many, even all, of these cases, the question of external variables, such as the success or failure of policy transfers or transpositions of EU law into domestic legal orders, necessitates specific attention. In Malawi, for example, the issue of same-sex marriage has become discursively linked as inevitably following from decriminalization of homosexuality, as gay marriage becomes a presumed international yardstick by which to measure state performance on LGBTIQ rights. That particular "policy transfer" has been emphatically rejected by the Malawian state. In Indonesia, the world's largest Muslim-majority country by population and often considered one of its more liberal ones—at least as concerns the (non-)imbrication of religion and politics—the external variables have been different, but with somewhat similar impacts. The global resurgence of hardline Islamism has interacted with local political and structural shifts (including decentralization) to result in the country moving away from, rather than toward, improvements for LGBTIQ populations.

Plan of the Book

Chapters 2 and 3 of this book cover Latin America, through comparisons between Argentina and Mexico (Jordi Díez) and Brazil and Chile (Tyler Valiquette and Daniel Waring). Adopting a primarily historical-institutionalist perspective, Jordi Díez provides an account of the differences between two types of federal systems, to make sense of two largely divergent processes of institutionalization in Argentina and Mexico, which otherwise share a number of features often seen as predictive of gay marriage institutionalization. Díez shows how constitutionalizing gay marriage can spark a backlash from conservative voices, ultimately reversing progress already made at the level of Mexican States, while regulating same-sex marriage *only* at the federal level initiated a more straightforward institutionalization in Argentina. Combining sociological and historical institutionalist approaches, Valiquette and Waring also address the impact of institutional design. Comparing a unitary state, Chile, with federal Brazil, they emphasize the opportunities offered by sub-national polities for judicializing same-sex marriage in the latter case, versus party politics preventing policy innovation in the former.

In Chap. 4, Miriam Smith adopts a predominantly historical-institutionalist perspective to make sense of the strong differences between the processes of legalization and recognition of same-sex marriage in Canada and the United States—countries that, due to their geopolitical proximity, share many features but nonetheless have important structural and historical differences. While in both countries, cases filed before courts by same-sex couples pursuing recognition were the main triggering factor, they encountered very different institutional landscapes, policy legacies, and dominant framings of constitutional rights. Smith discusses the respective nature of the two federal systems, the separation of powers versus parliamentarism, and the role of courts, and concludes with the role of ideational factors.

In Chap. 5, devoted to Malawi and South Africa, Ashley Currier and Julie Moreau develop a discursive institutionalist approach to account for regional variations with respect to the legalization of same-sex marriage. They explore how in Malawi, "discursive anxiety" about same-sex marriage—referring to the collective apprehension that same-sex marriage would overwhelm social, political, and religious institutions and displace heteronormative marriage practices—led to the adoption in 2015 of a law reinforcing marriage as a heterosexual institution. In South Africa also, they argue, the frame of "discursive anxiety" played a major role in shaping the same-sex marriage debate, although the political and social movement setting was far less favorable to homophobic discourses, limiting the power of the latter to influence the policy outcome.

Chapter 6, by Réjane Sénac, highlights the paradox of Spain, a constitutional monarchy where the Catholic Church still attempts to influence public debate and which embraced democracy only four decades ago, opening marriage to same-sex couples roughly a decade before France, a two-centuries-old secular Republic. Adopting a discursive institutionalist lens, the author explores two contrasting narratives: one of continuity in France, where the legal recognition of same-sex marriage in 2013 was presented as a logical consequence of the secularization movement of society and the marriage institution; and one of rupture in Spain, where granting equal marriage rights to same-sex couples reflected the rapid pace of the country's late modernization after it broke free of dictatorship upon Franco's death in 1975. Sénac also considers the impact of different institutional patterns, such as federalism in Spain versus centralism in France.

In Chap.7, Maxime Forest adopts a discursive and historical institutionalist approach to address the situation of Central and Eastern Europe with regard to the legal recognition of same-sex couples. First, he provides an account of the role of variables common to the region, such as the Sovietization process after World War II, the transition from state socialism to liberal (market) democracy, and the concurrent process of EU accession opened by the late 1990s. Second, the author highlights the respective weight of path-dependency and Europeanization. How they interplay is illustrated through four case studies, placed on a scale that goes from policy debates overshadowed by domestic nationalist and/or religious framing, to policy contexts where EU accession played a greater role. Yet, these patterns are also discussed so as to reflect variations over time. For example, Hungary, which had been a relatively liberal state with respect to LGBTIQ rights, converted to illiberal democracy where heterosexual marriage is protected by the Constitution.

Chapter 8, by Bronwyn Winter, adopts a broad focus, drawing transcontinental comparisons between Australia, Ireland, and the United Kingdom. What unites these three cases, beyond Westminster-style parliamentary democratic systems and shared (colonial) history, is the counter-intuitive paths taken in the institutionalization of gay marriage. Catholic-majority Ireland has been so far the only country in the world to legalize same-sex marriage through a referendum, with the support of some Catholic voices. In the United Kingdom, a conservative prime minister advocated gay marriage in the name of conservative values, while in Australia, which in many other areas has shown world leadership in both women's and LGBTIQ rights, a law was enacted in 2004 to explicitly heterosexualize marriage, while party politics are (at the time of writing) stalling further development. In all three cases, Winter combines discursive and sociological institutionalist approaches to discuss discursive strategies deployed by social and political actors, and their utilization of institutions. She also addresses the interplay between exogenous and endogenous variables.

Chapter 9, by Hendri Yulius, Shawna Tang, and Baden Offord, addresses the Indonesian and Singaporean cases, mainly combining discursive and historical institutionalist stances. Contrasting the largest Muslim country in the world with a neighboring global city-state and its dynamic twenty-first-century economy, this chapter highlights the dynamics created by the tension between the globalization of LGBTIQ movements and their claims on the one hand, and domestic patterns regarding the institutionalization of sex on the other. In both contexts, the globalized world of LGBTIQ identities and the growing number of countries where same-sex marriage has become legal have generated a series of counter-reactions, with unexpected outcomes. In Indonesia, the growing visibility of LGBTIQ identity has been used by (mainly Muslim) conservative groups to promote policies and laws that further exacerbate discrimination against LGBTIQ people, reasserting the nationalist imaginary and Islamic values perceived to be a response to globalization. In Singapore, LGBTIQ identities have long been silenced by a postcolonial imaginary recycling old legal provisions to condemn homosexual sexual intercourse. However, the demands of being a global city have included pressures to reconcile the state with local LGBTIQ communities, opening new windows of opportunity for publicly debating the issue.

The tenth and final chapter, by Elaine Jeffreys and Pan Wang, compares Taiwan and China, embracing historical, sociological, and discursive neo-institutionalist framing. Path-dependent features are given a great deal of attention, reflecting the opposite evolutions of both countries since 1949, and the characteristics of their respective political settings. In China, government control over civil society has so far prevented the emergence of any large-scale LGBTIQ movement, whereas the simultaneous promotion of Confucian traditions and core "Chinese" and "socialist" values such as democracy, civility, harmony, and equality, has proved ambiguous for supporting the rights of same-sex couples. In Taiwan, the emergence of demands in favor of same-sex marriage recognition developed in the context of democratization, with a measurable shift in public opinion toward more positive views on same-sex couples, strong social mobilization, and eventually a crucial role of the Constitutional Court, paving the way for same-sex marriage legalization.

References

Aloni, Erez. 2010. Incrementalism, Civil Unions and the Possibility of Predicting Legal Recognition of Same-Sex Marriage. *Duke Journal of Gender Law and Policy* 18: 105–161.

Alonso, Alba, María Bustelo, Maxime Forest, and Emanuela Lombardo. 2012. Institutionalizing Intersectionality in Southern Europe: Italy, Spain, and Portugal. In *Institutionalizing Intersectionality: The Changing Nature of European Equality Regimes*, ed. Andrea Krizsan, Hege Skjeie, and Judith Squires, 148–178. Basingstoke: Palgrave Macmillan.

Ayoub, Phillip M. 2016. *When States Come Out: Europe's Sexual Minorities and the Politics of Visibility*. Cambridge: Cambridge University Press.

Bacchi, Carole Lee. 1999. *Women, Policy and Politics: The Construction of Policy Problems*. London: SAGE.

Badgett, M.V. Lee. 2005. Predicting Partnership Rights: Applying the European Experience to the United States. *Yale Journal of Law and Feminism* 17(1), Article 4. Accessed April 20, 2017. http://digitalcommons.law.yale.edu/yjlf/vol17/iss1/4/

———. 2009. *When Gay People Get Married: What Happens When Societies Legalize Same-Sex Marriage*. New York: New York University Press.

Baisley, Elizabeth. 2016. Reaching the Tipping Point? Emerging International Human Rights Norms Pertaining to Sexual Orientation and Gender Identity. *Human Rights Quarterly* 38 (1): 134–163.

Bernstein, Mary, and Nancy A. Naples. 2015. Altared States: Legal Structuring and Relationship Recognition in the United States, Canada, and Australia. *American Sociological Review* 80 (6): 1226–1249.

Bernstein, Mary, and Verta A. Taylor. 2013. *The Marrying Kind? Debating Same-Sex Marriage within the Lesbian and Gay Movement*. Minneapolis: University of Minnesota Press.

Carstensen, Martin B., and Vivien A. Schmidt. 2016. Power Through, Over and in Ideas: Conceptualizing Ideational Power in Discursive Institutionalism. *Journal of European Public Policy* 23 (3): 318–337.

Díez, Jordi. 2016. *The Politics of Gay Marriage in Latin America: Argentina, Chile and Mexico*. Cambridge: Cambridge University Press.

DiMaggio, Paul J., and Walter W. Powell. 1983. The Iron Cage Revisited: Institutional Isomorphism and Collective Rationality in Organizational Fields. *American Sociological Review* 48 (2): 147–160.
Dolowitz, David, and David Marsh. 1996. Who Learns What From Whom? A Review of the Policy Transfer Literature. *Political studies* 14 (2): 343–357.
Dorf, Michael C., and Sidney Tarrow. 2014. Strange Bedfellows: How an Anticipatory Countermovement Brought Same-Sex Marriage into the Public Arena. *Law and Social Inquiry* 39 (2): 449–473. https://doi.org/10.1111/lsi.12069.
Duggan, Lisa. 2002. The New Homonormativity. In *Materializing Democracy: Toward a Revitalized Cultural Politics*, ed. Russ Castronovo and Dana D. Nelson, 175–194. Durham: Duke University Press.
Faderman, Lillian. 2016. *The Gay Revolution: The Story of the Struggle*. New York: Simon and Schuster.
Ferree, Myra Marx, William A. Gamson, Jürgen Gerhards, and Dieter Rucht. 2002. Four Models of the Public Sphere in Modern Democracies. *Theory and Society* 31 (3): 289–324.
Hellum, Anne, ed. 2016. *Human Rights, Sexual Orientation, and Gender Identity*. London and New York: Routledge.
Johnson, Carol, and Manon Tremblay. 2016. Comparing Same-Sex Marriage in Australia and Canada: Institutions and Political Will. *Government and Opposition* 36. https://doi.org/10.1017/gov.2016.36.
Joint Statement on Human Rights, Sexual Orientation and Gender Identity. 2008. Delivered by Argentina on Behalf of 66 States, December 18, 2008. New York: UN General Assembly. Accessed 15 September 2016. http://arc-international.net/global-advocacy/sogi-statements/2008-joint-statement/
Kantola, Johanna. 2006. *Feminists Theorize the State*. Basingstoke: Palgrave Macmillan.
Lennox, Connie, and Matthew Waites, eds. 2013. *Human Rights, Sexual Orientation and Gender Identity in the Commonwealth*. London: Institute of Commonwealth Studies, University of London.
Lombardo, Emanuela, and Maxime Forest, eds. 2012. *The Europeanization of Gender Equality Policies. A Discursive-Sociological Approach*. Basingstoke: Palgrave Macmillan.
Lombardo, Emanuela, Petra Meier, and Mieke Verloo, eds. 2009. *The Discursive Politics of Gender Equality: Stretching, Bending and Policy-Making*. London and New York: Routledge.
Mackay, Fiona, Meryl Kenny, and Louise Chappell. 2010. New Institutionalism Through a Gender Lens: Towards a Feminist Institutionalism? *International Political Science Review* 31 (5): 573–588.
March, James G., and Johan P. Olsen. 1984. The New Institutionalism: Organizational Factors in Political Life. *American Political Science Review* 78: 734–749.

Matía Portilla Francsico, J. 2013. Interpretación evolutiva de la Constitución y legitimidad del matrimonio formado por personas del mismo sexo. *Teoría y Realidad Constitucional* 31: 543.

Mello, Joseph. 2016. *The Courts, the Ballot Box, and Gay Rights: How Our Governing Institutions Shape the Same-Sex Marriage Debate.* Lawrence: University of Kansas Press.

Mezey, Susan. 2007. *Queers in Court: Gay Rights Law and Public Policy.* Lanham, MD: Rowman & Littlefield.

———. 2009. *Gay Families and the Courts: The Quest for Equal Rights.* Lanham, MD: Rowman & Littlefield.

O'Flaherty, Michael, and John Fisher. 2008. Sexual Orientation, Gender Identity and International Human Rights Law. *Human Rights Law Review* 8 (2): 207–248.

Offord, Baden. 2003. *Homosexual Rights as Human Rights: Activism in Indonesia, Singapore and Australia.* Oxford and New York: Peter Lang.

Outshoorn, Joyce, Radka Dudova, Ana Prata, and Lenita Freidenvall. 2015. Women's Movements and Bodily Integrity. In *European Women's Movements and Body Politics: The Struggle for Autonomy*, ed. Joyce Outshoorn, 1–21. New York: Springer.

Panizza, Francisco, and Romina Miorelli. 2013. Taking Discourse Seriously: Discursive Institutionalism and Post-structuralist Discourse Theory. *Political Studies* 61: 301–318.

Pierceson, Jason. 2014. *Same-Sex Marriage in the United States: The Road to the Supreme Court and Beyond.* Lanham, MD: Rowman & Littlefield.

Rydstrom, Jens. 2011. *Odd Couples: A History of Gay Marriage in Scandinavia.* Amsterdam: Amsterdam University Press.

Schmidt, Vivien A. 2008. Discursive Institutionalism: The Explanatory Power of Ideas and Discourse. *Annual Review of Political Science* 11: 303–326.

———. 2010. Taking Ideas and Discourse Seriously: Explaining Change through Discursive Institutionalism as the Fourth 'New Institutionalism'. *European Political Science Review* 2 (1): 1–25. https://doi.org/10.1017/S1755773909 99021X.

Slootmaeckers, Koen, Heleen Touquet, and Peter Vermeersch, eds. 2016. *The EU Enlargement and Gay Politics: The Impact of Eastern Enlargement on Rights, Activism and Prejudice.* Basingstoke: Palgrave Macmillan.

Smith, Miriam. 2008. *Political Institutions and Lesbian and Gay Rights in the United States and Canada.* New York: Routledge.

Stark, David, and Laszlo Bruszt. 1998. *Postsocialist Pathways: Transforming Politics and Property in East Central Europe.* Basingstoke: Palgrave Macmillan.

The Yogyakarata Principles. 2006. Accessed 13 May, 2010. www.yogyakartaprinciples.org

Tremblay, Manon, David Paternotte, and Carol Johnson, eds. 2011. *The Lesbian and Gay Movement and the State*. Farnham, Surrey & Burlington, VT: Ashgate.
UN Human Rights Council. 2011. Resolution on Human Rights, Sexual Orientation and Gender Identity,Geneva: A/HRC/RES/17/19, June 17. Accessed 15 September 2016. http://www.ohchr.org/EN/Issues/Discrimination/Pages/LGBTUNResolutions.aspx
———. 2014. Human Rights, Sexual Orientation and Gender Identity, Geneva: A/HRC/RES/27/32, September 26. Accessed 15 September 2016. http://www.ohchr.org/EN/Issues/Discrimination/Pages/LGBTUNResolutions.aspx
Verdrager, Pierre. 2014. *La France sur son 31. Ils/elles racontent leur "mariage pour tous"*. Paris: Des Ailes sur un Tracteur.
Verloo, Mieke, ed. 2005. Displacement and Empowerment: Reflections on the Concept and Practice of the Council of Europe Approach to Gender Mainstreaming and Gender Equality. *Social Politics* 12 (3): 344–365. https://doi.org/10.1093/sp/jxi019.
———. 2007. *Multiple Meanings of Gender Equality: A Critical Frame Analysis of Gender Policies in Europe*. Budapest: Central European University Press.
Waaldrijk, Kees. 2001. Small Change: How the Road to Same-Sex Marriage Got Paved in the Netherlands. In *Legal Recognition of Same-Sex Partnership: A Study of National, European and International Law*, ed. Robert Wintemute and Mads Andenæs, 437–464. Oxford: Hart Publishing.
Weiss, Meredith L., and Michael J. Bosia. 2013. *Global Homophobia: States, Movements, and the Politics of Oppression*. Urbana: University of Illinois Press.

Bronwyn Winter is Deputy Director of the European Studies Program at the University of Sydney, Australia. Her research addresses a range of global theoretical and political issues that lie at the intersections of gender, sexuality, ethnicity, religion, globalization, militarization, and the state. Publications include *Hijab and the Republic: Uncovering the French Headscarf Debate* (2008) and *Women, Insecurity and Violence in a Post-9/11 World* (2017). She is currently working on a monograph on the political economy of same-sex marriage. She holds the French title of *Chevalier dans l'Ordre des Palmes Académiques*.

Maxime Forest is research associate at Sciences Po Paris, France (OFCE). Previously, as a postdoctoral researcher at University Complutense, Madrid, he participated in the QUING project (Quality in Gender + Equality Policies), an EU-wide comparative analysis including the politics of intimate citizenship. His research interests cover the Europeanization of gender and anti-discrimination policies and neo-institutionalist approaches to the politics of gender in Central and

Southern Europe. Recent publications include *The Politics of Feminist Knowledge Transfer* (Palgrave 2016), coedited with Maria Bustelo and Lucy Ferguson, and *The Europeanization of Gender Equality Policies: A Discursive-Sociological Approach* (Palgrave, 2012), coedited with Emanuela Lombardo.

Réjane Sénac is a French National Centre for Scientific Research (CNRS) tenured researcher/lecturer at the Centre for Political Research at Sciences Po Paris, France (CEVIPOF). She is a member of the steering committee for Sciences Po's Gender Studies program, PRESAGE. Her research focuses on public justifications of equality policies (such as parity, diversity, and same-sex marriage). Publications include *L'ordre sexué: la perception des inégalités femmes-hommes* (2007); *L'égalité sous conditions: genre, parité, diversité* (2015); and *Les non-frères au pays de l'égalité* (2017).

CHAPTER 2

Institutionalizing Same-Sex Marriage in Argentina and Mexico: The Role of Federalism

Jordi Díez

INTRODUCTION

On 17 May 2016, a day that many countries mark as the International Day Against Homophobia (IDAHO), Mexico's president Enrique Peña Nieto (2012–2018) declared that his government would be submitting to Congress proposals which, among other things, would enshrine into the country's Constitution the right to same-sex marriage. The declaration, as I argued at the time (*The New York Times*, 18 May 2016, 3), was not only made with clear political objectives, but it was rather perplexing for those who had closely followed the country's politics of same-sex marriage. Indeed, the proposal amounted to what Manuel Ramírez termed a "constitutional tautology" (*Ala Izquierda*, 18 May 2016): a previous constitutional reform had already incorporated (into Article 4) the right not to be discriminated against based on sexual orientation, which meant that denying same-sex couples the right to marry was already constitutionally prohibited.

J. Díez (✉)
University of Guelph, Guelph, ON, Canada

The proposal was therefore redundant. Moreover, a year earlier, Mexico's Supreme Court had ruled that no judge in the country could deny *amparos* (legal injunctions) sought by same-sex marriage couples whose applications were denied by government officials. The ruling not only meant that same-sex marriage became constitutional, but it extended the right to marry to the entire country, provided gays and lesbians seek an *amparo* when civil servants refuse to approve their marriage applications. The ruling therefore made same-sex marriage a reality in the country, albeit with an additional administrative requirement. Peña Nieto's constitutional tautology not only contributed to the muddling of the debate over same-sex marriage in Mexico, given that it raised questions regarding its actual constitutional status, but it inadvertently sparked a significant backlash from conservative social forces, which have used the opportunity to challenge the constitutionality of same-sex marriage and reverse any progress already made on the issue, ultimately making it more difficult to institutionalize the *de jure* and *de facto* right.

Mexico's experience contrasts markedly with the politics of same-sex marriage in Argentina, the other country in the region which also began discussions on the issue in 2009. After an expectedly heated national debate that saw the Argentine Congress approve reforms to the national civil code allowing same-sex marriage, President Cristina Fernández de Kirchner (2007–2015) promulgated them into law in mid-2010, making the right to marry accessible to Argentines irrespective of gender. Argentina then became the second country in the hemisphere, after Canada, in which that right was universally extended. With only minor and isolated incidents, particularly involving the refusal of some administrators to issue marriage certificates for same-sex couples on moral and religious justifications, the implementation of these reforms in Argentina has been remarkably unproblematic.

The two countries' experiences with the politics of same-sex marriage point to one simple, yet important, puzzle: despite sharing several similarities, what accounts for the vast differences in the politics of same-sex marriage in the two countries? Specifically, why is it that, compared to Argentina, same-sex marriage in Mexico, where it is already a right, has been significantly more difficult to institutionalize? Both countries share several characteristics that, as extant research shows, tend to account for variance in policy outcomes, such as levels of industrialization and economic development, active and visible gay and lesbian mobilization, and relatively strong socially progressive political parties (Corrales 2015).

This chapter addresses these questions and argues that the answer to the policy puzzle is found in political institutions and, specifically, in the two countries' types of federalism. Argentina and Mexico are two of the four Latin American countries (the other two being Brazil and Venezuela) with institutional designs that divide power vertically along clearly demarcated federal systems of government. Yet, Mexico is the only one, similar to the United States, in which family law is enacted by sub-national jurisdictions (or federative entities) through civil codes: in this case the 31 states plus Mexico City. The fragmentation of family law through Mexican federalism has thus resulted in the judicialization of the process, making same-sex marriage more difficult to implement or institutionalize. In Argentina, on the other hand, family law is set by the country's national civil code, which means that the approval of same-sex marriage simply required a change in the definition of marriage in that legislation.

This chapter is divided into three sections. The first section briefly reviews the debates among institutionalists and focuses on federalism. The second section looks at the reform processes that led to the adoption of same-sex marriage in the two countries. The last section analyzes the relationship between federalism and the institutionalization of same-sex marriage in the two countries.

INSTITUTIONS, PUBLIC POLICY AND FEDERALISM

Institutions, generally understood as behaviour-bounding formal and informal rules, matter for understanding policy outcomes. Since scholars rediscovered institutions three decades ago through what is now generally known as neo-institutionalism, a great deal of work has relied on several institutional approaches to explain a variety of policy processes and outcomes in a variety of contexts (Koning 2015).

In the case of Latin America, however, scholars have traditionally been rather sceptical of the explanatory power of institutions in policy analyses given the region's state weakness and political instability. Within the earlier and broader discussions of democratization in Latin America, Guillermo O'Donnell argued that formal political institutions are of limited use in understanding the politics of the region given the wide socioeconomic disparities that characterize the region. He argued that they tend to concentrate power in the hands of a few, power that can override the rules of the game and benefit the privileged classes through the process of "informal institutionalization" (O'Donnell 1996). Writing specifically about the potential of institutions to explain policy outcomes, Judith Teichman has more recently argued that while institutions may possess some explanatory power, broader contextual "social forces" are more important in obtaining a full understanding of policy processes (2012). For Teichman, larger societal struggles are far more important in shaping policy outcomes than institutions.

Nevertheless, as most of the region's democracies have become more stable since the last phase of authoritarian rule, scholars have paid increased attention to the role institutions play in policy processes and outcomes. In some instances, the claimed weakness of some Latin American institutions has been challenged by more recent research. For example, in the early 1990s, O'Donnell famously coined the concept of "delegative democracy" to capture the deference with which Latin America's legislatures behaved vis-à-vis the executive branch (1994). Recent research has challenged those early assessments; in the most exhaustive study of its kind, Ernesto Calvo has shown that the Argentine Congress (which O'Donnell used as a reference for his concept) has in fact been rather active, and that presidents in post-transition Argentina have not always got their way (2014). In some other cases, such as judiciaries, constitutional reforms implemented in some countries have given rise to an unprecedented autonomy and policy assertiveness of the region's high courts in numerous policy areas, making institutional explanations indispensable in some public policy analyses (Smulovitz 2012). This does not mean that institutional approaches developed to study the Global North can be mechanically transported to the study of Latin American public policy. As Susan Franceschet and I have argued, the region's institutional weakness and the importance of informality in politics must be taken into account when relying on institutions in our explanations (Franceschet and Díez 2012, 17–18). However, much fewer mainstream political scientists working on Latin America today would deny that political institutions can be useful in explanations of public policy outcomes. In short, institutions matter in Latin American politics.

The scepticism over institutions that pervaded political science scholarship on Latin America until recently was similar in the study of sexual politics. Until the publication of Miriam Smith's groundbreaking comparison between Canada and the United States on gay rights (2008), most work on the subject, as she argued, favoured society-centred explanations of policy outcomes. Given that gay and lesbian rights is a policy area inextricably linked to social mobilization, and that it was until relatively recently dominated by sociologists, the scholarly focus on non-state actors was understandable. However, as an increasing number of political scientists have taken up the once-fringe study of gay and lesbian rights, institutions have figured among some of the sources of policy change and of broader explanations of policy processes.

The same has occurred in the study of gay and lesbian politics in Latin America. Even though there exists a debate over the extent to which some factors, such as international forces, are the drivers of policy change in gay and lesbian rights expansion (Encarnación 2016), recent research has shown that, while social mobilization is key in explaining variation in policy outcomes, institutions do play a role (Corrales 2015; Díez 2013, 2015; Schulenberg 2012). One of those institutions is the vertical separation of powers: federalism. While lagging behind work on gender policy and federalism (Piscopo and Franceschet 2013; Piscopo 2014), some political science research has looked at the role federalism plays in shaping the strategies pursued by gay and lesbian activism (Díez 2013) and the degree of openness of sub-national levels of government to pressures from such mobilization (Marsiaj 2012). Federalism thus appears to matter in explaining policy variance. It also matters in uncovering the puzzle this chapter identifies. The chapter takes the position that federalism helps explain variance in the degree of institutionalization of same-sex marriage in Argentina and Mexico. While in both countries activists pursued very similar strategies in their push for same-sex marriage, the implementation of the policy, once achieved, varied according to the type of federalism each country possesses.

Two Roads, One Destination: Sharing Policy Trajectories

The politics of gay and lesbian rights in Argentina and Mexico share striking similarities. Both countries have the region's oldest, and two of the most visible, gay and lesbian movements which, over the last three decades, have pushed for similar rights at very similar times. Their push has been conditioned by very similar political institutions, which meant that the two countries have shared very similar policy trajectories. However, after the enactment of same-sex civil unions in Buenos Aires and Mexico City, the two trajectories bifurcated as the two different types of federalisms have forced activists to seek different policy avenues. In Argentina, activists had to push for same-sex marriage at the national level given that the country's civil code, which defines marriage, is enacted by the national Congress. In Mexico, on the other hand, civil codes fall under the purview of sub-national governments, which forced gay and lesbian activists to focus their attention on Mexico City.

Gay and Lesbian Mobilization

In both countries strong mobilization forced the issue of same-sex marriage on the state after having conquered a variety of other rights. Argentina has the oldest movement in the region: it saw the foundation of the first homosexual organization in Latin America in 1967, Nuestro Mundo (Our World)—two years before the mythical beginning of the gay mobilization in the United States during the Stonewall Inn riots of New York City. In Mexico, homosexuals began to organize in the early 1970s and formed several underground organizations. In 1978, individuals "came out of the closet" and decided to take their demands onto the streets. Public activism in both countries during this time, which generally called for the liberation of social stigma and oppression then associated with homosexuality, allowed the movements to attract attention and visibility to their demands and were critical in provoking some of the first national discussions on homosexuality in Latin America.

In both cases, early gay and lesbian activism was short-lived, as the movements entered periods of weakness and essentially disappeared from the public sphere. In the case of Argentina, the military dictatorship (1976–1983) banned all social mobilization and political activity as the military junta attempted to "cleanse" society of "subversive" forces. Despite the political opportunities the acceleration of democratization in Mexico presented, the panic unleashed by the onset of the HIV/AIDS epidemic—largely fuelled by an aggressive accusatory discourse led by the Catholic Church blaming the appearance of the virus on the "unnatural" behaviour of homosexuals, as well as the 1982 economic crisis—reduced gay and lesbian mobilization mostly to cultural activities during the 1980s.

Nevertheless, both movements strengthened significantly after these periods of weakness. Despite the democratization of the two countries, transitions away from authoritarian rule did not automatically translate into the expansion of rights to gays and lesbians, thereby incentivizing them to undertake collective action. The end of military rule marked the end of a state-directed policy to exterminate homosexuals in Argentina, but police repression continued in the years following the return to democratic rule. An increasing number of individuals therefore decided to mobilize to halt police abuses, and the number of NGOs dedicated to the advancement of gay and lesbian rights grew steadily in the early 1990s (Brown 2002; Bazán 2010). In Mexico, even though the political leadership adopted a discourse framed around the need to protect human rights in the early 1990s and established a national human rights commission, police repression against homosexuals, especially males, continued during the 1990s (Díez 2011). Taking advantage of the opportunities for social mobilization presented by a democratizing political system, gays and lesbians also decided to organize themselves to demand the halt of state harassment. In both countries, these struggles contributed to the augmentation in the size of both movements (Brown 2002; Hiller 2010; Díez 2011).

Both movements continued to strengthen as they became professionalized during the 1990s due to an important increase of national and international financing available to fight HIV/AIDS. In both countries, governments were originally slow to react to the disease and failed to deliver information and medical support. But as the magnitude of the illness increasingly became apparent, and debates surrounding it were placed in national and international agendas, significant amounts of resources, both technical and financial, became available to activists during this time. In both Argentina and Mexico, state agencies were established to implement prevention and treatment programs. The movements thus became professionalized, or to pick up Sonia Álvarez's term, "NGOized" (1999). In other words, similar to what occurred in Latin America with other social movements, the Argentine and Mexican gay and lesbian movements underwent a process of institutionalization. Whereas by the late 1980s mobilization manifested itself as "street activism"—characterized by relatively fluid forms of protest and organization—by the mid-1990s financial and technical support allowed activists to acquire the necessary infrastructure to establish institutional operations and to recruit well-trained individuals to their organizations, many of whom became able to devote themselves fully to their causes.

During this period of professionalization, activism became for the most part agglutinated around two main organizations—the Argentine Homosexual Community (Comunidad Homosexual Argentina, CHA) in Argentina, and Letter S: HIV/AIDS, Sexuality and Health (Letra S: VIH/SIDA, Sexualidad y Salud, Letra S) in Mexico. Given their access to national and international financial resources, they were able to recruit professional staff to run their operations and, by 2000, became well-established organizations that had several paid staff. By the turn of the century, then, gay and lesbian activism in both countries was strong.

From Anti-Discrimination to Same-Sex Civil Unions

The strengthening of activism during the 1990s in both countries also witnessed a shift towards demanding the state to recognize same-sex partnerships. In both countries, constitutional reforms undertaken in 1994 devolved power to Bueno Aires and Mexico City, and activists sought, and obtained, the inclusion of anti-discrimination provisions in the Constitution of Buenos Aires and in Mexico City's by-laws in the late 1990s. The year 2000 in fact marked the beginning of well-organized efforts to demand the enactment of same-sex civil unions in Argentina and Mexico. Inspired by the ability of Spanish activists to secure the enactment of legislation establishing the recognition of these relationships in some of Spain's autonomous regions, they turned their attention to the pursuit of civil unions in both cities. While in Argentina marital relations are regulated by the national civil code, activists pushed for a type of civil union, modelled after the French civil union (Pacte Civil de Solidarité, Pacs) of 1999, which would not require a change of civil code because it was contractual, not marital, in nature. This meant that they could pursue civil unions at the Buenos Aires city level.

In the case of Mexico, the initiative, a draft bill, was originally conceived by three individuals: Enoé Uranga, Arturo Díaz and Claudia Hinojosa. Uranga and Díaz, both openly gay and visible members of the gay and lesbian movement, were elected to Mexico City's legislature as councillors in the 2000 elections and brought with them the objective of advancing the civil-union proposal. Once elected, they began to coordinate efforts with members of the gay and lesbian community and created the Citizens Network for the Support of the Cohabitation Law. In the case of Argentina, activists (César Cigliuti, Marcelo Suntheim, Pedro Paradiso and Alejandro Modarelli) held informal discussions in early 2000 and decided to begin the process to push for the adoption of civil unions (Díez 2013). They consequently elaborated a draft bill proposal and introduced it to the city's assembly.

Argentine activists undertook an intense campaign to meet every city councillor to convince them of their case and to present them with scientific, legal and academic arguments in favour of the bill. A central tactic of their lobbying efforts was to force every councillor to declare in public whether they were against or for the bill, thereby forcing them to engage in debates on legal, rather than moral, grounds. In order to achieve this, activists approached each lawmaker with journalists allied to their cause who would report in the media on the councillors that refused to take a position. After intense pressure, they were successful, and the first civil unions in Latin America were approved in 2002 (Díez 2013).

Unlike the Argentine experience, Mexican gay and lesbian activists were unsuccessful in obtaining support for their initiative from the city mayor and his allies in the city council because of the mayor's broader political and ideological calculations. Manuel Andrés López Obrador, who represented a more traditional and socially conservative wing of the Mexican left, and who was attempting to build a close relationship with the Catholic Church as he planned to run for the presidency in 2006, opposed the bill and gave instructions to city councillors not to support it. The bill was not reintroduced to the city council until 2006, when it finally obtained the necessary votes and support from a new mayor's office as more progressive leadership displaced López Obrador after the 2006 local elections.

To Same-Sex Marry or Not

The policy trajectories the two countries shared up until the adoption of civil unions in their two capital cities began to diverge once activists decided to pursue same-sex marriage. In Argentina, attempts at pursuing nationwide same-sex relationship recognition forced activists to focus their attention on the national Congress given that, in order to change the definition of marriage from one between a man and a woman to a non-gender specific one, the national civil code, which defines marriage, had to be reformed. The same applied to other types of unions that would change a person's marital status, such as civil unions.

In the years following the enactment of civil unions in Buenos Aires, some Argentine activists belonging to the CHA decided to pursue civil unions at the national level. For these activists, who had been in the movement since the 1980s, civil unions were a superior form of relationship to pursue, given that they did not have the religious and patriarchal connotations marriage has had. For younger activists belonging to the newly created Argentine Federation of Lesbians, Bisexuals and Transgendered People

(Federación Argentina de Lesbianas, Gays, Bisexuales y Trans, FALGBT), the objective was the pursuit of same-sex marriage. Influenced by Spanish activism, which had been successful in having the Spanish state recognize same-sex marriage by deploying the concept of "marriage equality," this group of activists believed that same-sex marriage should be the priority given that it meant full equality under the law. As such, in collaboration with allied members of the Argentine Congress, several initiatives to adopt civil unions and same-sex marriage were introduced to Congress in the years following the enactment of civil unions in Buenos Aires. However, none of these bills made it to the committee level given the lack of support they received outside a handful of members of Congress, and subsequently lost parliamentary status. As a consequence, FALGBT members decided that part of their strategy had to include the judiciary. Their failure at generating a parliamentary discussion convinced them that judicializing their strategy would help place the issue on the national agenda. As a result, FALGBT's legal team began to challenge in federal courts applications for marriage that had been denied at Civil Registries in Buenos Aires in early 2009.

Mexico's experience was very different because of its type of federalism. The Mexican Constitution confers upon the State the responsibility to protect the family, but, as mentioned earlier, the definition of marriage and its administration falls under the strict jurisdiction of the sub-national governments. In contrast to Argentina, then, Mexico's federalism offered activists not one but precisely 32 (31 states plus Mexico City) policy venues through which to pursue same-sex marriage. The push for same-sex marriage in Mexico consequently underwent a process of fragmentation. The adoption of civil unions in Mexico City in 2006 expectedly ignited a national debate on gay rights, which motivated activists and state legislators to replicate the capital city's experience. In mid-2006, state legislators in nine states publicly announced their desire to pursue similar reforms. Within the next five years, bills had been introduced in eight states (Coahuila, Guerrero, Guanajuato, Zacatecas, Yucatán, San Luis Potosí, Puebla and Jalisco), primarily by state legislators from the Party of the Democratic Revolution (Partido de la Revolución Democrática, PRD) (Díez 2015). With the exception of the northern state of Coahuila, which approved civil unions in 2007, none of these initiatives were successful.

Similar to Argentina, the approval of civil unions in Mexico City and in Coahuila prompted internal discussions among activists regarding their next objectives. Some activists continued to focus their efforts on HIV/AIDS prevention campaigns. For the most visible ones, those associated with the prominent organization Letra S, the documentation of hate crimes had to be a priority. Many of the discussions held among activists revolved around whether the next site of their struggle should be at the national level. Using the case of Mexico City as a beachhead, this group of people surmised that the push for additional rights could be taken to the national level and the 2009 mid-term federal elections represented an opportunity to do so. As such, these discussions led to the decision to advance the candidacy of Enoé Uranga, the main actor behind the push for civil unions in Mexico City in 2000 (see above), for a seat in the lower house on the PRD ticket. With the support of the numerous activists, Uranga formulated a platform that included several objectives, but could not obviously include either civil unions or same-sex marriage. Uranga was successful in her candidacy and elected deputy on 5 July 2009.

For other activists, the gains made in Mexico City and the opportunity offered by the administration of the very socially progressive Marcelo Ebrard meant that a further expansion of rights in the city was possible. Activist Lol Kin Castañeda was the main proponent of this view. Influenced by the tradition of Mexican gay activism to advance gay rights through partisan politics, she decided to pursue a seat in the city's assembly for the 2009 mid-term elections. Castañeda included same-sex marriage in her platform. While she shared some of the reservations activists had on marriage given that, she thought, it had deeply patriarchal and religious roots, she also believed that it could have a powerful symbolic effect on social ideas regarding social norms on sexuality and equality.

Castañeda's decision to begin pushing for gay marriage in Mexico City, by adopting it as a campaign promise, divided Mexico's gay movement. While in Argentina such division happened between those who supported civil unions and those who preferred gay marriage, in Mexico the division occurred because of the fragmented nature of moral politics in the country.

For other activists, such as Uranga, pursuing gay marriage in Mexico City could potentially bring about a backlash similar to what had occurred with the decriminalization of abortion two years earlier. Uranga argued that should gay marriage be approved in the capital, conservative forces elsewhere would similarly try to shield their states from the adoption of gay marriage by changing state constitutions to define marriage as one between a man and a woman, thereby making it more difficult to reform civil codes. According to Uranga, the pursuit for gay marriage at the national level had to take place through the judiciary. In what she called

Plan B, her idea was to challenge heteronormative definitions of marriage at the sub-national level through the courts and to force the issue up the judiciary to the Supreme Court. Given that on moral policy issues the Court had ruled favouring the expansion of sexual and reproductive rights (Madrazo and Vela 2011), Uranga reckoned that should the same-sex marriage issue reach the Court's docket, it would likely rule favourably on that matter as well. In an extensive interview, Uranga detailed her strategy. While in Mexico, similar to Argentina, court rulings only affect the parties involved (*inter partes*), inducing five *amparos* in three states would be sufficient to force the Court to pronounce itself in a way that would set national precedence. It would then invalidate provisions in sub-national civil codes that defined marriage as being between a man and a woman (Interview, Mexico City, 3 July 2010). The two different types of federalism in the two countries thus forced activists into two different ways to pursue same-sex marriage.

Parting Ways: The Bifurcation of the Road

The two countries' policy trajectories diverged widely after activists decided which objectives and strategies to pursue. In Argentina, the push for same-sex marriage took off in the fall of 2009 as political opportunities opened up and as activism coalesced around them. The Fernández de Kirchner administration was ambivalent to legislating on the issue when FALGBT members first proposed the idea in late 2007. While some members of her cabinet were supportive, the president remained non-committal until mid-2009. As a result, FALGBT's legal team judicialized the process through the deployment of "strategic litigation." The idea was to have numerous same-sex couples request marriage certificates and, once denied, file *amparos* to appellate courts. By late 2009, approximately 60 cases had been submitted to courts and had begun their upward percolation towards the Supreme Court (Interview, Carolina von Opiela, FALBGT lawyer, 30 November 2010, Buenos Aires). At the same time, activists agreed to join forces and to make same-sex marriage the top priority. After several meetings held in the fall of 2009 with allied members of Congress, the leaders of the two main organizations agreed to join forces and, in addition to continuing through the judiciary, began a coordinated campaign to pressure Congress to approve reforms to the civil code to allow for "equal marriage."

As detailed elsewhere (Díez 2015; Schulenberg 2012), activists relied on the very extensive networks they had built with state and non-state actors to mount a campaign for marriage equality through the latter's framing it as a human rights issue, which was ultimately successful within a remarkably short period of time. Soon after activists agreed to join forces, and the debate heated up by the end of 2009, a ruling declared the unconstitutionality of denying same-sex couples the right to marry. While the ruling was followed by a complex judicial process that involved jurisdictional disputes, it sparked a broad national debate. Although opposition mounted from socially conservative groups, mostly led by the Catholic Church leadership, activists began to win as an increasing number of public figures and members of Congress decided to support the campaign. Deploying a well-coordinated effort to lobby members of Congress, a bill to reform the civil code to allow for same-sex marriage was voted favourably at the committee level in April 2010 and on the floor of the Chamber of Deputies a month later. After a 12-hour debate, the pro-gay marriage forces won the debate with 126 votes cast in favour, 110 against and 4 abstentions. The bill moved on to the Senate right after the vote. The debate expectedly intensified, but replicating the campaign activists had pursued in the lower house, they managed to get enough support at the committee level to allow for a vote on the Senate floor. After a marathon, 14-hour long debate, the vote was held at 4:30 a.m. on July 15, with 30 votes in favor and 27 against.

In a carefully choreographed ceremony held at the Casa Rosada (presidential palace) on 21 July 2010, surrounded by the numerous gay and lesbian activists, legislators, provincial governors, judges and artists, President Fernández de Kirchner promulgated the law. She delivered a speech that made references to previous expansions of rights and on the importance of building a more equal society (Presidencia de la Nación). Argentina thereby became the first country in Latin America, the second in the Western Hemisphere and the tenth in the world to approve same-sex marriage.

The Mexican experience departed from the Argentinean one, as its institutional framework fragmented the process. Whereas in Argentina the pursuit of same-sex marriage focused on its national Congress, in Mexico the focus was on Mexico City. As activists became divided over objectives, so did their subsequent efforts. Uranga was elected to the national Congress and Castañeda lost her bid for a seat in the Mexico City

Legislative Assembly in the mid-term elections of 2009. However, through discussions and negotiation, Castañeda managed to convince a newly elected, very progressive city councillor to include in his legislative agenda the adoption of same-sex marriage and to begin the drive of convincing his fellow councillors to support the initiative. A detailed account of the process that led to a vote in the Assembly is available elsewhere (Díez 2015) and so the details ought not to detain us here. Suffice it to say that the push for the approval of same-sex marriage in Mexico City shared some characteristics with the national effort in Argentina. In both cases, and in spite of the Mexican movement's internal divisions, activists wove extensive networks of allies made up state and non-state actors to help them convince a majority of councillors to vote in favour. Also similar to Argentina, activists framed the demand for same-sex marriage as an issue of human rights, democracy and equality, even though their campaign did not refer to it as "equal marriage." In yet another similarity, the process unfolded very rapidly: the bill to reform Mexico City's civil code to change the definition of marriage was introduced to the Assembly on 23 November 2009, a favourable vote was held on 11 December, and a vote on the Assembly's floor 10 days after that. After a very intense debate that consumed the national media for weeks, with a two-vote majority, Mexico City's Legislative Assembly became the first in Latin America to approve same-sex marriage. The City's progressive mayor, Ebrard, supported the bill throughout the process and signed it into law on 29 December 2009. The new law became effective on 4 March 2010.

Unlike Argentina, however, the vote enactment of same-sex marriage in Mexico City not only failed to settle the issue, but instead forced a national debate which has fragmented the process, forcing it into judiciary. The process has not yet stopped. Less than a month after the vote, the Felipe Calderón administration (2006–2012) decided to challenge the reform before Mexico's Supreme Court on the grounds that: it violated the State's constitutionally enshrined responsibility to protect the (assumed heteronormative) family; it affected the rights of children (placing them at a disadvantage vis-à-vis those living with heterosexual parents); and it infringed the jurisdictional delineation on social security protection established by federalism (*Milenio*, 28 January 2010). The constitutional challenge was but the first among many that followed; six state governments (Morelos, Guanajuato, Sonora, Jalisco, Baja California and Tlaxcala) governed by the conservative National Action Party (Partido de Acción Nacional, PAN) challenged before the Court the reform undertaken in

Mexico City with the argument that it could potentially have an effect on the legal frameworks of the states which define marriage as one between a man and a woman. In February 2010, the Court decided to hear only two of these cases (Jalisco and Baja California).

The national debate raged on until late in the summer of 2010 as the Court heard arguments from both sides around the federal government's constitutional challenge. On 5 August it handed down a rather extensive ruling upholding the reform. In a majority ruling (nine of eleven justices) it ruled that both same-sex marriage and adoption were constitutional. Five days later, it handed down another majority ruling stating that, according to Article 121 of the Constitution, all states in the federation must recognize gay marriages contracted in the capital. In regard to the challenges argued by the states of Baja California and Jalisco, on 23 January of the following year, in a 7–4 decision, the Court rejected the states' arguments declaring that they could not constitutionally challenge reforms approved in a different jurisdiction. These rulings would have appeared to have settled the debate, but they did not.

Continued Challenges to Institutionalization in Mexico

The implementation of same-sex marriage in Argentina after its enactment in 2010 settled the issue. Following its promulgation, opponents to the law attempted to pass legislation at the provincial level to allow judges and public servants to refuse marrying same-sex couples on religious grounds, and in Santa Fe Province a judge refused to officiate at a wedding on the same grounds (*La Nación*, 3 August 2010). However, after the assertive intervention of the National Anti-Discrimination Institute, none of the provincial bills was passed, and the Santa Fe judge was forced to transfer to a different court district. Unlike Canada, in which the Stephen Harper government (2006–2015) held a vote (that it lost) in 2006 in the Canadian Parliament to repeal marriage equality, no efforts have been made in Argentina's Congress to do the same, and the issue of conscientious objection has fizzled out. Same-sex marriage has therefore become fully institutionalized.

The same is not true for Mexico, as its federal system has fragmented and judicialized the process following jurisdictional conflict. A key area of conflict has been social security. While the second 2010 Court ruling forced all states to recognize marriages performed in Mexico City, conflict arose between couples who married in Mexico City and resided in other states and the deferral government as they tried to access federal social services. In numerous cases, officials from the national public health care system denied them care. The issue thus turned to the judiciary as couples throughout the country began to seek *amparos*. Some of these cases began to work their way to the Supreme Court. The Court ruled on the first case to reach its docket in early 2014 and granted an injunction to a couple from the state of Puebla who had been denied spousal benefits. The ruling not only ordered the national health care system to recognize the marriage, but also ordered the (highly conservative) state of Puebla to do the same. Issues regarding social security also arose within the federal system for public servants. Cases were filed in many states arguing that the federal law regulating the system was discriminatory towards same-sex couples. In yet another ruling in late 2016, the Court declared that several articles of that law were unconstitutional because they were discriminatory.

The second, and clearly more profound, conflict has regarded the constitutionality of same-sex marriage, an issue that, despite their clarity, the 2010 rulings do not appear to have solved. Following these rulings, *amparos* were filed in every state challenging traditional definitions of marriage in sub-national civil codes. The *inter partes* character of Mexico's civil law system notwithstanding, the Mexican Supreme Court can set a precedent in a jurisdiction once it grants five *amparos* from that jurisdiction. This, of course, has incentivized litigation throughout the country. The issue came to a head in 2012, when the Supreme Court granted an *amparo* to a couple from the southern state of Oaxaca, which argued that the traditional definition of marriage in the state's civil code was unconstitutional and further arguing that *amparos* should be granted to same-sex couples regardless of whether a state has reformed its civil code. Conflict over the constitutionality of same-sex marriage has further arisen through a backlash from conservative states. Despite the clear 2010 Supreme Court rulings on same-sex marriage in Mexico City, several states governed by the conservative National Action Party (Partido Acción Nacional, PAN) shielded their jurisdictions from changes in the civil code by explicitly defining marriage between a man and a woman in state constitutions. Addressing this issue in its clearest ruling so far, the Supreme Court ruled in June 2015 that those provisions were unconstitutional, ordered every judge in the country to grant *amparos*, and established guidelines on how to do so.

Despite the consistency with which Mexico's Supreme Court has ruled on the constitutionality of same-sex marriage, and in an attempt to restore a deeply damaged image of his administration's record on human rights,

Peña Nieto decided to reignite the debate by proposing his "constitutional tautology": to reform the Constitution to allow for same-sex marriage. The proposal fuelled the crystallization of a nationwide movement against same-sex marriage that has reawakened a fierce debate, a debate that has re-entered electoral politics. Within weeks of his announcement, a national organization, the National Family Front, was formed. This umbrella organization is made up of social conservative state and non-state actors, which include the National Parents Union, several deputies from the lower house, wealthy donors, far-right political group El Yunque (The Anvil), and Mexico City's cardinal (*Proceso*, 9 September 2016). Ten days after the president's announcement, these conservatives declared publicly that his proposal amounted to a "lethal coup" to the family (*El Universal*, 25 May 2016) and that they would mobilize to stop the measure. Arguing against the imposition of "gender" and "LGBT ideology," they followed up on their statements: the organization grew to 140,000 members within two weeks, and, with the direct encouragement of Pope Francis (*Proceso*, 12 September 2016), organized strong protests in 19 states across the country (*La Jornada*, 19 September 2016). These have been some of the largest protests the country has seen in recent years.

This conservative backlash has not stayed on the street, however, and the Family Front's activities have assumed clear political aims. The first one was to stop the president's constitutional reform proposal at the committee level. After obtaining support from the PAN's leadership as well as other conservative state and non-state actors, they organized a campaign to stop discussion of the bill through the submission of 500, 000 petitions to stop it (*El Universal*, 11 September 2016). The Chamber of Deputies Constitutional Committee voted against the initiative soon after, stopping the bill. The organization also began a campaign to reform Article 4 of the Constitution in order to "protect" children by banning same-sex couples from adopting them (*Proceso*, 8 September 2016). A bill to such effect was introduced to the lower house in September 2016. Finally, while the fate of such bills is not very promising, they have more recently entered electoral politics, with the objective of having an effect on the 2018 presidential and general elections. In the lead-up to the 4 June 2017 state elections in Mexico State (the largest sub-national jurisdiction after Mexico City, in which 11 million people are eligible to vote, and the last election before the 2018 presidential one), the PAN candidate, Josefina Vásquez Mota, signed a public agreement with the Family Front in which she pledged to fight for the various elements in the Front's manifesto (*El Universal*, 14

May 2017). All this while the constitutionality of same-sex marriage has time and again been established by the country's highest court, which has the last word on the matter.

Conclusion

Rarely are political scientists offered the opportunity to carry out comparative work on cases in which variables can be controlled in order to isolate the dependent variable. Frequently, comparative work includes a series of qualifiers on possible independent or intervening variables. The politics of sexual rights in Argentina and Mexico offer us one of those rare opportunities. Both countries share numerous striking similarities as shown in their LGTB policy trajectories. Yet, those similarities appear to have stopped in 2010 once same-sex marriage was approved in both countries. As this chapter has detailed, the two countries' sexual policy trajectories bifurcated when the Argentine Congress and the Mexico City Legislative Assembly enacted same-sex marriage. In Argentina, the new right became institutionalized without a problem. In a region known for the disparities that exist between legal formalism and compliance with the law, this is no small feat. The case of Mexico, as we have seen, has been markedly different. Despite the fact that the Supreme Court has consistently ruled on that right, the political discussion gives the impression that the matter is not yet settled and same-sex marriage clearly has not yet been institutionalized. The answer to explain the bifurcation of the policy trajectories rests in institutions. Mexico's rare type of federalism makes the administration of family law the responsibility of sub-national levels of government, which has fragmented and judicialized the process. Argentina's institutional design is the opposite, which has resulted in opposite outcomes. In these two cases, then, institutions have definitely mattered.

References

Álvarez, Sonia. 1999. Advocating Feminism: The Latin American Feminist Boom. *International Feminist Journal of Politics* 1 (2): 181–209.
Bazán, Osvaldo. 2010. *Historia de la homosexualidad en la Argentina*. Buenos Aires: Editorial Marea.
Brown, Stephen. 2002. 'Con discriminación y represión no hay democracia': The Lesbian and Gay Movement in Argentina. *Latin American Perspectives* 29 (2): 119–138.

Calvo, Ernesto. 2014. *Legislator Success in Fragmented Congresses in Argentina: Plurality Cartels, Minority Presidents, and Lawmaking.* Cambridge: Cambridge University Press.

Corrales, Javier. 2015. The Politics of LGBT Rights in Latin America and the Caribbean: Research Agendas. *European Review of Latin American and Caribbean Studies* 100: 53–62.

Díez, Jordi. 2011. Argentina: A Queer Tango between the LG Movement and the State. In *The Lesbian and Gay Movement and the State: Comparative Insights into a Transformed Relationship*, ed. Carol Johnson, David Paternotte, and Manon Trembaly, 13–25. Surrey: Ashgate.

———. 2013. Explaining Policy Outcomes: The Adoption of Same-Sex Unions in Buenos Aires and Mexico City. *Comparative Political Studies* 46 (2): 212–235.

———. 2015. *The Politics of Gay Marriage in Latin America.* New York: Cambridge University Press.

El Universal. Various Issues. Mexico City: Mexico.

Encarnación, Omar. 2016. *Out on the Periphery: Latin America's Gay Rights Revolution.* New York: Oxford University Press.

Franceschet, Susan, and Jordi Díez. 2012. Thinking about Politics and Policymaking in Contemporary Latin America. In *Comparative Public Policy in Latin America*, ed. Jordi Díez and Susan Franceschet, 3–33. Toronto: University of Toronto Press.

Hiller, Renata. 2010. Reflexiones en torno a la Ley de Matrimonio Igualitario. In *Matrimonio Igualitario: Perspectivas sociales, políticas y jurídicas*, ed. Renata Hiller, Rafael de la Dehesa, Ernesto Meccia, and Mario Pecheny, 85–130. Buenos Aires: Eudeba.

Koning, Edward. 2015. The Three Institutionalisms and Institutional Dynamics: Understanding Endogenous and Exogenous Change. *Journal of Public Policy*, first published online July 20.

La Jornada. September 19, 2016. Mexico City: Mexico.

La Nación. August 3, 2010. Mexico City: Mexico.

Madrazo, Alejandro, and Estefanía Vela. 2011. The Mexican Supreme Court's (Sexual) Revolution? *Texas Law Review* 89(7). México, DF: CIDE.

Marsiaj, Juan P. 2012. Federalism, Advocacy Networks, and Sexual Diversity Politics in Brazil. In *Comparative Public Policy in Latin America*, ed. Jordi Díez and Susan Franceschet, 126–149. Toronto: University of Toronto Press.

Milenio. January 28, 2010. Mexico City: Mexico.

O'Donnell, Guillermo. 1994. Delegative Democracy. Kellog Institute of International Studies, Notre Dame University, South Bend, IN.

———. 1996. Illusions about Consolidation. *Journal of Democracy* 7: 34–51.

Piscopo, Jennifer M. 2014. Female Leadership and Sexual Health Policy in Argentina. *Comparative Political Studies* 47 (1): 86–111.

Piscopo, Jennifer M., and Susan Franceschet. 2013. Federalism, Decentralization, and Reproductive Rights in Argentina and Chile. *Publius: The Journal of Federalism* 43 (1): 129–150.

Proceso. Various Issues. Mexico City: Mexico.

Schulenberg, Shawn. 2012. The Construction and Enactment of Same-Sex Marriage in Argentina. *Journal of Human Rights* 11 (1): 106–125.

Smith, Miriam. 2008. *Political Institutions and Lesbian and Gay Rights in the United States and Canada*. New York: Routledge.

Smulovitz, Catalina. 2012. Public Policy by Other Means: Playing the Judicial Arena. In *Comparative Public Policy in Latin America*, ed. Jordi Díez and Susan Franceschet, 105–125. Toronto: University of Toronto Press.

Teichman, Judith. 2012. The New Institutionalism and Industrial Policy-Making in Chile. In *Comparative Public Policy in Latin America*, ed. Jordi Díez and Susan Franceschet, 54–77. Toronto: University of Toronto Press.

Jordi Díez is Professor of Political Science at the University of Guelph, Canada. Díez has taught at numerous universities in the Americas and Europe and has written extensively on a variety of topics, including environmental politics and policy, civil-military relations, sexual and reproductive rights and public opinion formation. His most recent book *The Politics of Gay Marriage in Latin America* (Cambridge UP 2016) is due for publication in 2018 in Spanish by the Fondo de Cultura Económica. He held the 2014–2015 Peggy Rockefeller Visiting Scholarship at Harvard University.

CHAPTER 3

A Tale of Two Congresses: Sex, Institutions, and Evangelicals in Brazil and Chile

Tyler Valiquette and Daniel Waring

INTRODUCTION

In May 2011, the Brazilian Supreme Court voted unanimously to legalize same-sex civil unions. Following that decision, 10 states went even further and legalized same-sex marriage. Building on the patchwork of marriage laws emerging throughout Brazil, another unanimous decision by the Federal Supreme Court in May 2013 forced the state to place homosexual and heterosexual relationships on the same legal footing. In Chile, while same-sex civil unions have been legal since October 2015, the judiciary has ruled against same-sex marriage twice, in September 2010 and then again in June 2016. Following its second ruling, the Santiago Court of Appeals stated that the definition of marriage is a matter that should be taken up by Congress, not the courts.

Literature on LGBT rights and same-sex marriage has traditionally stressed the roles of strong social movements in enacting or influencing such policy (Encarnación 2016; Díez 2015; Corrales 2015). However, while social movement organizations are important in the adoption of controversial policy, they are not the sole actors involved in the policymaking process. In order for social movement organizations to be successful, they need political allies in parliaments and the executive branch. The role

T. Valiquette (✉) • D. Waring
University of Guelph, Guelph, ON, Canada

of politicians and political elites thus strongly impacts the debate. This chapter makes the argument that Brazil and Chile both have strong social movements that have allies with the legislative and executive branches of government. However, those connections are muted by the overwhelming influence of conservative actors.

This chapter will use historical institutionalism and Political Opportunity Structure (POS) approaches to demonstrate the importance of institutional design in enacting same-sex marriage. The importance of our analysis lies in the difference in the institutional framework and the role of the courts in each country. The federal system has aided in enacting same-sex marriage in Brazil, while the unitary system of Chile presents significant barriers. The Brazilian Supreme Court rulings in favor of same-sex marriage and the negative rulings in Chile have also affected the way social movements operate in each country. What we have seen in Brazil is the "judicialization" of LGBT rights, whereas in Chile the debate remains in Congress.

The chapter opens with an overview of gay and lesbian mobilization in the two countries and suggests that, some differences notwithstanding, social mobilization does not solely explain the lack of policy reform. The chapter then moves on to look at institutional variables. Both the Brazilian and Chilean congresses contain influential conservative voting blocs, which makes passing pro-sexual rights legislation challenging in both states. Such representation, we show, amounts to veto power. The Chilean and Brazilian LGBT social movements were each effective in lobbying and framing the issue of same-sex marriage in order to gain presidential support. Finally, the chapter will utilize historical institutionalism and POS to demonstrate the role of institutional design, more specifically the judiciary, in providing avenues to enhancing LGBT rights.

Social Movement Mobilization

While they originated differently, the Brazilian and Chilean LGBT movements are both strong. In Brazil, LGBT activism found its strength in the early 1990s in response to the HIV/AIDS epidemic. Yet, in Chile, LGBT activists struggled to gain political momentum until the early 2000s. Despite their differences, activists have become important political forces in their respective countries. However, their strength has not equally translated into policy success for same-sex marriage.

Social Movement Strength in Brazil

The Brazilian LGBT movement experienced tremendous growth during a time of liberalization within the country (Marsiaj 2006). In the early 1990s, during a time of democratization and at the peak of the HIV/AIDS epidemic, pro-LGBT NGOs expanded rapidly. This expansion was a result of an unprecedented formal relationship between the LGBT social movement and the Brazilian government. However, the movement's expansion and success during the HIV/AIDS epidemic did not translate into congressional success for the movement's next focus: civil unions and same sex marriage.

The Brazilian LGBT movement's origins are generally traced to the creation of the Nucleo de Ação pelos Direitos dos Homosexuias (Action Nucleus for Homosexual Rights) in May 1978, later known as SOMOS (We are: Group of Homosexual Affirmation) (Green 1999; de la Dehesa 2010). In 1980, Luiz Mott formed the Grupo Gay da Bahia (GBH), making it the oldest association for the defense of human rights for homosexuals still functioning in Brazil. In 1987, GBH was granted legal status making it the first gay organization in Latin America to be recognized by a state's government.

Beginning in the 1980s, the focus of Brazilian LGBT activism was to combat the growing HIV/AIDS epidemic (Marsiaj 2006). The tragedy of the HIV/AIDS epidemic mobilized the LGBT movement, as organizations such as the GBH began working with AIDS prevention programs, creating an unprecedented alliance between the state and gay activists (Encarnación 2016). By the early 1990s, HIV/AIDS began expanding to the general population, with Brazil having the fastest infection rate of any country outside Africa. In 1994, the World Bank famously warned Brazilian public officials to brace for nothing short of a catastrophe (Encarnación 2016). International pressure, coupled with the HIV/AIDS virus spreading to the general population, contributed to the government's willingness to work with LGBT organizations.

In 1983, Sao Paulo's Ministério da Saúde (Health Ministry) in combination with gay leaders, local politicians, and health professionals created the Grupo de Apoio à Prevençã à AIDS (AIDS Prevention Support Group, GAPA). GAPA is credited with transforming national policy and the gay movement itself by becoming the prototype for the Programa Nacional DST/AIDS (PNDA), a program renowned by international health organizations for passing a federal law guaranteeing antiretroviral therapy through the national healthcare system to anyone infected with HIV (Encarnación 2016).

The PNDA approach was successful and by the mid-2000s the AIDS total infection rate was close to 800,000, which although still high, was only half of the World Bank's 1994 prediction. The success of PNDA is attributed to the social movement's ability to press the state into action. The movement used the provision in the 1988 Brazilian Constitution regarding universal healthcare as a human rights issue, applying it to HIV/AIDS treatment. Scholars credit the success of this mobilization with reshaping the Brazilian gay movement, demonstrating how state policies can transform social movements and their activism (Marsiaj 2006; Encarnación 2016). By 2007, the government's engagement with the HIV/AIDS epidemic led to the "NGO-ization" of the LGBT movement with the creation of over 700 NGOs involved in HIV/AIDS. The funding available from the state led to the centralization of the LGBT movement with the creation of the Associação Brasileira de Gays, Lésbicas, Bissexuais, Travestis, e Transexuais (ABGLT). ABGLT is a national network of over 300 LGBT groups, making it Latin America's largest gay rights confederation. Its collaborative relationship with the state extends beyond health care policies to other ministries, which has been essential for the movement's organization (Carrara 2012).

Marsiaj (2012) argues that a strong social movement is necessary in order for minority groups to advance progressive policy in Latin America. Brazil has one of the oldest and most visible gay rights movements in the Global South (Goméz 2010; De la Dehesa 2010; Encarnación 2016). The LGBT movement effectively collaborated with the government in order to fight the pandemic of HIV/AIDS.

However, the movement's ability to impact policy outside HIV/AIDS within the Brazilian Congress has yet to succeed. Its attempts at enacting same-sex marriage and pro-LGBT legislation through its national congress have failed. To date, the Brazilian Congress has passed no pro-LGBT policy at the federal level. This is because of the growing countermovement to LGBT rights, permeating the legislative arena, as discussed later in this chapter.

Social Movement Strength in Chile

Historically, the Chilean state has not had a positive relationship with the LGBT community (Contardo 2011). Oppression of the LGBT community existed under both democratic and authoritarian regimes. Prior to the Pinochet dictatorship (1973–1990), there was little to no LGBT mobilization against state oppression. The movement failed to crystallize even within the atmosphere of social mobilization that took place in the 1960s and 1970s (Díez 2015). Nor did gays and lesbians form the same civil society connections as other movements in the region did (Argentina, Brazil, and Mexico). There was little chance for mobilization during the repression of civil society that occurred under the Pinochet dictatorship, although some commercial spaces for socialization emerged toward its end.

It was not until after the dictatorship ended that a formal movement began to emerge in 1991. The main organization that was formed at this time was the Movimiento de Integración y Liberación Homosexual (Homosexual Movement for Integration and Liberation, Movilh). However, even then, internal divisions over priorities left the movement poorly organized. HIV/AIDS policy offered little treatment or education under the Pinochet dictatorship and had not changed significantly since the transition to democracy. However, unlike in Brazil, the HIV/AIDS crisis did not lead to any cohesive mobilization. In fact, there was further division over whether activists should focus on the HIV/AIDS crisis or lobby solely for civil rights.

The Chilean movement did not pursue the same strategies as successfully as its counterparts in some Latin American countries. Unlike activists elsewhere, in Chile the movement did not launch a public awareness campaign to halt homosexual repression. Rather surprisingly given the context, Movilh chose not to partake in the broader post-dictatorship human rights discussion taking place at that time. The leadership of the organization thought that LGBT rights issues should be kept separate from other human rights concerns, specifically women's rights. Due to this lack of connections with other civil society groups, Movilh was unable to find governmental allies to introduce policy initiatives (Dawn King 2013; Frasca 2010). Therefore, the movement remained weak until the early 2000s. At this point, Movilh became more influential. The group raised awareness of LGBT discrimination and repression through political protest (Ramón Gómez Roa, Interviewed by Daniel Waring, July 8, 2016). In doing so, the group also raised their political profile.

The evolution of Chilean LGBT mobilization changed significantly in 2011 with the establishment of Fundación Iguales (Equals Foundation), an organization that has gained great prominence in Chile. Iguales was founded by members of the Chilean elite, a characteristic that has given it important strength in securing political allies due to the strongly classist nature of Chilean society. Politicians tend to favor working with members of society's elite over individuals from more humble backgrounds, which have characterized Movilh members. As a result, Iguales has become an important organization in the fight for LGBT rights in Chile.

The combined strength of these two organizations was the driving force behind the inclusion of LGBT categories in the anti-discrimination law that Congress passed in 2012. Even though they lobbied separately, sustained pressure from Movilh and Iguales was key to the passage of the bill, according to Members of Congress. They were clear that Movilh was central to the introduction of the bill to the Chamber of Deputies. Movilh and Iguales continued to raise consciousness of the bill in the Senate when it was faced with strong conservative opposition (Maria Antonieta Saa, Guillermo Cernoi, Marcelo Drago, Nicolas Dualde, Interviewed by Daniel Waring, Santiago, and Valparaíso July 14–July 25, 2016).

Movilh and Fundación Iguales also played important roles in the adoption of civil unions. Both organizations worked closely with politicians and the executive branch to introduce proposals. Movilh and their political allies introduced two different bills, but both were archived due to a lack of executive support. While neither bill was passed, they led to important public debate and political response. After President Sebastian Piñera (2010–14) withdrew his initial support for civil unions, Fundación Iguales intensely pressured the government to make civil unions a legislative priority. They were eventually legalized in October 2015.

While Chile's LGBT movement came from weak beginnings, it has grown into a powerful political force: from a small organization to a movement with national visibility. Both Movilh and Fundación Iguales played a crucial role in the adoption of the anti-discrimination law and civil unions through intense and calculated political lobbying (Waring 2017). Yet, the absence of presidential support for LGBT rights has made that lobbying even more difficult. A lack of executive backing for moral policy initiatives, through a need to satisfy conservative actors, ultimately limits the success that civil society lobbying can achieve.

An exploration of the history of LGBT mobilization in Brazil and Chile demonstrates that the success or failure of same-sex marriage legalization initiatives cannot solely be explained by social movements. Both countries possess strong, effective LGBT social movement organizations. In Brazil, the movement has found strength in lobbying on health policy but has been unable to translate that strength into power within the Brazilian Congress. In Chile, LGBT activists have had serious legislative victories in Congress, but same-sex marriage has still not been passed. A social movement analysis is insufficient to explain same-sex marriage in these two countries.

Conservative Opposition

Brazil and Chile are both characterized by the conservative nature of their legislative houses. The Brazilian context demonstrates a powerful countermovement emerging from the growing Evangelical-led LGBT opposition in both society and politics. The Chilean example highlights the power of conservative control of the legislative agenda, regardless of the ruling coalition.

The Countermovement to LGBT Rights in Brazil

Evangelicals, rather than the larger and more longstanding Catholic Church, are the main actors driving the countermovement to LGBT rights in Brazil. The Evangelical Church is an export from United States missionaries, who arrived in 1911 and began targeting poor communities in rural regions of Brazil. Presently, the two main Evangelical Churches in Brazil are the Universal Church, which was founded in the 1970s, and the Assembly of God, founded in 1911. Universal alone has more than 35,000 churches and close to 12 million followers in Brazil (Espinosa 2004). In 1950, three percent of the population identified as Evangelical, while by 2016 that number had risen to 26 percent (Espinosa 2004; Ogland 2014; Encarnación 2016). As membership grew, so did the Church's interest in electing politicians.

Since the early 1980s, the Evangelical Church in Brazil has been actively seeking to elect politicians to pursue its moral agenda (Oro 2003; Reich and Dos Santos 2013). In 1986, the Universal Church of the Kingdom of God successfully mobilized to elect its first federal deputy (Oro 2003). From here, it organized to elect deputies and senators representing various regions across the country. This was the start of what led to the "Evangelical bench" within the Chamber of Deputies. Allesandra Ramos, a policy advisor for Congressman Jean Wyllys, states that during the early "1990s and 2000s, [the Evangelicals'] political influence started to grow, and they started to enter parties, they realized that numbers are power and that politics and religion are a perfect marriage" (Interviewed by Tyler Valiquette, Rio de Janeiro, July 27, 2016). Deputy Maria do Rosario of the Partido dos Trabalhadores (Workers Party, PT) elaborates that Evangelicals chose to "elect people from small councils, with some Churches electing deputies so that they could stop bills, such as the same-sex marriage or anti-discrimination" (Interviewed by Tyler Valiquette,

Brasilia, September 14, 2016). By doing so, they ensure that their moral agenda is met within Congress and they are able to influence legislation.

This countermovement led by the Evangelical Church and their elected politicians has proven to be a formidable opponent to LGBT rights. It has amassed a tremendous amount of political influence. Alone, this countermovement controls 15 percent of the seats in the lower house, making it the second largest voting bloc after PT (Encarnación 2016). In an alliance with the União Democrática Ruralista (the Democratic Association of Ruralists), a far-right party representing farmers and activists, the military, and the Catholic Church, the Evangelical voting bloc is a symbol of conservative power in Congress. These caucuses, or the BBB (Bullets, Bibles, and Beef), make up almost 60 percent of the 515 seats in the Chamber of Deputies (Encarnación 2016), demonstrating a conservative takeover of the Brazilian Congress and, with conservative voting blocs often voting in lockstep, a significant barrier for socially progressive legislation. This takeover in Congress granted significant power to the countermovement, extending to an influence over the executive branch.

As Javier Corrales argues (2015), an important factor for the successful advancement of LGBT rights at the state level is creating strong connections with national-level parties and obtaining support from the executive branch. We saw above that outside HIV/AIDS policy, the Brazilian LGBT movement has had difficulty in framing sexual minority rights in a way that leads to legislative support from the executive branch. Lula da Silva's election to the presidency in 2003 brought hope to the LGBT community given his party's (PT) position on sexual rights; it was the first party in Latin America to recognize LGBT rights as a priority in its official mandate (Keck 1995; Marsiaj 2012). For activists, the stage was set for a major advancement in LGBT rights.

With much anticipation but limited progress, the Lula presidency frustrated the LGBT community. Lula's lack of support is attributed to the growing countermovement. Worried about political survival, Lula reached out to the Evangelical Church, mainly Universal, for support (Oro 2003). Gerson Scheidweiler Ferreira of the Secretariat of Women states that "during the last two legislatures, there has been an important presence of organized conservatism ideology because of the Evangelical benches during the presidential elections creating the understanding that if you don't work with Evangelicals, you won't be elected" (Interviewed by Tyler Valiquette, Brasilia, September 6, 2016). Lula consequently backed away from his promises to LGBT people and extended his arm to the Evangelicals.

Dilma Rouseff, Lula da Silva's protégée, was elected president in 2011. Under Rouseff, significant steps for LGBT rights were made, such as the rulings of civil unions in 2011 and same-sex marriage in 2013. Despite such progress, Rouseff was not seen as an LGBT rights champion. Like Lula, she was beholden to the congressional Evangelical-led countermovement. According to Marina Bosso Lacerda, a policy advisor for the Human Rights Commission: "Dilma gave up on the LGBT mandate and gender issues because of Evangelical pressure in Congress" (Interviewed by Tyler Valiquette, Brasilia, September 8, 2016). Indeed, Rouseff essentially became a veto-player against LGBT rights, vetoing legislation for anti-homophobia tool-kits in schools when presented in Congress. LGBT rights were not a mandate for the Rouseff administration, and thus same-sex marriage received no executive support.

However, the LGBT movement in Brazil has been successful in engaging with politicians and implementing policy at the sub-national level (Marsiaj 2008). This is a result of some state-level governments being highly progressive in comparison to the national congress. In terms of success at the federal level, however, no bill has been passed through the Brazilian Congress protecting or enhancing LGBT rights. With no executive support and limited congressional support, the only ally for the LGBT movement at the federal level has been the Brazilian courts.

Conservative Opposition to LGBT Rights in Chile

In her second presidential campaign, Michelle Bachelet (2006–10, 2014–) openly supported same-sex marriage. She was the first major presidential candidate in Latin America to endorse the issue during a campaign. However, since the election, the only mention of same-sex marriage from the president has been a commitment that the executive branch would introduce a bill by the end of 2017. This late introduction would thus follow a similar pattern to Bachelet's support for civil unions. During her first presidential campaign, she openly supported civil unions for same sex couples, yet only introduced a bill in late 2009 at the end of her first term.

To understand these political dynamics, one must contextualize Chilean politics. The Chilean policymaking process is based on broad political consensus. The president's agenda-setting powers in the Constitution are very broad. Yet, in practice, the policy process is characterized by wide cooperation and consultation. The system involves negotiations to ensure that the government's agenda has support from within its own coalition and the opposition (Olavarria-Gambi 2016; Aninat et al. 2008; Carey 2002; Siavelis 2002). There is a system of "supermajority thresholds" to pass special legislation that limits the president's agenda-setting powers (Aninat et al. 2008). Laws on issues ranging from education, banking, and social security require a high threshold of votes in both chambers. As a result, the opposition is in a position to block reform. If the bill requires a supermajority, the executive branch must cooperate with members across the aisle to ensure their support. This forces an administration to negotiate with the opposition and within their coalition in both chambers. The president must ensure that bills introduced at one point are not so controversial that they will cost them supermajority support on social or fiscal reforms.

The Chilean Congress is composed of two coalitions: New Majority (formally Coalition of Parties for Democracy or Concertación) and Let's Go Chile (formally the Coalition for Change or Coalición por el cambio). New Majority is the center-left coalition and comprises four main political parties: the Christian Democratic Party, the Socialist Party, Party for Democracy, and the Radical Social Democratic Party. Let's Go Chile is the center-right coalition. It also comprises four parties: Independent Democratic Union, National Renewal, Independent Regionalist Party, and Political Evolution. As a result of the ideological spread, negotiations frequently take place within coalitions and with the opposition in order to secure the necessary number of votes. The executive branch has to ensure that legislation will pass not only the opposition but its own coalition as well. The inclusion of the socially conservative Christian Democrats (DC) in the New Majority can make it difficult to pass progressive legislation, especially regarding moral policy (Blofield 2006).

Consensual politics mean that controversial bills must have executive support. However, given the need for cooperation, the president cannot force a bill through Congress, but must depend on support from the coalition and the opposition as well. If the president depended on conservative support for a more substantial bill, then he/she must work with the opposition to ensure the latter's ongoing support. Concertación followed consensual politics which led to the delays in LGBT rights advancement. The first civil union bill introduced in 2003 failed despite having support within Concertación, because President Ricardo Lagos (2000–06) did not support the bill. In Bachelet's first term, the bill tabled in 2009 was archived due to lack of support. Bachelet's lack of movement for LGBT rights can be traced to the role of the Christian Democratic Party in

Concertación. The Catholic Church is strongly involved with DC, which means that they have a direct influence into the agenda-setting process.

A lack of support was evident in the anti-discrimination bill. Politicians from then Concertación and Coalición por el Cambio explained that the president did not lobby in favor of or against the bill (Maria Antonieta Saa, Guillermo Ceroni, Nicolas Dualde, Marcelo Drago, Interviewed by Daniel Waring, Santiago and Valparaiso, July 18–July 25, 2016). They confirmed that it was not on the president's agenda because he/she was beholden to the conservative wing of Concertación. Civil unions were not discussed until the end of Bachelet's first term because she depended on DC support. Anti-discrimination and civil unions were executive priorities, but the socialist presidents were unable to risk alienating conservative factions within their coalitions. DC politicians held such power that moral policy reform did not even reach discussions over the agenda (Díez 2015). Therefore, members of the executive branch did not seriously discuss civil unions until the end of her term. Real change did not take place until Sebastian Piñera's administration.

What was ultimately successful for civil unions was the departure from consensual politics. In his presidential campaign, Sebastian Piñera (2010–14) openly supported civil unions, which was a departure from past rhetoric from the right-wing Coalición por el Cambio (Coalition for Change), to which Piñera's National Renewal party belonged. The open endorsement of civil unions was a campaign strategy. By endorsing civil unions, the National Renewal and Piñera established themselves as an open and liberal right-wing party as opposed to other, more extreme members of the Coalición por el Cambio (Díez 2015). His endorsement of civil unions created serious tensions within the coalition, but he did not waver. After being elected president he introduced a proposal to legalize same-sex civil unions into the Senate in June 2010. This proposal was reviewed twice, and his support faded during his presidency due to the lack of support for the bill from within his own coalition. Yet, the proposal introduced during his administration ultimately became law in October 2015. Piñera's decision to break consensus on the issue of civil unions was what ultimately allowed his administration to make serious progress on civil unions.

Bachelet's style of governance in her second term has been much like her first. She has sought to maintain consensus with her coalition and the opposition. The centrist DC holds the balance of power in the New Majority. Bachelet has tried to maintain consensus between this party and more progressive actors in the coalition. Therefore, she has avoided significant moral policy reforms. Her desire to maintain consensus gives conservative actors veto power, resulting in no action on same-sex marriage.

An analysis of the Brazilian and Chilean congresses demonstrates the impact of conservative actors in vetoing the advancement of LGBT rights. The powerful countermovement to LGBT rights in Brazil, led by Evangelicals, provides an overwhelming barrier to pro-LGBT policy, while also creating fear in the executive branch regarding political survival. Conservative opposition to same-sex marriage and the executive branch's desire to maintain consensus with conservative actors in Chile has meant little executive support for same-sex marriage once elected. A withdrawal of executive support has caused policy stasis on same-sex marriage. The composition of institutional design and parameters of the Brazilian and Chilean congresses have led to significant roadblocks within the legislative branch. This is where the unitary system of Chile and the federal system of Brazil matter for our analysis. In Chile, the conversation on same-sex marriage has been limited to Congress, whereas in Brazil, another avenue is available: the courts.

The Courts

The major difference between these two states lies in the ability of the court system to impact same-sex marriage. The issue of LGBT rights has become judicialized in Brazil, which has led to the Supreme Court, and other high courts, ruling in favor of progressing LGBT rights. Subnational politics have aided in this advancement, applying pressure on the federal courts to respond. Chilean activists also attempted to judicialize same-sex marriage but were unsuccessful. Because there are no subnational political avenues, the Chilean judiciary did not have to respond to any significant pressure the same way it did in Brazil.

An Ally in the Courts

Under the PT administration of Dilma Rouseff, significant progress was made regarding LGBT rights. However, Rouseff herself provided little support for the LGBT community in the matter of same-sex marriage. In fact, in both her 2010 and 2014 successful presidential campaigns, she is on record opposing it. In a 2014 interview, on the TV show *Roda Viva* of

TV Cultural of São Paulo, Rouseff stated: "I am in favor of gay civil unions, since I think marriage is a religious issue. I as an individual would never tell a religion what it can and cannot do."

Despite a lack of executive support, the Brazilian judiciary ruled in favor of enshrining several civil rights for same-sex couples with a series of rulings beginning in 2010. First, the Brazilian Superior Court of Justice, the top appellate court, ruled unanimously that gay couples have the right to adopt. Second, in 2011, another unanimous decision by the Federal Supreme Court forced the state to put homosexual and heterosexual relationships on the same legal footing. This ruling deemed all homosexual couples to be awarded the same rights given to heterosexual couples. Finally, in 2013, the National Council of Justice (a body that oversees the judicial system) ordered the federalization of same-sex marriage. The Council did this by ordering all notary publics to issue marriage certificates to same-sex couples requesting them. The ruling was seen as important because of the growing number of states that had legalized same-sex marriage without judicial approval. Chief Justice Joaquim Barbosa, who headed the National Council of Justice, stated on the Council's website in 2011 that "the Supreme Court affirmed that the expression of homosexuality and heterosexual affection cannot serve as a basis for discriminatory treatment, which has no support in the Constitution."

There was considerable frustration and impatience with the inability of Congress to progress any sort of gay issue through the two legislative houses. The endless deliberation and lack of action by Congress was a key factor in the Court's becoming involved and making a ruling in Brazil. The Federal Supreme Court's 2011 decision on civil unions was provoked by the "legal lacuna" brought about by the stagnation of Congress (Encarnación 2016). Same-sex couples were in legal limbo, so the Court felt it had a responsibility to protect gay couples (Encarnación 2016).

Courts as a Dead-End Road

Due to the unitary structure of the Chilean state, the judiciary is not an option for LGBT activists there. There are no state courts at which LGBT activists could argue in favor of same-sex marriage nor are there subnational legislatures that can approve it. Therefore, they are unable to build momentum before arriving at the Supreme Court. LGBT activists have tried to win rights through the judicial route in the past, but they have been unsuccessful.

The Court has not been friendly to LGBT rights. In 2004, the Supreme Court upheld a lower court decision to remove children from the custody of Karen Atala because she was a lesbian. That same year, the Supreme Court removed Judge Daniel Calvo from his position on the Santiago Court of Appeals when it became known that he visited a gay sauna. The first challenge on same-sex marriage was in July 2011. In September 2010, three same sex couples went to the Civil Registry Office to request marriage licenses. They were denied because the Chilean Civil Code defines marriage as being between one man and one woman. They took their case to the Court of Appeals of Santiago and then the Supreme Court. The Court voted 9-1 in favor of upholding the traditional definition of marriage. The next challenge was in June 2016. The Santiago Court of Appeals ruled against a challenge from Movilh on the language on marriage being between one man and one woman. The court also stated that it should not be in a position to change the definition of marriage; that power remains with the government.

That statement, combined with their earlier judgments, demonstrates that same-sex marriage will not come through the courts in Chile. This means that the judicialization of LGBT rights is highly unlikely. Unlike in Brazil, the judiciary has demonstrated that they are unfriendly to LGBT rights and do not believe it is their place to regulate the definition of marriage. Change will have to come through Congress.

HISTORICAL INSTITUTIONALISM AND JUDICIALIZATION

Both Chile and Brazil have social movements which are established and strong. They are able to penetrate institutions, as well as interact with political elites. Additionally, both Brazil and Chile have strong conservative fronts which influence each country's Congress. Religious conservatism in the legislative houses impacts the executive branch and supersedes the LGBT movement's attempts at enacting pro-LGBT policy, such as same-sex marriage. As we have seen, the main difference between the two countries lies in the judiciary.

In order to understand policy divergence on same-sex marriage between Chile and Brazil, a historical institutionalist lens can be applied. Historical institutionalism theory argues that policy choices made when an institution is being formed, or when a policy is initiated, will have a continuing and largely determinate influence over the policy into the future (Skocpol 2017; King 1995; Pierson and Skocpol 2002). Thus, it is vital to begin by examining state structures, with the field of political institutions and the legacies of previous policies, to explain divergence in policy outcomes.

To highlight the major difference between the two policy structures, it is important to analyze the state as the most important actor in influencing policy, as the state can ultimately choose to remain autonomous to outside forces in the practice of human rights (Skocpol 1985). From this perspective, it is vital to look at the policy legacies between the two countries and how these legacies exert influence on contemporary political battles by closing off certain policy choices or making them more difficult, less feasible, or difficult to envision. Ongoing policy discussions center around the weight of current policies and the political, bureaucratic, administrative, and legal apparatuses that have been created by them (Pierson and Skocpol 2002).

With both countries having a countermovement that controls more power in the congress and over the executive branch, the social movements' ability to overcome opposition and enact policy within the legislative houses remains insurmountable. The difference lies in the federalist state of Brazil vs. the unitary state of Chile. Brazil's Supreme Court began advocating for the rights of LGBT folk beginning in 1998, with Chief Justice Celso Mello commenting in the newspaper *O Estado do São Paulo*:

> it is of no use commemorating the fiftieth anniversary of the Universal Declaration of Human Rights if unjust practices which deny homosexuals their basic human rights continue to exist ... judicial bodies need to take note of these cruelties and acknowledge our need to confront the conditions of grave adversaries in which members of these extremely vulnerable groups are forced to exist.

This resulted in a critical juncture in which the Supreme Court became a possibly favorable arena for progressing LGBT rights. As a result, the high courts of Brazil have been pushed, resulting in setting judicial precedence in regard to adoption, civil unions, and same-sex marriage.

The Chilean Supreme Court has been much less favorable to the development of LGBT rights. It has ruled against every major LGBT case that has come before the Court. Thus, this policy avenue is unavailable for the progression of LGBT rights.

Finally, the role of institutions in Brazil and Chile has shaped the political opportunity structures for LGBT movements. In Brazil, there are various avenues for movement penetration. In Chile, the Congress remains the only avenue for same-sex marriage legalization.

POLITICAL OPPORTUNITY STRUCTURES

The institutional framework and designs of the political systems in Brazil and Chile have ultimately shaped the avenues available for social movements. The recent involvement of the high courts in Brazil has altered the movements' strategy in regard to political opportunity.

In being outspokenly in favor of LGBT rights in 1998, the Brazilian Supreme Court provided an early window of opportunity for the movement. The social movement used this window to forge opportunities through the sub-national level, forcing the high courts of Brazil to rule on issues of LGBT rights. In Chile, that window has never been available. The Supreme Court has demonstrated its opposition to LGBT rights. Due to the lack of sub-national units, it is unlikely for that policy avenue to open.

In comparing the two congresses, the window of opportunity is closed in Brazil, whereas it remains somewhat open in Chile. No pro-LGBT policy has ever passed through the Brazilian Congress. In Chile, by contrast, sexual orientation and gender identity were included in the 2012 anti-discrimination law and a bill recognizing civil unions for same-sex couples was passed in 2015. An increase in opportunity within the Brazilian judiciary nonetheless demonstrates more space and fewer constraints for the movement, and in comparison with the Congress, demonstrates a more favorable system to its demands (Gamson and Meyer 1996). In turn, the judiciary's response then shapes the social movement's strategies for enacting its agenda.

Through judicialization, some countries in Latin America have changed the procedures for constitutional review, while others have expanded the scope of rights that are legally protected, and yet others have broadened the identity of the actors that are authorized to make claims Smulovitz 2012. In its 1988 Constitution, Brazil expanded the bills of rights and introduced provisions that make it easier for individuals or collective organized actors to access constitutional courts and demand both concrete and abstract protection of certain rights (Smulovitz 2012). Social actors in Brazil have also been using and filing claims in lower courts demanding the enforcement and expansion of social and economic rights (Gauri and Brinks 2008). This includes the Court's decisions regarding LGBT rights.

In Brazil, the Court's rulings acted as a sign of indignation for sexual minorities. The rulings also mirror a shifting trend by the Brazilian LGBT movement in the perception that the emphasis and focus on impacting change through Congress had run its course and the executive branch is in fact not an ally to the movement. This shift has led to a changing opportunity structure and a new wave of activism in Brazil. The focus now lies on changing and enhancing legislation through the court system (Encarnación 2016). For, the core agenda of the Groupo de Advogados pela Diversidade Sexual e de Genero (Group of Lawyers for Sexual and Gender Diversity), or GADvS, founded in 2012, is not to lobby the legislature but to develop legal strategies for enhancing LGBT rights. The president and founder of GADvS, Paulo Iotti, demonstrates the window of opportunity developing in the judiciary as well as the one closing in Congress. He argues that the political and judicial climate has changed dramatically since the 1990s; while Congress has grown more conservative, the judiciary has become more liberal as suggested by the competition of the Federal Supreme Court causing activists to shift their attention from the Congress to the courts. Gay activists are now going so far as to turning to the courts to enact laws already blocked by Congress.

Politics in Chile, on the other hand, have not become judicialized in the same way that they have in Brazil. The courts remain in deference to Congress (Couso 2005), and the system is less welcoming than the Brazilian judicial system to any human rights issue, regardless of its nature. When the Supreme Court did hear arguments in favor of same-sex marriage, it ruled against them. Due to the conservative Supreme Court, LGBT rights have not progressed through that avenue, which leaves activists to pursue policy through Congress.

While conservative actors have been a major obstacle in the past, activists have found strength in the windows of opportunity that come through division among political elites. Chile's political system favors consensus between the president and his/her coalition. This is the system Bachelet has followed, resulting in little action as we have seen. Sebastian Piñera, by contrast, used civil unions to differentiate his party from other members of the coalition. Therefore, divisions emerged that activists could exploit to pursue policy goals. These divisions have not yet emerged in Bachelet's second term.

Conclusion

The institutional framework of Brazil and Chile has been crucial in the adoption of same-sex marriage. The Brazilian federalist state and its more open judicial system have provided avenues that are unavailable to the Chilean unitary state. This has led to momentum in regard to the Brazilian court system becoming involved in enacting rights for sexual minorities, while in Chile, activists remain focused on passing policy through congressional avenues. The judiciary has proven itself to be a conservative institution that is unfriendly to LGBT rights.

Moving forward, judicialization will continue to occur in Brazil with Congress maintaining a conservative majority and a mobilized countermovement. However, the Supreme Court is susceptible to a conservative front as well. The countermovement is beginning to acknowledge the significance of the court system. With a conservative president and Congress, appointment of future judges can remove this avenue for LGBT activists. In Chile, politics has not been judicialized to the same extent that it has been in Brazil. LGBT issues are confined to Congress. While faced with strong conservative opposition, activists have benefitted from divisions among political elites in the past. Unfortunately, President Bachelet shows no signs of breaking ranks from the New Majority. Presidential elections at the end of 2017 can bring the issue of same-sex marriage onto the legislative agenda again. Yet, the Chilean courts show no sign of becoming more favorable to LGBT rights. Consequently, institutions are less favorable for enacting same-sex marriage in Chile than in Brazil.

References

Aninat, Cristóbal, John Londregan, Patricio Navia, and Joaquín Vial. 2008. Political Institutions, Policymaking Processes, and Policy Outcomes in Chile. In *Policymaking in Latin America: How Politics Shapes Policies*, ed. Ernesto Stein and Mariano Tommasi. Washington, DC: Inter-American Development Bank.

Blofield, Merike. 2006. *The Politics of Moral Sin: Abortion and Divorce in Spain, Chile, and Argentina*. San Diego: University of California.

Carey, J.M. 2002. Parties, Coalitions, and the Chilean Congress in the 1990s. In *Legislative Politics in Latin America*, ed. S. Morgenstern and B. Nacif. Cambridge: Cambridge University Press.

Carrara, Sergio. 2012. Discriminação, políticas e direitos sexuais no Brasil. *Cadernos de Saúde Pùblica* 28 (1). https://doi.org/10.1590/S0102-311X2012000100020.

Contardo, Oscar. 2011. *Raro: Una Historia gay de Chile*. Santiago: Editorial Planeta.
Corrales, Javier. 2015. The Politics of LGBT Rights and the Caribbean: Research Agendas. *European Review of Latin American and Caribbean Studies* 100: 53–62.
Couso, Javier A. 2005. The Judicialization of Chilean Politics: The Rights Revolution That Never Was. In *The Judicialization of Politics in Latin America*, ed. Rachel Sieder, Line Schjolden, and Alan Angell, 105–131. New York: Palgrave Macmillan.
Dawn King, M. 2013. The Role of Societal Attitudes and Activists' Perceptions on Effective Judicial Access for the LGBT Movement in Chile. *Interface* 5 (1): 183–203.
De la Dehesa, Rafael. 2010. *Queering the Public Sphere in Mexico and Brazil: Sexual Rights Movements in Emerging Democracies*. Durham: Duke University Press.
Díez, Jordi. 2015. *The Politics of Gay Marriage in Latin America*. New York: Cambridge University Press.
Encarnación, Omar. 2016. *Out in the Periphery: Latin America's Gay Rights Revolution*. New York: Oxford University Press.
Espinosa, G. 2004. The Pentecostalization of Latin America and U.S. Latino Christianity. *The Journal of the Society for Pentecostal Studies* 26 (2): 270–271.
Frasca, Tim. 2010. Chile: Seizing Empowerment. In *Politics of Sexuality in Latin America*, ed. Javier Corrales and Mario Pecheny. Pittsburgh: University of Pittsburgh Press.
Gamson, William, and Stephen Meyer. 1996. Framing Political Opportunity. In *Comparative Perspectives on Social Movements: Political Opportunities, Mobilizing Structures, and Cultural Framings*, ed. Doug McAdam, John D. McCarthy, and Mayer N. Zald. New York: Cambridge University Press.
Gauri, Varun, and Daniel M. Brinks. 2008. *Courting Social Justice: Judicial Enforcement of Social and Economic Rights in the Developing World*. New York: Cambridge University Press.
Goméz, Eduardo. 2010. Friendly Government, Cruel Society: AIDS and the Politics of Homosexual Strategic Mobilization in Brazil. In *The Politics of Sexuality in Latin America*, ed. J. Corrales and M. Pecheny, 233–250. Pittsburgh: University of Pittsburgh Press.
Green, James. 1999. *Beyond Carnival: Male Homosexuality in Twentieth Century Brazil*. Chicago: University of Chicago Press.
Keck, Margaret. 1995. *Democratization and the Workers Party in Brazil*. New Haven: Yale University Press.
King, Desmond. 1995. *Actively Seeking Work: The Politics of Unemployment and Welfare Policy in the United States*. Chicago: University of Chicago Press.

Marsiaj, Juan. 2006. Social Movements and Political Parties: Gays, Lesbians and *Travestis* and the Struggle for Inclusion in Brazil. *Canadian Journal of Latin American and Caribbean Studies* 31 (62): 167–196.

———. 2008. Social Movements and Political Parties: Gays, Lesbians, and Travestis. In *The Politics of Sexuality in Latin America*, ed. J. Corrales and M. Pecheny, 197–212. Pittsburgh: University of Pittsburgh Press.

———. 2012. Federalism, Advocacy Networks, and Sexual Diversity Politics in Brazil. In *Comparative Public Policy in Latin America*, ed. Jordi Díez and Susan Franceschet, 126–149. Toronto: University of Toronto Press.

Ogland, Curtis. 2014. Religion and the Rainbow Struggle: Does Religion Factor into Attitudes Toward Homosexuality and Same-Sex Civil Unions in Brazil? *Journal of Homosexuality* 61 (9): 1334–1349.

Olavarria-Gambi, Mauricio. 2016. Agenda and Public Policy: Evidence From Chile. *International Journal of Public Administration* 39 (2): 157–172.

Oro, A.P. 2003. A Política da Igreja Universal e Seus Reflexos Nos Campos Religioso e Politico Brasileiros. *Revista Brasileira de Ciências Sociais* 18 (53): 579–607.

Pierson, Paul, and Theda Skocpol. 2002. Historical Institutionalism in Contemporary Political Science. In *The State of the Discipline*, ed. Ira Katzenelson and Helen Milner, 693–792. New York: Norton.

Reich, Gary, and Pedro dos Santos. 2013. The Rise (and Frequent Fall) of Evangelical Politicians: Organization, Theology and Church Politics. *Latin American Politics and Society* 55 (4): 1–22.

Siavelis, Peter M. 2002. Exaggerated Presidentialism and Moderate President's: Executive-Legislative Relations in Chile. In *Legislative Politics in Latin America*, ed. Scott Morgenstern and Bentio Nacif. Cambridge: Cambridge University Press.

Skocpol, Theda. 1985. Bringing the State Back In: Strategies of Analysis in Current Research. In *Bringing the State Back in*, ed. Theda Skocpol, Peter B. Evans, and Dietrich Rueschmemeyer, 3–37. Cambridge: Cambridge University Press.

Skocpol, Theda. 2017. State Formation and Social Policy in the United States. *American Behavioral Scientist* 35 (4–5): 559–584.

Smulovitz, Catalina. 2012. Public Policy by Other Means: Playing the Judicial Arena. In *Comparative Public Policy in Latin America*, ed. Jordi Díez and Susan Franceschet, 105–125. Toronto: University of Toronto Press.

Waring, Daniel. 2017. *A Question of Priorities: Variance in LGBT Protections in Anti-discrimination Legislation in Argentina and Chile*. MA thesis, University of Guelph.

Tyler Valiquette is an MA student in political science at the University of Guelph, Canada. His research focuses on LGBT rights in Brazil. Specifically, he looks at the role of the LGBT movement and the countermovement to LGBT rights and how they impact public policy. He is also the co-founder and director of Vote Savvy, a non-partisan Canadian organization that aims to promote political literacy and increase youth voter turnout.

Daniel Waring recently submitted his master's thesis in Latin American and Caribbean studies at the University of Guelph, Canada, on the topic of variance in LGBT protections in anti-discrimination legislation in Argentina and Chile. He has previously worked as a junior research fellow at the NATO Association of Canada.

CHAPTER 4

Historical Institutionalism and Same-Sex Marriage: A Comparative Analysis of the USA and Canada

Miriam Smith

INTRODUCTION

This chapter provides a comparative analysis of the evolution of same-sex marriage rights in the USA and Canada. Building on my previous work comparing lesbian, gay, bisexual, and transgender (LGBT) rights in Canada and the USA (Smith 2008), which was grounded in a historical institutionalist approach to understanding policy change, I emphasize the importance of federalism, the separation of powers versus a parliamentary system, and the role of courts in shaping the institutional structure of political opportunity for LGBT movements in the two North American neighbors. The relative concentration of power and the nationalization of rights protections through judicial empowerment in Canada provide a stark contrast to the state-by-state struggle for same-sex marriage that occurs in the USA. At the same time, the impact of the recent US Supreme Court ruling in *Obergefell v. Hodges* (2015) demonstrates the impact of national-level judicial decision-making. Comparing two countries with strong courts highlights the factors that condition judicial impact in this policy area. Centralized decision-making and federal jurisdiction over marriage

M. Smith (✉)
York University, Toronto, ON, Canada

are key factors affecting the reach of judicial power in Canada, while decentralized decision-making and state jurisdiction over marriage play an important role in the USA.

In addition to this comparison of the structural features of political institutions in facilitating or blocking political opportunity for social movement actors, this chapter reflects on the ideational turn in historical institutionalism, linking the recent development of discursive institutionalism to the older concept of the policy legacy, originally used in historical institutionalist scholarship.

In this chapter, I suggest some of the ways in which social movement activists and political actors have deliberately mobilized ideational power in the debate over same-sex marriage in both countries. In particular, I stress the ways in which the current debate over same-sex marriage is situated in specific ways in relation to the legacy of previous policies. I consider the matrix of social policy that provides discursive resources for arguments over equality and rights and gives same-sex marriage a different meaning in the two countries. In addition, I discuss the ways in which specific legal rights, such as freedom of religion, have been deliberately linked to marriage debates in the USA, benefitting same-sex marriage opponents, while, in Canada, the strong positive association between LGBT rights and nationalisms (both Charter-based nationalism in English-speaking Canada and progressive nationalism in Quebec) have provided ideational resources for same-sex marriage supporters. While other recent scholarship has explored the transnational and global dissemination of same-sex rights (Kollman 2009), these global and transnational factors play a negligible role in the USA because of its preeminent role in the world and its relatively insular political debates, while the timing of same-sex marriage in Canada occurred before the recent explosion of global discussion on sexuality.

In sum, from a comparative perspective, while both countries have now adopted same-sex marriage, they did so through different pathways, pathways which were structured in important ways by the political institutional configurations including federalism, the separation of powers versus parliamentarism, and the role of courts. The impact of political institutions is a key factor in explaining the rapidity of policy change in Canada and the delay in same-sex marriage in the USA compared to Canada and other countries. Despite the fact that both countries permit same-sex marriage, the policy outcome has a different meaning in the two countries. In Canada, including Quebec, the achievement of same-sex marriage is seen in homonationalist terms as an element of Canadian and Quebec nationalism.

In contrast, in the USA, marriage equality is linked to the Democratic Party and to the progressive politics of the "blue states." It is also linked to the backlash politics against the larger shifts in social policy that have occurred since the 1960s. Hence, despite the *Obergefell* decision, there is ongoing resistance to same-sex marriage in some states and regions, while this resistance has petered out in Canada. The ideational turn and the emphasis on the political agency of collective actors provides a richer discussion of same-sex marriage that sheds light on the process as well as the outcome of policy change.

Historical Institutionalism, the Ideational Turn, and Same-Sex Marriage

Historical institutionalism was developed to explain policy change in the welfare state in developed capitalist countries of the Global North. The call to "bring the state back in" was a reaction to the dominance of pluralist, neo-Marxist, and power resources approaches that, in different ways, argued that social and economic power was at the root of policy development. In contrast, historical institutionalism conceptualized the state not as a unitary actor, but as a complex set of political institutions that facilitated and impeded the actions of political actors operating within the structure. Further, historical institutionalism emphasized that the interaction of structures and agents unfolded over historical time (hence *historical* institutionalism) and that, therefore, time was a variable in the equation of explanation (Pierson and Skocpol 2002; Pierson 2004). The terms of discussion of the welfare state in the USA, for example, were strongly influenced by the group interests reinforced through the legacies of previous policies and through political discourse whose terms were in part established by the parameters of what was considered to be feasible and possible. Despite the focus on political institutions, policy legacies, and historical time, historical institutionalism did not neglect social power.

In general, however, the mainstream of historical institutionalist analysis has not specifically focused on sexuality or the politics of the LGBT policies such as same-sex marriage. Nonetheless, historical institutionalist analysis offers powerful tools for understanding policy outcomes in this, as in other areas, and acts as an antidote to analysis that sees the discussion of gay marriage as another form of morality politics, along with abortion and prayer in the schools. In contrast, however, same-sex marriage, like abortion and the role of religion in public life, is not just a question of morality or public opinion. Political outcomes vary over time, and there is no one to one relationship between public opinion and policy outcomes on same-sex marriage. If same-sex marriage is framed as a question of morality or a question of identity (or even national identity), then our task is to ask why it is framed this way, and not to simply take the frame as the independent variable that explains all. The danger with taking ideas too seriously as an approach to LGBT rights is that the discussion quickly transforms into one that focuses on loose ideas of political culture rather than tighter discussions of the role of framing and discourse. In the literature on comparative analysis of LGBT public policies, political culture and religiosity are often cited as important factors shaping the debate. Some scholars see "gay rights" as one of a number of issues that fall into the category of morality politics—that is, policies on which the public has different moral beliefs and values (Engeli et al. 2013). I strongly reject this approach, as it creates a false dichotomy between the equality interests of LGBT people as well as intersecting groups such as people of color, people with disabilities, Indigenous peoples, and linguistic minorities, among others. It also suggests that questions of economic and social policy, which are defined as outside the frame of "morality," do not concern morals and values. Rather than analyzing same-sex marriage through a morality lens, I view same-sex marriage as subject to the same factors that might explain policy change in any other area.

Despite the weaknesses of an analysis based solely on ideas in the form of public opinion and/or religiosity as the only factors in explaining comparative outcomes on same-sex marriage, a more delimited concept of ideational power, as developed in discursive institutionalism (Béland 2009), is a useful complement to an analysis based solely on institutional factors. Like the concept of political will, recently developed in the work of Johnson and Tremblay (2016), the concept of ideational power draws attention to the decisions of political actors in making decisions that affect the course of the same-sex marriage debate. Unlike structural institutionalist analysis, which tends to see actors' strategies and decisions as shaped by delimited institutional pathways, an ideational approach permits agency for political actors in making decisions about how to frame the same-sex marriage debate. Two such examples are the decision of same-sex marriage opponents to emphasize arguments based on religious freedom, on the one hand, and the decision of same-sex marriage proponents to emphasize arguments based on marriage equality.

This analysis views such ideational power through the lens of historical institutionalism's original concept of the policy legacy—that is, the ways in which current and past policies share current policy debates, and the importance of paying attention to the ways in which policy concepts and discourse unfold over time. The concepts of religious liberty and equality that are deployed by the two sides in the US marriage debate are obviously not new in US law and politics. Political and social movement actors on both sides of the debate draw on these frames that have longstanding resonance as the legacies of previous debates over other issues such as civil rights and the welfare state. By tracing these policy debates and linking them to institutional structures and policy legacies, the analysis will move beyond a purely instrumental approach to the impact of political institutions and consider institutions in their discursive context. In doing so, the analysis will account for some of the concerns of those who argue for the importance of ideational factors in the same-sex marriage debate.

POLITICAL INSTITUTIONS IN CANADA AND THE USA

The USA and Canada are similar systems that share a common legal heritage. They are both developed capitalist societies with stable and longstanding democratic political institutions. The two are relatively similar in sociological terms, and saw the rise of second-wave feminism in the 1960s and 1970s along with the rise of the gay liberation movements in the same period. In the 1980s and onward, both countries suffered under the AIDS crisis while, at the same time, a new generation of out queer couples undertook the project of parenthood. In particular, lesbian couples established families with children and increasingly sought the legal recognition of their relationships and their parental rights, while many gay men, having lived through the experience of HIV/AIDS, recognized the importance of spousal rights following the illness or death of a partner or having watched friends and members of the community suffer from lack of spousal recognition. As a result of these sociological trends, same-sex couples filed legal cases seeking recognition of their rights as partners, spouses, and parents in both countries. It is important to note that connections between LGBT organizations and the plaintiffs in these cases are complex and that, therefore, LGBT organizations are not responsible for litigation directly, nor can they be held responsible for the fact that same-sex marriage became a goal that was pursued in both countries. Same-sex couples who filed cases seeking spousal recognition and parental rights were the drivers of the same-sex marriage issue in both countries. However, these sets of plaintiffs encountered very different institutional landscapes in the two otherwise similar countries, and these differences contributed to very different processes of legalization and recognition of same-sex marriage. Further, their claims to what came to be framed as "marriage equality" were differently situated in relation to policy legacies and the dominant framings of constitutional rights.

In the next section, I outline three main structural features of political institutions that have shaped the political process and outcome of the same-sex marriage debate in the USA and Canada: federalism, the separation of powers versus parliamentarism, and the role of courts. This is followed by a discussion of the role of ideational factors in relation to the legacies of previous policies that were encountered by LGBT movements and plaintiffs in the two countries.

Federalism

The USA and Canada are federal systems with a division of jurisdictions between the federal and subnational levels of government, set out in a written constitution and enforced by the courts. The division of jurisdiction has important effects on same-sex marriage. In the USA, in part because of the legacy of slavery, the states have jurisdiction over who can marry. However, these laws are subject to constitutional law, enforced by courts. Over time, civil rights in the US have been nationalized and federalized as state infringements of citizen rights have been struck down by the US Supreme Court. Until 1967, it was constitutional for states to prohibit interracial marriage. In the *Loving* case (1967), the US Supreme Court struck down these laws as an unconstitutional violation of the Fourteenth Amendment, which enshrines the right to equal protection of the laws. The same pattern occurred with same-sex marriage. As same-sex marriage was legalized in some of the states, beginning with Massachusetts in 2003, other states could decline to recognize those marriages, thus limiting the areas in which same-sex spouses could live as married couples. Moreover, the federal government did not have to recognize same-sex marriages in the states, meaning that the legalization of marriage in one state did not lead to the recognition of marriage in federal law. This led to a situation of legal pluralism for same-sex couples in which their union was a legal marriage in the eyes of their state, but unrecognized in federal law for purposes such as income tax or immigration. In the 2015 *Obergefell v.*

Hodges case, the Supreme Court ruled that states' refusal to recognize same-sex marriages from other states was unconstitutional and that the federal refusal to recognize same-sex marriage was also unconstitutional. The strong majority ruling recognizing the positive right of same-sex couples to legal recognition had the effect of forcing all states to recognize and implement same-sex marriage (see the discussion on *Obergefell* in Pierceson 2015).

The effect of the federal division of powers in the USA is that the LGBT movement(s) and, specifically, the marriage equality movement, focused initially on state-by-state battles, rather than on changing policy at the federal level. The lesbian and gay movement requires vast resources of organization and coordination to compete on a state-by-state playing field in order to change policies that are within the jurisdiction (Kane 2007). This has meant that US lesbian and gay organizations have required formidable financial and organizational resources in order to press legal and lobbying campaigns across the USA, state by state. Following on the initial state court decisions recognizing same-sex marriage, federal legislation was passed to ban the recognition of same-sex marriage in federal jurisdiction and to provide that states did not have to recognize the same-sex marriage laws of other states. This 1996 Defense of Marriage Act (DOMA), signed by President Bill Clinton, indicated that federal action was blocked. In any case, from a constitutional perspective, the federal government could not compel the states to recognize same-sex marriage without using other policy levers (e.g. tying federal funding to state implementation of same-sex marriage). It took a court decision to set out the legal requirement for states to establish the right to same-sex marriage because of state control over the question of who can marry.

In contrast, in Canada, as in many other countries, the jurisdictional question is very different. The federal government has control over who can marry (Hogg 2006), meaning that the question of marriage rights was entirely under the control of one government, not 50 states and the federal government as in the USA. This concentrated jurisdiction facilitated the legalization of same-sex marriage as only one government was involved; at the same time, as the example of Australia shows, the allocation of jurisdiction to one level of government can also lead to blockage rather than to change. Nonetheless, in either case, the centralization of authority over the decision means that politicians must develop a strategy for managing blame avoidance. While the government's decision may be shaped by judicial power, there is no question that the federal level of government has the jurisdiction to decide the question and LGBTQ marriage activists can direct their efforts to one level of government, rather than running state-by-state campaigns as occurred in the USA. Therefore, federalism is an important structural institutional factor that shapes the process of political debate over same-sex marriage.

Separation of Powers

The US system of government is notoriously fragmented at the center. Since the 1990s when same-sex marriage arose as a public policy issue following the decision in *Baehr v. Lewin* (1993), there have been many years of divided government. Because of the separation of powers, the executive cannot command the legislature in the US system, meaning that even if the federal government had wanted to recognize same-sex marriage, its hands were tied. In the 1990s when the first legal cases arose, Congress was dominated by Republicans, facilitating the passage of DOMA, which was then signed by President Clinton.

When President Obama decided to support same-sex marriage, he withdrew federal government opposition to plaintiffs who claimed that the federal DOMA was unconstitutional. In other words, the Justice Department and Attorney General did not oppose the plaintiffs in *Windsor* (2013), signaling to the courts that the federal government did not oppose a strike-down of the 1990s–era legislation. However, unlike the leader in a parliamentary system, the president could not institute comprehensive same-sex marriage reform, even if the federal government had possessed sole constitutional jurisdiction over the issue.

The rise of executive power in the USA may have incrementally altered this institutional balance. Under President Obama, 245 executive orders were signed and, although none of them affected same-sex marriage directly and nor could they in the wake of *Obergefell*, this shift demonstrates that the US executive can fight back against legislative gridlock and judicial power, if the political will is there. In 2014, President Obama signed a presidential order that prohibited discrimination on the basis of gender identity in the federal public service, as well as prohibiting discrimination on the basis of sexual orientation and gender identity by federal contractors (*Harvard Law Review* 2015). However, the election of Trump shows the dangers of proceeding by this route. Executive orders can be unilaterally rolled back by the next president without legislative consent.

In the Canadian case, major breakthroughs on LGBT rights issues occurred under Liberal governments, which used their parliamentary majorities to pass legislation decriminalizing homosexuality in 1969 and to institute same-sex marriage in 2005. They also passed or amended legislation to include LGBTQ people in rights protections at the federal level, such as the Canadian Human Rights Act. With regard to anti-discrimination measures and same-sex marriage, the federal government was prodded to act by court rulings; however, once decided, a determined federal government did not face obstacles from a legislative opposition. The fusion of executive and legislative powers facilitated concerted action from the center and enabled the government to implement policy change. In contrast, in the US system, the executive's authority is limited, limits that are compounded by the division of powers between the federal government and the states.

Judicial Power

One of the main questions in comparative analysis of LGBT policy issues concerns the way in which policy change occurs. Are laws changed through legislative or judicial action (Sommer et al. 2013)? What is the role of supranational norms, including supranational courts (Paternotte and Kollman 2013; Helfer and Voeten 2014)? Both the USA and Canada have strong judicial branches with the power to enforce constitutional rights that specifically include equal treatment under the law. In exploring the role of courts in blocking or facilitating same-sex marriage in the USA and Canada, the role of courts must be read in relation to the broader political institutional structures of which they are a part. As we shall see, court rulings both reflect and contribute to the framing of same-sex marriage. Therefore, it is not only a question of the impact of courts in bringing about same-sex marriage; it is also a question of the process through which courts act and the stories that courts tell about how same-sex marriage is linked to constitutional rights.

Courts in the USA are divided between federal and state, while Canada has a unified court system. In addition, states in the USA have their own state constitutions which provide levers for same-sex marriage opponents to stop same-sex marriage, as well as providing legal ammunition for same-sex marriage advocates. The first same-sex marriage cases in the USA were brought in state courts in the 1970s. At that time, the courts stated that there was no legal issue as marriage by definition took place between a man and a woman. The next round of same-sex marriage cases in state courts began in the early 1990s in Hawai'i with the *Baehr* case, which challenged Hawai'i's exclusion of same-sex couples from marriage as a violation of the state and federal constitutions. The bill of rights in Hawai'i's state constitution specifically banned discrimination on the basis of sex. These tools were not available to Canadian same-sex couples as Canadian provinces do not have standalone constitutions. While there is provincial and territorial human rights legislation in each province, there is no analogue to the state bills of rights found in state constitutions in the USA.

In the wake of the *Baehr* ruling, there was a mobilization of lawyers and LGBT rights advocates in the USA to consider its legal and political implications. At the same time, there was also a mobilization of same-sex marriage opponents to plan their next steps. Advocates focused on keeping the issue of same-sex marriage out of federal courts as it was thought that conservative courts—especially the US Supreme Court—would rule against marriage and the movement would be stuck with a precedent akin to *Bowers v. Hardwick* (1986), which had upheld the constitutionality of state sodomy laws, a precedent that was overturned much later in *Lawrence v. Texas* (2003). Same-sex marriage opponents developed a political and legal campaign that took advantage of state constitutions and state jurisdiction over marriage at the state level to pass laws and state constitutional amendments banning marriage equality, a process that allowed for the mass mobilization of same-sex marriage opponents, and a process that does not exist in most Canadian provinces. These direct democracy measures played an important role in the evolution of the same-sex marriage debate in the USA, and many of the laws and state constitutional amendments passed in the electoral cycles following *Baehr* still stood in 2015 at the time that the *Obergefell* case was heard. Therefore, state constitutions both provided fodder for equality claims while they also provided tools for same-sex marriage opponents. With a different institutional context, things would have evolved differently in the wake of *Baehr*.

The Canadian case demonstrates how differences in institutional context condition the impact of courts on public policy outcomes. The unified nature of the Canadian court system and the strong constitutional protections for equality rights in section 15 of Canada's constitutionally entrenched bill of rights (the Charter of Rights and Freedoms) meant that cases which began their lives in trial courts at the provincial level ended up in the Supreme Court of Canada, ensuring that they applied across Canada. Just as plaintiffs in the USA could draw on bills of rights at the state level in some states to make legal claims for rights recognition, so too Canadian plaintiffs drew on compelling precedents from previous legal challenges. In particular, an important previous Supreme Court of Canada case on common law relationship recognition—*M v. H* (1999)—set the stage for same-sex marriage. In *M v. H*, the Ontario Court of Appeal ruled that it was unconstitutional under the Charter to exclude same-sex couples from spousal status in provincial law. Given that the Ontario court found that it was unconstitutional to exclude same-sex couples from common law or de facto recognition, it remained to be seen if this decision would be appealed to the Supreme Court of Canada. As it was not, this Ontario decision applied across Canada, and other provinces began to change their legislation on de facto (common law) spousal status to include same-sex couples. On this basis, a number of plaintiff couples from across Canada began to challenge their exclusion from marriage and, in 2003 and 2004, courts in Quebec, British Columbia, and Ontario ruled that the exclusion of same-sex couples from marriage was unconstitutional.

In response, the Liberal government of Paul Martin declined to appeal against these rulings and designed a reference question for the Supreme Court of Canada to establish whether or not the federal government was required to change the law on marriage to permit same-sex couples to wed. The government drafted legislation to legalize same-sex marriage and then asked the Supreme Court to rule on its constitutionality in 2004. Through this means, Canada avoided appeals by same-sex couples to the Supreme Court. The concentrated power of the Westminster system provided the institutional structure for the government to act alone in making this decision. The federal government had a majority in the legislature and the opposition did not have the votes to defeat the bill even if they had been so inclined. The government could have chosen to oppose same-sex marriage by using the notwithstanding clause to pass legislation upholding the traditional definition of marriage, even in the face of court rulings in favor of same-sex marriage. However, the notwithstanding clause option was not seriously canvassed (Smith 2008).

While institutional factors facilitated the swift passage of same-sex marriage legislation in Canada and conditioned the back and forth swings of law and policy between American courts, legislatures, and, ultimately, courts again, culminating in *Obergefell v. Hodges*, the reaction of governments and legislators to court decisions also raise questions about what Johnson and Tremblay (2016) call "political will" in making decisions about same-sex marriage. Tremblay and Johnson argue that institutional factors alone cannot explain the failure of Australia to adopt same-sex marriage in comparison with Canada and that, to explain the divergence between the two countries, we must consider political will or electoral strategies of partisan political actors. While my analysis does not consider partisanship per se, the ideational turn is compatible with a focus on electoralism, as framing and defining ideas, and being able to impose ideas in terms of agenda-setting and voter preferences, are key capabilities in contemporary media-saturated elections.

Policy Legacies and Ideational Factors

The legacy of previous policies makes certain options thinkable and others unthinkable. Activist actors on both sides of the same-sex marriage debate have drawn on specific dimensions of law and social policy in seeking ideational resources for their positions on same-sex marriage. These include the idea of legal equality in US and Canadian jurisprudence, the different relationship between marriage and the welfare state in the two countries, the unique legal power of religious liberty in the USA, and the relationship between marriage and nationalism in the two cases.

The formulation of the concept of "marriage equality" was an important shift in activist framing of same-sex marriage in the USA, a deliberate antidote to the "special rights" rhetoric of gay rights' opponents. Throughout the 1980s and 1990s, anti-gay organizations had claimed that the "homosexual agenda" sought "special rights" for an already privileged minority. The framing of marriage as a question of equality for same-sex couples compared to opposite sex couples was a key discursive shift for the same-sex marriage movement in the USA. By comparing couples with couples, this shift moved away from the idea of the LGBT communities as a minority group, which could be easily turned into a "special interests" group.

The framing of "marriage equality" also drew its ideational strength from the legacies of previous policies as well as from the legal framing of rights. Marriage laws exist within a matrix of preexisting policies, institutions, and discourse, which are somewhat different between the two countries. In Canada, cohabiting unmarried couples have a wide range of rights and obligations; by the 1990s, litigation and legislation had greatly reduced the legal differential between married and unmarried cohabiting couples. In some US states, the legal status of marriage entails much more extensive benefits and obligations than simply living together. As the law changed in Canada, same-sex couples came to enjoy the same status as opposite-sex couples who were living together but not married. While these changes began in the USA as well, obtaining parity with opposite-sex couples did not afford the same level of rights and obligations as did the Canadian change, due to the lesser status of common law relationships under the laws of many US states.

Moreover, marriage fits into the broader structure of social policy in each case. In the USA, prior to the passage of the Affordable Care Act in 2010, public health care played a limited role through Medicare and Medicaid. Employer-based health care benefits were critically important and legal marriage afforded a route to those benefits. In contrast, in Canada, the public health care system reduces the role of employer-provided benefits. In both cases, however, employer-based health care provides benefits to couples, not solely to individuals. This is a policy choice. In other countries, full state benefits are provided based on individual citizenship, not civil status. This same point applies to many other areas of public policy. For example, in some US states, unmarried couples are not subject to laws on domestic violence. Only married couples may claim enhanced protections in state penal codes for spousal abuse. In a nutshell, obtaining a right of legal marriage is more important for American same-sex couples in many states than it is for Canadian same-sex couples because of the privileged place of marriage in US social policy. This strengthens the hand of claimants for "marriage equality," who can point to concrete material benefits that are denied to same-sex couples specifically because of their lack of access to legal marriage (on the relationship between same-sex marriage and care, see Wilson 2014).

The centrality of marriage in US social policy is reflected in the racialization of debates over marriage (Kandaswamy 2008), a debate that is not present in the same form in Canada. Debates over marriage and family in the USA uphold the idea that the protection of these institutions is centrally important to social stability. Social conservatives in the USA have deliberately mobilized to shift opinion and framing on social issues over the last 40 years. The rise of the conservative legal academy (Teles 2010) and the professionalization of anti-queer nongovernmental organizations (NGOs) have had important impacts on the debate over same-sex marriage. This policy discourse has positioned marriage as an institution of stability, one that is emerging as highly racialized and classed in the USA. This might seem to reinforce the homonationalist claims of marriage equality advocates who seem to link the recognition of gay marriage to conservative values on family stability and statements that "we're just like you," while marginalizing queer voices and voices of people of color. Moreover, the structure of marriage laws in the USA is a legacy of slavery. The role of the states in recognizing or not recognizing marriage, and in refusing to recognize marriages from other states, has its historical parallel in anti-miscegenation laws which were left to the control of the states, in part to ensure white control of southern states. Even in the contemporary period, social conservatives in the USA can call upon the legacy of states' rights as a racially encoded discourse that can be deployed against queer rights. Recent social movement organizing in the US such as Black Lives Matter, which was co-founded by queer-identified women, indicate the linkages that are currently made in US social movement politics among queer people of color (Black Lives Matter 2015).

Social conservative activists in the USA have deliberately drawn on distinctive US legal doctrines on religious freedom to push against same-sex marriage. The critically important US Supreme Court ruling in *Burwell v. Hobby Lobby* (2014) is the culmination of a long legal and political campaign to secure religious exemptions for corporations. In finding in favor of the craft store chain Hobby Lobby in the case, the Supreme Court opened the door to private sector discrimination against same-sex couples wanting to marry in cases, for example, in which such businesses refuse to provide accommodation and services for same-sex weddings. In contrast, in Canada, analogous questions have been raised about the right of government employees to refuse to perform same-sex ceremonies. To date, Canadian courts have denied marriage commissioners in the provinces the right to refuse performing such a ceremony (e.g. *Marriage Commissioners* 2011) and the implementation and institutionalization of same-sex marriage has proceeded smoothly. While, in the USA, government employee objections to performing same-sex marriages have made news headlines, the impact of the Supreme Court's decision in *Obergefell* make such actions ultimately unconstitutional, and implementation of same-sex marriage has occurred through the USA in the wake of the decision (Pinello 2016). Nonetheless, beyond the role of states in issuing marriage licenses and changing federal law to recognize same-sex married couples, the role of private companies in accommodating same-sex couples remains controversial. While these debates have occurred in other countries, the idea that private companies have religious liberty rights is unique to US debates. The strength of this legal and constitutional argument in US courts cannot be understood without reference to the broader framing of race, gender, and class in US politics.

The drive for religious liberty is an expansion of racialized backlash against civil rights, the perceived expansion of the welfare state, and structural shifts in gender roles as women's labor force participation increased. Social conservatives have expanded the scope of religious liberty to the private sector to roll back reproductive rights as well as same-sex rights. In this way, social conservatives have succeeded in imposing particular ideas of religious liberty as legal doctrine which, in turn, influences policy debates over same-sex marriage and other LGBT civil rights issues, such as passing a federal legislative prohibition against employment discrimination on the basis of sexual orientation and gender identity. Therefore, in order to understand the same-sex marriage debate in the USA, it is important to consider how the issue is placed in relation to the social conservative universe.

In contrast, in Canada, the recognition of same-sex marriage is linked to nationalism in both English-speaking Canada and in Quebec (Stychin 1998). In turn, nationalism has been linked to Charter rights to equality, of which LGBT people have been the emblematic symbol. Judicial empowerment led to rapid change in Canadian laws on marriage from above, thus obviating the need for sustained political battles and well-resourced LGBT NGOs. Canadian LGBT groups are much weaker than US organizations, especially at the pan-Canadian level. Because of the link between the Charter of Rights and Freedoms, which is viewed as linked to Canadian nationalism, it is difficult for same-sex marriage opponents to find ideational resources to deploy against same-sex marriage. Similarly, Quebecers have long considered themselves to be more progressive on social matters than English-speaking Canada, and the early passage of human rights legislation that protects gays and lesbians from discrimination is often taken as an indicator of Quebec's front-runner status on gay rights. Therefore, whether Canadian nationalism or Quebec nationalism, same-sex marriage is tied to both political projects, providing powerful ideational resources for same-sex marriage advocates. While there is strong religious objection to same-sex rights in Canada, it has not taken the legal form of expanding religious rights for the private sector. The Canadian Civil Marriage Act (2005) specifically recognizes the right of religious organizations not to perform same-sex marriages, but otherwise obliges the legal recognition of such relationships.

Social movement activists in the marriage equality movement in Canada and the USA have exploited the political opportunities provided by institutional openings such as the centralization of power in the Canadian system, the role of empowered courts, and the political and legal constructions of civil rights (USA) and human rights (Canada). In doing so, they have drawn on the available discursive toolkit formed by past policies and cultural resources. In Canada, both Quebec and Canadian nationalisms have played a key role in relation to queer rights while, in the USA, same-sex marriage advocates have faced framings of the issue of marriage that are anchored in the politics of racial backlash against the welfare state and its alleged role in undermining the family. These framings in the USA reflect the impact of social conservative activism as well as the impact of policy legacies. In contrast, social movement activists in Canada and Quebec have framed their demands for marriage equality in terms that vaunt the tolerant nature of citizens (e.g. Quebec) or the importance of shared Canadian citizenship through the Charter (Canada). In both cases, claims for marriage equality are linked to progressive nationalism, while, in the USA, they have been shaped in reaction to the politics of racial backlash.

Conclusion

Historical institutionalism offers a powerful lens on policy change, not only in relation to the welfare state and social policy, the traditional topics of historical institutionalist scholarship, but also with regard to LGBT policies such as same-sex marriage. The approach sheds light on the ways in which policies change over time or the "how" of policy debates, as well as on policy outcomes at a given point in time. Looking to the future under the Trump presidency, the executive orders issued by President Obama in areas such as LGBT employment discrimination could easily be reversed and religious exemptions could be widened, negatively affecting LGBT rights. An institutional analysis calls our attention to the importance of the binding nature of the Supreme Court decision in *Obergefell*, while a consideration of the intersection of federalism and LGBT rights shows the ways in which the privileges enjoyed by same-sex married couples in the USA today could be incrementally eroded through federal or state actions to limit the access of same-sex couples (even married couples) to benefits. While all this could be litigated by same-sex marriage advocates, it would mean another round of political struggle to ensure the full maintenance of same-sex marriage in the USA.

Despite the importance of institutional factors, they are not the only ones at play in explaining the comparative politics of same-sex marriage. Ideational and discursive factors can play a role in the explanation, especially in the most recent incarnation of discursive institutionalism that highlights the link between ideas and political power (Carstensen and Schmidt 2016). The agency of political actors, including politicians and social movement activists, as emphasized in the work of Johnson and Tremblay (2016) as well as Jordi Díez (2015), complement an approach based solely on the structural power of institutions. Historical and discursive institutionalisms offer a superior approach to understanding the comparative politics of the LGBT social movements and public policy, especially when compared with a broad political cultural approach that labels entire societies as "conservative" or "liberal" or to a public opinion approach, which defines policy failure and success in these "morality policy" areas as pure questions of "opinion" or "moral conscience." Public opinion and moral conscience are shaped by structural factors and through political struggles. In this sense, historical and discursive institutionalism offer much potential for future scholarship on LGBT politics in general and same-sex marriage in particular.

References

Legal Cases

Baehr v. Lewin, 74 Haw. 645, 852 P.2d 44 (1993).
Bowers v. Hardwick 478 US 186 (1986).
Burwell v. Hobby Lobby, 573 U.S. ___ (2014).
Lawrence v. Texas, 539 U.S. 558 (2003).
Loving v. Virginia, 388 US 1 (1967).
M v. H [1999] S. C. J. No. 23.
Marriage Commissioners Appointed Under The Marriage Act (Re), 2011 SKCA 3 (CanLII).
Obergefell v. Hodges 576 U.S. ___ (2015).
United States v. Windsor, 570 U.S. ___ (2013).

Other Sources

Béland, Daniel. 2009. Ideas, Institutions, and Policy Change. *Journal of European Public Policy* 16 (5): 701–718.
Black Lives Matter. 2015. Herstory. http://blacklivesmatter.com/herstory/. Accessed 15 January 2017.

Carstensen, Martin B., and Vivien A. Schmidt. 2016. Power Through, Over and in Ideas: Conceptualizing Ideational Power in Discursive Institutionalism. *Journal of European Public Policy* 23 (3): 318–337.

Díez, Jordi. 2015. *The Politics of Gay Marriage in Latin America: Argentina, Chile, and Mexico.* Cambridge: Cambridge University Press.

Engeli, Isabelle, Christoffer Green-Pedersen, and Lars Thorup Larsen. 2013. The Puzzle of Permissiveness: Understanding Policy Processes Concerning Morality Issues. *Journal of European Public Policy* 20 (3): 335–352.

Editors of the Harvard Law Review. 2015. Recent Executive Order. *Harvard Law Review* 1304–1311.

Helfer, Laurence R., and Erik Voeten. 2014. International Courts as Agents of Legal Change: Evidence from LGBT Rights in Europe. *International Organization* 68 (1): 77–110.

Hogg, Peter W. 2006. Canada: The Constitution and Same-Sex Marriage. *International Journal of Constitutional Law* 4 (3): 712–721.

Johnson, Carol, and Manon Tremblay. 2016. Comparing Same-Sex Marriage in Australia and Canada: Institutions and Political Will. *Government and Opposition* 1–28. doi:10.1017/gov.2016.36.

Kandaswamy, Priya. 2008. State Austerity and the Racial Politics of Same-Sex Marriage in the US. *Sexualities* 11 (6): 706–725.

Kane, Malinda. 2007. Timing Matters: Shifts in the Causal Determinants of Sodomy Law Decriminalization, 1961–1998. *Social Problems* 54 (2): 211–239.

Kollman, Kelly. 2009. European Institutions, Transnational Networks and National Same-Sex Unions Policy: When Soft Law Hits Harder. *Contemporary Politics* 15 (1): 37–53.

Paternotte, David, and Kelly Kollman. 2013. Regulating Intimate Relationships in the European Polity: Same-Sex Unions and Policy Convergence. *Social Politics* 20 (4): 510–533.

Pierceson, Jason. 2015. From Kameny to Kennedy: The Road to the Positive Rights Protection of Marriage Equality in Obergefell v. Hodges. *Politics, Groups, and Identities* 3 (4): 703–710.

Pierson, Paul. 2004. *Politics in Time: History, Institutions, and Social Analysis.* Princeton: Princeton University Press.

Pierson, Paul, and Theda Skocpol. 2002. Historical Institutionalism in Contemporary Political Science. In *Political Science: The State of the Discipline*, ed. Ira Katznelson and Helen Milner, 693–721. New York: Norton.

Pinello, Daniel R. 2016. *America's War on Same-Sex Couples and Their Families: And How the Courts Rescued Them.* New York: Cambridge University Press.

Smith, Miriam. 2008. *Political Institutions and Lesbian and Gay Rights in the United States and Canada.* New York: Routledge.

Sommer, Udi, Victor Asal, Katie Zuber, and Jonathan Parent. 2013. Institutional Paths to Policy Change: Judicial versus Nonjudicial Repeal of Sodomy Laws. *Law & Society Review* 47 (2): 409–439.

Stychin, Carl F. 1998. *A Nation by Rights: National Cultures, Sexual Identity Politics, and the Discourse of Rights*. Philadelphia: Temple University Press.

Teles, Steven M. 2010. *The Rise of the Conservative Legal Movement: The Battle for Control of the Law*. Princeton: Princeton University Press.

Wilson, Angelia R. 2014. *Why Europe Is Lesbian and Gay Friendly*. Albany: State University of New York Press.

Miriam Smith is a professor in the Department of Social Science, York University, Canada. She has published widely on lesbian, gay, bisexual, and transgender (LGBT) politics and policy in Canada and the USA. Among other works, she is the author of *Political Institutions and Lesbian and Gay Rights in the United States and Canada* (2008).

CHAPTER 5

Understanding Same-Sex Marriage Debates in Malawi and South Africa

Ashley Currier and Julie Moreau

Introduction

Taking a discursive institutionalist approach, we explore the connection between dominant discourses of same-sex sexuality and institutional outcomes around same-sex marriage in Malawi and South Africa. We compare two different country cases to understand regional variation in same-sex marriage policy and the interaction of discourses about same-sex marriage and social and political institutions. Beginning in the mid-2000s, politicians in Malawi began politicizing and maligning same-sex sexualities, whereas in South Africa, lawmakers, at the behest of the judiciary, investigated legalizing same-sex marriage. Most Malawian political elites regard same-sex marriage negatively, but many South African political elites and activists favorably view same-sex marriage as a right in this post-apartheid nation.

"Discursive anxiety" around same-sex marriage in Malawi conflated same-sex marriage with any lesbian, gay, bisexual, transgender, and intersex (LGBTI) rights campaign and ultimately resulted in the 2015 passage of the Marriage, Divorce, and Family Relations Act, which defines marriage as

---

A. Currier (✉)
University of Cincinnati, Cincinnati, OH, USA

J. Moreau
University of Toronto, Toronto, Canada

© The Author(s) 2018
B. Winter et al. (eds.), *Global Perspectives on Same-Sex Marriage*, Global Queer Politics, https://doi.org/10.1007/978-3-319-62764-9_5

involving one cisgender man and one cisgender woman (Chiumia 2015). A feature of "homosexuality-is-un-African" discourse (Currier 2012, 121–122), "discursive anxiety" about same-sex marriage refers to how elite constructions and interpretations of same-sex sexualities escalate quickly into collective apprehension that same-sex marriage will overwhelm social, political, and religious institutions and displace heteronormative marriage practices. Homophobic discourses that conflated the decriminalization of sodomy with same-sex marriage and marked same-sex sexuality as a threat to national wellbeing generated a negative institutional outcome, which makes the passage of same-sex marriage law unlikely in the near future.

In the South African case, LGBTI activists strategically amplified a discourse that framed marriage in terms of human rights to satisfy Constitutional Court judges of its importance in building South Africa's nascent democracy. "Homosexuality-is-un-African" discourse also played a significant role in the same-sex marriage debate, and the marriage campaign provoked a similar anxiety. As such, though the law was passed, this discourse shaped the policy adoption process and is evident in the legislation itself, which contains a religious exemption. Further, the predominance of a rights-based discourse came at the cost of suppressing intramovement discourses that critiqued rights and marriage from queer and feminist standpoints.

Our comparison of these two cases highlights the interaction between competing discourses and preexisting institutional configurations. In both cases, homophobic discourses dominated public discussion of same-sex marriage and sexualities. However, in Malawi, social and political institutions, including the media, the president, political parties, and some nongovernmental organizations (NGOs), deployed homophobic discourses to deter activists from mobilizing for LGBTI rights and same-sex marriage. Political elites portrayed same-sex marriage as an unwanted foreign intrusion. Malawian social and political elites created a context in which same-sex marriage became impossible to imagine. In the South African context, human rights discourse "won" because it resonated with a judicial branch, granted relatively significant authority in the postapartheid era, to achieve a policy outcome. Framed in terms of human rights, the realization of a "rainbow nation" became impossible to imagine without equal access to marriage. By illuminating this interaction between discourse and institutions, we call attention to "the role of discourse in generating and legitimizing ideas about political action" related to same-sex marriage and sexualities (Freidenvall and Krook 2011, 43). Additionally, we consider the role institutions play in same-sex marriage law and policy.

Discursive Institutionalism and Same-Sex Marriage

Currently, there are at least four strands of new institutionalism: historical, rational choice, sociological, and discursive (Chappell and Waylen 2013; Hall and Taylor 1996). While each strain provides a lens for understanding institutional creation, change, and persistence, we adopt a discursive institutionalist approach to understanding variation in same-sex marriage policy in Malawi and South Africa. Discursive institutionalism (DI) is useful for our analysis because it (1) highlights contests of legitimacy in politics; (2) considers institutional context; and (3) accommodates multiple levels of analysis for producing political outcomes.

A DI approach thus allows us to focus on the process by which ideas become legitimate or illegitimate (Schmidt 2010). Discourse "is not just ideas or 'text' (what is said) but also context (where, when, how, and why it was said)" and "refers not only to structure (what is said, or where and how) but also to agency (who said what to whom)" (Schmidt 2008, 305). DI examines the "interactive processes of discourse through which ideas are generated and communicated to the public" (Mackay et al. 2010, 575). The DI approach is compatible with perspectives that treat political institutions not as "monolithic," but as a "number of institutional areas or spaces" (Krook and Mackay 2011, 3). Institutions both constrain and enable "constructs of meaning" (Schmidt 2010, 4), and any discussion of discourse and institutional change must be embedded in the broader institutional context. This is vital for comparative work aimed at understanding variation in institutional change and political outcomes.

Finally, the DI approach is useful for examining same-sex marriage across African contexts because it can accommodate analysis of both domestic and transnational levels of analysis (Mackay et al. 2010). Considering discourse allows us to account for variation in the adoption and reception of same-sex marriage law and policy and to recognize the influence of transnational discourses about same-sex sexualities on a variety of domestic institutional configurations. For instance, recent research that builds on new institutionalist theory establishes the importance of "exogenous" factors influencing cross-national variation in laws governing sex (Frank and Moss 2017, 941). Such exogenous factors affecting laws governing sex include laws inherited from former European colonial powers and the presence of international NGOs that introduce new legal templates in different countries. These exogenous factors feature prominently in discourses of politicized homophobia, which are anchored in "homosexuality-is-un-African" logics

(Currier 2012, 121–122). "Politicized homophobia" refers to public hostility toward same-sex sexualities, gender variance, and gender and sexual diversity activism. Emphasizing the foreignness of same-sex sexualities, some African political elites use politicized homophobia to bolster their authority, to impugn political opponents, and/or to deflect attention away from political controversies (Currier 2010; McKay and Angotti 2016).

Debates about same-sex marriage and sexualities in southern Africa constitute an interesting subject for a DI investigation, given the presence of homophobic discourses and vibrant LGBTI organizing in the region (Currier 2012, 2014; Moreau 2017; Msibi 2011). In particular, homophobic discourses in Malawi and South Africa about same-sex marriage highlight what Joseph Massad (2002, 374), borrowing from Michel Foucault (1978, 17–35), calls the "incitement to discourse." We understand the "incitement to [homophobic] discourse" in southern Africa as stemming from political elites' worries that westerners were introducing same-sex sexual practices, including same-sex marriage, into African cultural and political repertoires, which threatened to displace African heteronormative traditions. In response to the perceived foreign encroachment of same-sex marriage, some governments may repress same-sex sexualities, although authorities may not have previously enforced colonial-era prohibitions against same-sex sexual practices (Massad 2002). Many postcolonial African governments left colonial anti-sodomy laws intact (Frank and Moss 2017). We treat discursive anxiety concerning same-sex marriage and state institutional prohibition of same-sex marriage in Malawi and ambivalent reception and state embrace of same-sex marriage in South Africa as emblematic of the "politicization of sexuality" in contemporary African societies that are still contending with the aftermath of colonialism and/or apartheid rule (Posel 2005, 127).

Methodology

To trace negative discourses about same-sex marriage and sexualities in Malawi, we draw on analyses of 1921 articles from Malawian newspapers from 1995 to 2016 that mention homosexuality or homophobia. Our goal in analyzing newspaper articles is to identify how, when, and why same-sex marriage and sexualities entered political discourse in Malawi and to classify different meanings that have become associated with same-sex marriage and sexualities. We augment these analyses with interviews

Currier conducted in the summer of 2012 with feminist, HIV/AIDS, human rights, and LGBTI rights activists in Malawi about how politicized homophobia affected their organizing.

The South African LGBTI movement has produced a significant amount of primary documentation and secondary scholarship. The data presented here come from secondary sources and interviews with six activists from different organizations, many of whom participated in the same-sex marriage campaign. Moreau conducted interviews in and around Cape Town, Johannesburg, and Durban over 11 months, from May 2011 to May 2012. She recruited activists with long histories in the movement, who had participated in many organizations, to gain a comprehensive picture of the history of LGBTI organizing and the contemporary social movement field. The main purpose of Moreau's research was to understand how lesbian organizations were articulating citizenship demands at the local, national, and transnational level; she interrogated the nature of social movements and the law more broadly and asked questions about the passage and reception of same-sex marriage in South Africa. Where deemed appropriate, we assign Malawian and South African interview subjects pseudonyms to protect their anonymity.

Discursive Anxiety About Same-Sex Marriage in Malawi

As same-sex sexualities slowly entered the political vernacular in Malawi in the 2000s, political, religious, and traditional leaders began assuming that the growing public visibility of same-sex sexualities would ultimately result in demands for the legalization of same-sex marriage in the near future. In the early 2000s, same-sex sex concerned police and prison officials as a criminal offense, but most journalists, politicians, and citizens ignored same-sex sexualities. Sporadic news coverage treated gender and sexual diversity as oddities, aberrant practices to be deplored, or acts to be ignored. Exogenous factors in the form of western LGBTI movements pushing for same-sex marriage partly influenced Malawian political elites, who began construing same-sex marriage as a foreign threat to cultural and political institutions. Such assumptions overlook the fact that lawmakers would have to decriminalize same-sex sex before taking up the issue of marriage equality. Elites perceived discussions about same-sex sexualities and LGBTI rights as ultimately culminating in demands for marriage equality even when no Malawian group had publicly made this request. When elites failed to distinguish between different forms of same-sex sexualities and activist claims for LGBTI rights and presumed that debates or demands about same-sex sexualities were only about same-sex marriage, they created discursive anxiety about same-sex marriage.

In Malawi, discursive anxiety about same-sex marriage was a feature of politicized homophobia. First, political elites and ordinary Malawians conflated efforts to decriminalize same-sex sex with nonexistent campaigns to legalize same-sex marriage in the country. The assumption that LGBTI rights activists who were mobilizing to decriminalize same-sex sex were instead secretly trying to legalize same-sex marriage, which political elites construed as a foreign practice, increased collective anxiety about same-sex sexualities. Second, political elites exploited social concerns about same-sex marriage to repress efforts by different social movements to challenge President Bingu wa Mutharika's authoritarian rule. Political elites alleged that large-scale protests in July 2011 were not about demanding that the government provide basic necessities to Malawians and respect the rule of law and human rights but were about legalizing same-sex marriage.

Journalistic accounts of same-sex sexualities in Malawi have long conflated gay rights and the decriminalization of same-sex sex with same-sex marriage. A 2000 news article presented evidence of same-sex relationships in Malawi and approached different civil society leaders for comment. Shyley Kondowe, the executive director of the Malawi Institute for Democratic and Economic Affairs, speculated that same-sex relationships might become legal under the "marriage by repute" statute, which recognized common-law relationships (Kamlomo 2000, 2). In this embryonic phase of public discussion about same-sex sexualities, some NGO leaders were willing to contemplate the possible legality of same-sex marriage. Discourses about same-sex sexualities were malleable and open to both negative and positive meanings, a finding that is consistent with other research on politicized homophobia.

Catalyzing events can reshape discourses governing gender and sexual politics (Plummer 2004). Malawian political elites and journalists may have treated gay rights and the decriminalization of same-sex sex as same-sex marriage because conflicts over LGBTI rights and same-sex marriage within the Anglican Church saturated Malawian Anglican leaders' perceptions of same-sex sexualities. Beginning in the late 1990s, African Anglican leaders started objecting to same-sex sexualities, most notably at the 1998 Anglican Conference of World Bishops (Hassett 2007, 71–101; Hoad 2007, 48–67).

Political elites and journalists perceived discussions about same-sex sexualities and LGBTI rights as culminating in demands for marriage equality even when no group publicly issued this assertion. This treatment lumped gay rights and the decriminalization of sodomy together with same-sex marriage.

Civil society and political leaders began conflating nascent LGBTI rights organizing in Malawi with marriage equality in 2004 when the Malawi Human Rights Resource Centre (MHRRC) asked lawmakers to consider decriminalizing same-sex sex and enshrining a sexual-orientation nondiscrimination clause in the Constitution. Many NGO leaders distanced themselves from MHRRC's request. Warning Malawians about the possible influence of US marriage-equality activism on MHRRC, Reverend Ian Longwe, the director of the Forum for Peace and Reconciliation, asserted that Malawi "should be on alert with [sic] the gay community who declared war on [the] USA" (Namangale 2005, 4). According to Longwe, when gay rights militancy surfaced in the country, ordinary Malawians would have to defend local cultural practices from foreign influence. As MHRRC asked lawmakers to guarantee constitutional protections for sexual minorities, political elites translated this request into efforts to legalize same-sex marriage, which citizens and lawmakers in the US and European nations were debating in 2004 and 2005 (Badgett 2009; see also Phiri 2004). Like Longwe, Idriss Ali Nassah imagined that nascent LGBTI organizing in Malawi would inevitably seek to "marry man-to-man, woman-to-woman" (Nassah 2005, 4).

However, these objectors never considered the necessary initial steps involved, in particular repealing anti-sodomy laws that barred legal recognition of (male) same-sex relationships. In 2005, a group named the Lesbian and Gay Movement of Malawi (LGMM) petitioned lawmakers to rescind anti-sodomy statutes (Khunga 2005). Their call to "legalise homosexuality" is a case of how political elites rushed to conflate the decriminalization of same-sex sex with the legalization of same-sex marriage (Khunga 2005, 3). Whereas LGMM mentioned no interest in legalizing same-sex marriage, the group's demand for the rescission of anti-sodomy laws coincided with the marriage-equality lawsuit that the South African Constitutional Court was hearing. Malawian political elites were primed to interpret requests for legalizing same-sex sex as demands for marriage equality, as decriminalizing same-sex sex would legalize same-sex relationships. They assumed that legal same-sex relationships amounted to legal same-sex marriages. Subsequent coverage of responses to LGMM's request also conflated decriminalizing same-sex sex with legalizing same-sex marriage. Andrina Mchiela, Principal Secretary for the Ministry of Gender, Child Welfare, and Community Services, assigned marriage a heteronormative, reproductive-oriented mandate: "Marriage is to 'perpetuate offspring'" (Mapondera 2005, 24). Alongside journalists and pundits (Kanyinji 2006), Christian and Muslim leaders also conflated legalized same-sex sex with legalized same-sex marriage (Banda 2005; Batolo 2005).

Anxiety about the potential legality of same-sex marriage motivated anti-gay vitriol and prompted some political elites to suggest revisiting marriage law. In the mid-2000s, some political elites expressed consternation about the possibility that activists could exploit existing marriage laws to permit same-sex marriage. Mandala Mambulasa (2007, 13), a lawyer, admitted that although laws "at the moment do not recognise the concept of same sex marriages," the Constitution did not unequivocally "state the kind of marriage that the constitutional fathers envisaged" as being "homosexual or heterosexual unions. It is therefore arguable that in its current state, our Constitution does not prohibit same sex marriages or partnerships." At a 2006 conference dealing with constitutional reform, Mchiela exhorted lawmakers to revise the Constitution and "define 'family' and 'marriage' to remove the ambiguities brought by its lack of definition as a marriage could also stand for same sex marriage" (Nyangulu 2006, 5). The legal ambiguity afforded by loosely defined concepts like "marriage" contributed to the discursive anxiety that the conflation of decriminalizing same-sex sex with legalizing same-sex marriage created.

The 2010 trial of Tiwonge Chimbalanga, a transgender woman, and Steven Monjeza, a cisgender man, for violating the anti-sodomy law concentrated political attention on same-sex marriage (Biruk 2014). Police arrested the couple after they held a public engagement ceremony celebrating their relationship (Somanje 2009). Police interpreted the engagement ceremony as confirmation that Chimbalanga and Monjeza had consummated their relationship, which police construed as a same-sex relationship. Throughout the trial, political elites deployed politicized homophobia to promote heteronormative nationalism, to attack the credibility of LGBTI rights activists who came to the aid of Chimbalanga and Monjeza, and to deplore sexual minorities' aspirations to marry. Some pundits argued that the couple only staged a public engagement ceremony "for money," an example of the argument that same-sex sexualities fueled economic prosperity. Steven Nhlane (2010, 15) stated that it was possible that someone ... promised them huge amounts of money to test the waters [on the legality of homosexuality]. He or she must have convinced them that after the Chinkhoswe [engagement ceremony], they would be arrested, prosecuted, convicted, and sentenced. They would serve jail. Finish the sentence. Come out of prison and find their largesse. Then live happily ever after—after properly [getting] married, of course.

Nhlane (2010, 15) concluded that Chimbalanga and Monjeza must have been "crazy" as "no sane person living a normal life would stoop so low even if lured by whatever amount of money as to pretend to be gay, risk arrest and prosecution and conviction and imprisonment." This commentary popularized toxic ideas about same-sex marriage and sexualities.

Despite national and international objection to their prosecution (Chipalasa 2010; Muwamba 2010), the court convicted the couple, and the presiding judge sentenced them to 14 years in prison with hard labor, the harshest penalty permitted under the law. When delivering his sentence, Chief Resident Magistrate Nyakwawa Usiwa Usiwa exploited political hostility toward same-sex marriage and sexualities. Invoking the "national readiness" argument that Malawians were unprepared for same-sex sexualities to become legal and commonplace in society, Usiwa Usiwa claimed that Malawian "society" was not "ready ... to see its sons getting married to other sons or conducting engagement ceremonies" or "its daughters marry each other" (Nkhoma-Somba 2010, 1). He intended the harsh penalty as a "scaring sentence" so that others would not practice same-sex sex (Nkhoma-Somba 2010, 1). Ultimately, Mutharika pardoned the couple after receiving pressure from United Nations Secretary-General Ban Ki-moon to vacate their sentences (Khunga 2010).

After the trial, Mutharika's government continued to use politicized homophobia to buttress and consolidate political authority. State leaders used politicized homophobia to repress different social movements that demanded that Mutharika address his undemocratic governance, shortages of petrol, foreign currency, and medicine, and lack of respect for human rights and the rule of law. In May 2011, representatives of the Council for Non-Governmental Organisations advised Mutharika not to use same-sex sexualities "to divert attention from real issues affecting the country" (Munthali 2011b, 2). This warning came as NGOs planned nationwide protests, dubbed the July 20 protests (Cammack 2012). In the run-up to the protests, Mutharika attacked sexual minorities and their defenders. At a political party rally, he ranted, "You will never see dogs marry each other. These people [sexual minorities] want us to behave worse than dogs. I cannot allow it" (Munthali 2011a, 2). At a June 2011 event celebrating the elevation of chiefs, Mutharika reproached NGO leaders for "selling the country by getting money to champion foreign cultures" and practices like same-sex sexualities (Nyirongo 2011, 4). Mutharika deplored LGBTI rights as an aid conditionality, stating, "Yes, we rely on donors but what is happening is like giving a beggar more money than he or she usually gets and spit[ting] on him or her. Sometimes it is fair to tell them to take their money so that we keep our culture" (Nyirongo 2011, 4). Commenting on Mutharika's use of politicized homophobia, a journalist observed, "Government spin doctors have recently intensified the campaign to isolate NGO leaders that want government to remove laws that make same-sex relationships illegal" (Nyirongo 2011, 4).

To deter Malawians from joining the July 20 protests, government officials portrayed them as trying to legalize same-sex marriage. This tactic was consistent with other government ploys to discredit NGOs that supported LGBTI rights as trying to legalize same-sex marriage. Jackson, a former employee of the Centre for the Development of People (CEDEP), a leading LGBTI rights NGO, noted that the media helped stoke opposition to organizations' defense of LGBTI rights. Malawian journalists reported that "NGOs were advocating for gay marriages" (Jackson, interview with Ashley Currier, July 4, 2012, Blantyre, Malawi). Senior Chief Kaomba, an influential traditional leader, claimed that July 20 protest organizers wanted "Malawi to allow men [to] marry fellow men that is why they are marching" (Chimgwede 2011). Despite government efforts to use politicized homophobia to discourage the July 20 protests, activists and ordinary people took to the streets in protest. Police used violence to disperse and punish protestors; police repression resulted in the deaths of 19 protestors and bystanders and gunshot injuries to 58 others (Cammack 2012).

Until his unexpected death in April 2012, Malawian President Bingu wa Mutharika portrayed same-sex marriage and sexualities as endangering the Malawian government and society. After Vice-President Joyce Banda, the leader of the People's Party (PP), became president, she named laws criminalizing same-sex as "bad laws" in need of legislative review and repeal in her first "State of the Nation" address in May 2012 (Mponda 2012). LGBTI rights activists welcomed her announcement. For instance, Gift Trapence, CEDEP's executive director, wanted lawmakers to overturn these laws, but he rejected the "politicisation" of same-sex sexualities

(Mizere 2012, 2). One outcome of politicized homophobia involved "how the issue of decriminalisation of anti-homosexuality laws is mistaken for legalisation of gay marriages" (Mizere 2012, 2). Trapence clarified that decriminalizing same-sex sex would not summarily legalize same-sex marriage because the "Marriage Act ... recognizes marriage as being between a man and a woman" (Mizere 2012, 2). In addition, Trapence explained, there are many "different steps to be taken to reach the level of recognising gay marriages. What is important is not to discriminate against someone based on sexual orientation. This is the issue of equality and that's what we are talking about on the need to repeal the sodomy laws" (Mizere 2012, 2). Trapence's statement constituted a much-needed reminder that decriminalizing same-sex sex did not automatically legalize same-sex marriage.

Despite Trapence's distinction between decriminalizing same-sex sex and legalizing same-sex marriage, Banda conflated the two actions, much like anti-gay opponents did. Soon after her "State of the Nation" speech, Banda succumbed to pressure from political elites who objected to decriminalizing same-sex sex and declared that she would not ask lawmakers to pursue this law reform (Mmana and Singini 2012). One columnist portrayed Banda as "dancing an undanceable dance. She is damned if she repeals anti-gay laws and damned if she doesn't" (Chipiri 2012, 7). Justifying her changed position, Banda stated:

> [A]s a president I do not make laws. The bill about same sex marriages has not gone to parliament; it is yet to be discussed even at cabinet level. Even if it were tabled for debate, I will not force MPs to pass it. If the people of Malawi do not want same sex marriages MPs will not pass the law. (Kasakura 2012, 2)

Admitting her office's limitations, Banda submitted to the will of anti-gay opponents. Her equation of the decriminalization of same-sex sex with the legalization of same-sex marriage gave credence to widespread misperceptions that decriminalization would grant same-sex couples the right to marry. Ralph Kasambara, a former attorney general, worked to dispel Banda's conflation of the decriminalization of same-sex sex with same-sex marriage. In an interview the day after Banda's confusing comments, he stated, "The issue is not about allowing or not allowing same-sex marriages ... we have not yet started talking or debating same-sex marriages in Malawi, but we are discussing minority rights of lesbians and gays" (Sharra 2012, 4).

Anti-same-sex marriage discourses culminated in 2015 with the passage of the Marriage, Divorce, and Family Relations Act, which defines marriage as involving one cisgender man and one cisgender woman (Chiumia 2015). Although feminist and child rights activists praise the Act for raising the minimum age for boys and girls to marry to 18 years, the Act prohibits same-sex marriage and forbids transgender people, particularly those who have undergone gender-confirming surgery, from "marrying a person, prior to that sex-changing surgery [who] was of the same sex [as] them" (Payton 2015). Lawmakers took preemptive action to prevent marriage equality, even though no activist group emerged to demand access to same-sex marriage. Same-sex marriage continues to incite anti-gay opposition in Malawi. In December 2016, Christian and Muslim leaders staged protests in major cities against abortion and same-sex marriage (Michael 2016).

SAME-SEX MARRIAGE AND HUMAN RIGHTS DISCOURSE IN SOUTH AFRICA

In 2006, South Africa became the first and only country on the continent to adopt national legislation recognizing same-sex marriage. Despite the persuasiveness of human rights discourse in newly democratic South Africa, gay rights framed as human rights produced discursive anxiety around same-sex marriage. This anxiety stifled alternative discursive constructions of same-sex relations that did not involve human rights, including feminist and broader social justice framings. As a result, we argue that the discourses that surfaced in the debate around marriage—and those that did not surface—played a significant role in shaping the institutional process of same-sex marriage adoption and the LGBTI movement itself. As in Malawi, LGBTI rights were embedded in broader human rights discourses. However, in contrast to Malawi, rather than an autocratic regime using the imbrication of gay rights and same-sex marriage to discredit a larger human rights movement, in South Africa, activists took advantage of the government's amenability to human rights to achieve their desired policy outcome.

The petition for marriage of a lesbian couple, Marie Adriaana Fourie and Cecelia Johanna Bonthuys, arrived at the Constitutional Court in May 2005. The Equality Project, an NGO based in Johannesburg, along with other NGOs and several same-sex couples, launched an application seeking to change marriage law as well (Judge et al. 2008, 2). In December of that year, Justice Albie Sachs delivered a judgment in the *Fourie* case, finding existing marriage law in violation of the Constitution. In an unusual move, the court sent the issue back to parliament; justices asked lawmakers to draft a new marriage law, giving them one year to complete this task, or the court would change section 30(1) of the existing Marriage Act to replace the Act's gender-specific language with the gender-neutral "spouse" (Judge et al. 2008, 3). After a first draft of the law created only civil unions for same-sex couples and kept marriages for opposite-sex couples, lawmakers faced allegations that they were not acting in the spirit of the court's ruling. Lawmakers amended the bill to allow same-sex couples access to marriage. The bill also created civil unions for both same-sex and opposite-sex couples. The bill passed in the National Assembly with a vote of 230 to 41 (Thoreson 2008, 682).

The strength of the judiciary in South Africa made it an appealing institutional focal point for LGBTI activists. Patrick Heller (2009, 129) describes the South African judiciary as "highly autonomous" and argues that it has "played a proactive role in supporting the constitution (in particular its social rights clauses)." Given its importance, it is no surprise that Edwin Cameron, now a justice, devised a litigation strategy for achieving a host of LGBTI rights—a veritable "shopping list"—and brought it to the attention of the National Coalition for Gay and Lesbian Equality (NCGLE) in 1994 (Berger 2008, 18). Guided by the shopping list, the NCGLE pursued a strategy that mobilized discourses of rights to target the relatively strong and amendable judiciary.

Prior to the marriage campaign, activists from the NCGLE mobilized a human rights discourse to persuade the drafters of the Constitution to include a clause to prohibit discrimination on the basis of sexual orientation (Cock 2003). This relatively small group of well-organized activists continued to capitalize on dominant discourses of human rights and democracy in the postapartheid era to persuade the Court that denying same-sex couple access to marriage violated the Constitution. Sheila Croucher (2002, 324) argues that to understand the South African LGBTI movement, one must account not only for the role of formal institutions but also the "extremely influential ... symbolic, discursive or ideational realm." Conservative organizations in the minority wanted to ensure their continued influence in the postapartheid period and invested in "protecting minority rights" (Croucher 2002, 324). Croucher (2002, 324) contends that activists mobilized human rights to "galvanise gays and lesbians and to legitimate their demands in the eyes of politicians and society as a whole," and that "the struggle for gay and lesbian rights cannot be separated from the struggle for freedom for all South Africans." The post-apartheid state's discursive commitment to human rights led to and was institutionalized in the LGBTI movement's legal victories (Cock 2003).

LGBTI activists succeeded in arguing for the same-sex marriage law, despite a counter discourse that blended religion, tradition, and anti-colonialism to assert that "homosexuality is un-African" (Croucher 2002; Currier 2012; Hoad 2007). In this discourse, homosexuality and lesbian and gay identities are threatening to traditional culture, national culture (Currier 2012), and Christianity (Hoad 2007). Despite the importance of prior legal victories to the movement, same-sex marriage was the first to garner such a degree of public attention. "[T]he same-sex marriage debate became far broader than the question of whether same-sex couples should have the right to marry: it went to the heart of beliefs about and attitudes to gender, sexuality, power, democracy, religion, culture and the like" (Judge et al. 2008, 5). The previous success of the LGBTI movement in embedding anti-discrimination in the Constitution created the sense that the transition to democratic governance jeopardized religion and traditional culture. In this way, the appearance of same-sex marriage for judicial consideration provoked discursive anxiety about homosexuality.

Discursive anxiety around same-sex marriage and the tension between discourses of rights and discourses of religion and tradition became apparent in the 2005 hearings of the National House of Traditional Leaders (NHTL) in six provinces (Reid 2010). The public hearings were designed to provide a forum for the public to express opinions regarding proposed same-sex marriage legislation (Reid 2010). The main objection to same-sex marriage, expressed at all six provinces visited, was "the non-procreative nature of same-sex coupling" (Reid 2010, 40). Graeme Reid (2010, 43) argues that the apparent overnight emergence of gay people seemed to "coincide with the dawn of democracy" and to be "inextricably tied with human rights" that were understood to undermine religion, culture, and tradition. The hearings revealed two competing discourses around what marriage was and the appropriate relation of LGBTI people to it: the religious/cultural discourse that "homosexuality is un-African" and a human rights discourse.

Several activists spoke about the prevalence of the religious and cultural discourse and how it shaped the marriage campaign and the resultant legislation. In response, Sharon Ludwig from the Capetonian Triangle Project explained her desire to give a "voice" to the Christian LGBTI community. She said,

> I think it's important to have a voice … otherwise the religious right dominates. That's the reason why I became involved in the same-sex marriage case and was part of the [campaign and application to the Court for the right to marry] … And did it, not because I wanted to get married … because I didn't. I did it only because I knew I was a Christian voice … So, you know, when the community or society were given opportunities to engage with this in town halls and whatever, you knew what you were up against … Every single person who spoke out against it came from a perspective of religion. And Cape Town is predominantly Islamic and Christian fundamentalism. And it's the reason that I did invest energy in that. (Interview with Julie Moreau, February 22, 2012, Cape Town, South Africa)

Ludwig details her motivation to participate in the marriage campaign: the opportunity to supply an LGBTI Christian voice to the debate over marriage. Her perspective complicates and challenges the fundamentalist discourses that insist that homosexuality is antithetical to marriage.

Despite Ludwig's and other activists' presence at the public forums, the adoption of same-sex marriage cannot be attributed to a public victory of human rights discourse over religious discourse. Andile (pseudonym), from the Lesbian and Gay Equality Project, questioned the manner in which rights and religion were pitted against each other in the meetings:

> I remember attending some public hearings. And those public hearings, they did depress me a lot … The way they were conducted because then parliament created a space where homophobes could be homophobic freely and openly … We are always the minority and we had to follow the meetings. But then parliament would say, "We already heard you." (Interview with Julie Moreau, March 5, 2012, Johannesburg, South Africa)

Rather than creating a space for the free exchange of ideas, the public hearings were dominated by what Andile calls "homophobic" speech, and LGBTI voices remained in the minority.

The influence of cultural and religious discourses is also evident in the resultant legislation. The Civil Union Act did not repeal the Marriage Act of 1961, which only permits marriage between opposite-sex couples (Judge et al. 2008). South Africa therefore has two marriage laws: an older one that affords both civil and religious marriage only to opposite-sex couples and the Civil Union Act, through which same-sex and opposite-sex couples can access civil marriage (de Vos 2008). While the new Act is progressive in addressing gender inequities present in the older law, many object to the Civil Union Act because the LGBTI movement failed to eliminate the older, more gender inequitable and exclusively heterosexual marriage law. One institutional legacy of the same-sex marriage campaign is thus the double institution of marriage and civil union. Elise (pseudonym), of the Cape Town Lesbians, said,

> It's kind of "separate but equal" ... I think the only reason I'd get married is for legal purposes, you know, so my partner and I can buy things as a couple, you know, and be married in community of property or not in community of property ... and for like, adopting children ... But I think because I'm gay and I can't get married in the church that I grew up in, I don't see it as the religious kind of ceremony. (Interview with Julie Moreau, July 7, 2011, Cape Town, South Africa)

Elise's denomination has not applied to be allowed to officiate weddings under the Civil Union Act, though they are allowed under the Marriage Act. Despite the law's passage and Elise's access to the institution of marriage, her inability to get married in a religious ceremony diminishes the significance of the legislation. Elise's comments reveal that the discourses of rights and religion were not reconciled during the marriage campaign, but rather their distinctness was institutionalized in the Civil Union Act itself, along with the persistence of the Marriage Act.

Finally, as evidence of the power of religious discourses of marriage, government officials can refuse to perform marriages between same-sex couples on moral grounds, which may mean that certain couples may not be able to get married in rural areas with limited governmental staff. Section 13(2) of the law excludes civil unions from recognition under the Customary Marriage Act, meaning that same-sex couples cannot obtain customary marriages. This was likely the result of vocal opposition to same-sex marriages by the NHTL and Congress of Traditional Leaders of South Africa (Mkhize 2008). This separation of customary marriage law and civil marriage law (and the lack of will on the part of LGBTI activists to ensure their reconciliation) evinces the hierarchy of legal systems in South Africa, which has consistently subjugated customary law. In this way, the legal privileging of civil law instantiated a western model of marriage and sexual identity that obscures South Africa's own historical and cultural models of kinship relations that could potentially be "more liberatory" (Bonthuys 2008, 172). The relative privilege granted to civil law in this case also produces and imposes westernized sexual identity categories.

Thuli Madi, former director of the Johannesburg organization Behind the Mask, raised this issue. "We've got this legislation that organises same-sex relationships," she said, "and I don't know, people have actually packaged themselves in boxes and I don't feel it's necessary. It's good, maybe initially it was, but no, not now" (Interview with Julie Moreau, March 5, 2012, Johannesburg, South Africa). Madi considers that the use of westernized identity categories by the movement may have helped with the passage of the law but worries that the cost of this choice unnecessarily places limits on South Africans' sexual subjectivities. Despite the "success" of human rights discourse in convincing the judicial branch of the constitutional basis of same-sex marriage, human rights carried with it the baggage of western identity categories.

The discourses that circulated around marriage also influenced the movement itself. The movement was not single-minded with respect to same-sex marriage; many different opinions existed on the issue but did not make their way into the public (Currier 2012, 96). Many activists took issue with how marriage as an institution reproduced heteronormative gender roles (Hames 2008). Yet, despite the existence of this critique, there was little queer/feminist discourse on marriage during the campaign. Carrie Shelver, from People Opposing Women Abuse, said:

> Out of all the things that we [the LGBTI movement] did, that's probably the thing I hated the most. I think this is really just my own view. I think one of the things that you do, when you ascribe to a human rights framework ... is that you start saying things like: "We're all just the same. And we're the same as you and we want the same things as you. Let's all just slip back into mainstream." So I think the marriage thing for me is very much part of that. Yes, I understand the socioeconomic dimensions of marriage ... and I understand that so many people did want that... [but] the people who were at the forefront of that marriage campaign ... if you speak to most of them most of them will say they don't agree with marriage ... So I think a far stronger critique should have been made of marriage, rather than looking for inclusion. We should have been critiquing the institution of marriage, which I don't think we did. (Interview with Julie Moreau, March 7, 2012, Johannesburg, South Africa)

Shelver's comments denounce the absence of a critical discourse on marriage during the campaign. She specifically pointed out the homogenizing effects of the human rights discourse of marriage. Though activists had personal reservations, they did not make these public enough to cohere into an intramovement dissenting discourse. For Shelver, there was "an absence of feminism within that area of work," reflected in the movement's discourse on marriage.

While the movement for same-sex marriage was successful in terms of policy, it did not generate a discourse capable of adequately addressing South Africa's complex socioeconomic inequality, of which sexual inequities are only one element. Social justice activist Zackie Achmat, whose leadership in the NCGLE in the 1990s was integral to their judicial strategy (Berger 2008), reflected on the development of the LGBTI movement. He lamented a lack of mainstream queer leadership able to advance an intersectional discourse to address questions of hate and violence:

> The question that we all have to ask is not whether the marriage campaign was the right one. The question we have to ask is: What happened between the coalition and now? Why do we have this ... widespread hate? Not widespread, but we have very serious hate problems. Why is it that we don't have a really strong clearly identifiable queer leadership that is also active in the huge problems of the country? The worst people that are going to be treated are immigrants and refugees, race crimes at schools where public schools are integrated ... But queer people don't think like that. Rather, professional queer people don't think like that. They think: "Let me go and deal with hate crimes against queers." (Interview with Julie Moreau, February 28, 2012, Cape Town, South Africa)

"Professional queers" focus narrowly on hate crime, unable to advance a discursive strategy that addresses South Africa's complex situation of racialized inequality. For example, activists have grappled with how to conceptualize sexual assaults against lesbians. Activists have attempted to visibilize the homophobic nature of these assaults with the term "corrective rape," referring to stated motivation of some attackers to "correct" the sexuality of those they assault (Muholi 2004). Using this terminology, activists have demanded that the South African state protect lesbians' human rights (One in Nine Campaign 2013). However, working within the discourse of human rights has separated discussions of anti-lesbian rape from broader discussions of misogyny and socioeconomic injustice (One in Nine Campaign 2013). According to the One in Nine Campaign (2013, 3):

> [t]he human rights paradigm—focusing on participatory rather than socioeconomic and distributive aspects of democracy and on legal remedies for

socio-economic problems—requires every problem to be articulated as a rights claim; an exclusively legalistic view of self-determination and agency necessarily trades in the discourse of victimisation and entitlement, a discourse that is unable to address structural causes of inequality and violence and which effectively disables alliance building and the formulation of multi-issue politics.

As a result, the mainstream LGBTI movement has not succeeded in framing violence against lesbians effectively. Regardless of the policy outcome of same-sex marriage, then, a discourse did not emerge from the movement capable of changing the social landscape on questions of violence and socioeconomic inequality.

In sum, the discourses that surfaced in the debate around marriage and those that did not shaped both the process and outcome of the same-sex marriage debate. Rights discourses triumphed in formal institutions, though popular discourses of tradition and culture emerged in the marriage debate and influenced the legislation itself. Despite the LGBT movement's policy success, the discourses that did not emerge are evident in lingering intramovement schisms.

Conclusion

We employed a DI approach to understand variation in the adoption of same-sex marriage in southern Africa. What lessons can we draw from comparison between Malawi and South Africa for the rest of the continent? Based on these two cases, we argue that the interaction between competing discourses and preexisting institutional configurations is integral for understanding the fate of same-sex marriage policy in each country. In both cases, homophobic discourses dominated public discussion of same-sex sexuality. However, in Malawi, homophobic discourses could be coopted by media, the president, political parties, and NGOs. In the South African context, human rights discourse triumphed because it resonated with the powerful judicial branch to achieve a policy outcome. Discursive framings of same-sex sexuality have a significant impact on what policy outcomes are possible.

Further, we introduced the concept of "discursive anxiety" to understand how apprehensions around same-sex sexuality can become embedded in political discourse to provide them with legitimacy and may be mobilized in service of homophobic policy outcomes. Given the resurgence of right-wing populism transnationally, alongside the strengthening of norms around LGBTI rights, we expect our framework to continue to provide insight into variation in marriage policy globally. Based on fieldwork in other countries in Africa and the Americas, we suspect that preemptive anxiety around same-sex marriage and the suppression of feminist and queer critiques of marriage are broader phenomena that merit further comparative analyses.

References

Badgett, M., and V. Lee. 2009. *When Gay People Get Married: What Happens When Societies Legalize Same-Sex Marriage*. New York: New York University Press.

Banda, Keith. 2005. Same-Sex Marriages Unbiblical. *Sunday Times*, December 11: 7.

Batolo, Taonga. 2005. Clergy Say Big 'No' to Homosexuality. *Sunday Times*, December 11: 5.

Berger, Jonathan. 2008. Getting to the Constitional Court on Time. In *To Have and to Hold: The Making of Same-Sex Marriage in South Africa*, ed. Melanie Judge, Anthony Manion, and Shaun de Waal, 17–28. Auckland Park, South Africa: Fanele.

Biruk, Crystal. 2014. 'Aid for Gays': The Moral and the Material in 'African Homophobia' in Post-2009 Malawi. *Journal of Modern African Studies* 52 (3): 447–473.

Bonthuys, Elsje. 2008. Civil Union Act: More of the Same. In *To Have and to Hold: The Making of Same-Sex Marriage in South Africa*, ed. Melanie Judge, Anthony Manion, and Shaun de Waal, 171–192. Auckland Park, South Africa: Fanele.

Cammack, Diana. 2012. Malawi in Crisis, 2011–12. *Review of African Political Economy* 39 (132): 375–388.

Chappell, Louise, and Georgina Waylen. 2013. Gender and the Hidden Life of Institutions. *Public Administration* 91 (3): 599–615.

Chimgwede, Wisdom. 2011. The Only July 20, 2011. *Zodiak Online*, July 18. http://www.zodiakmalawi.com/index.php?option=comcontent&view=article&id=1118:the-only-july-20-2011

Chipalasa, Mike. 2010. Norway Comments on Gay Arrest. *Daily Times*, March 8: 3.

Chipiri, Chipiri wa. 2012. Criticism of JB's Stance on Gay Rights Unfair. *Malawi News*, May–26 June 1: 7.

Chiumia, Thom. 2015. Malawi Marriage Bill Spurns Same-Sex Liaisons. *Nyasa Times*, February 17. http://www.nyasatimes.com/malawi-marriage-bill-spurn-same-sex-liasons/

Cock, Jacklyn. 2003. Engendering Gay and Lesbian Rights: The Equality Clause in the South African Constitution. *Women's Studies International Forum* 26 (1): 35–45.

Croucher, Sheila. 2002. South Africa's Democratisation and the Politics of Gay Liberation. *Journal of Southern African Studies* 28 (2): 315–330.

Currier, Ashley. 2010. Political Homophobia in Postcolonial Namibia. *Gender & Society* 24 (1): 110–129.

———. 2012. *Out in Africa: LGBT Organizing in Namibia and South Africa.* Minneapolis: University of Minnesota Press.

———. 2014. Arrested Solidarity: Obstacles to Intermovement Support for LGBT Rights in Malawi. *Women's Studies Quarterly* 42 (3–4): 142–159.

de Vos, Pierre. 2008. Difference and Belonging: The Constitutional Court and the Adoption of the Civil Union Act. In *To Have and to Hold: The Making of Same-Sex Marriage in South Africa*, ed. Melanie Judge, Anthony Manion, and Shaun de Waal, 29–41. Auckland Park, South Africa: Fanele.

Foucault, Michel. 1978. *The History of Sexuality, Volume 1: An Introduction.* Translated by Robert Hurley. New York: Vintage.

Frank, David John, and Dana M. Moss. 2017. Cross-national and Longitudinal Variations in the Criminal Regulation of Sex, 1965 to 2005. *Social Forces* 95 (3): 941–969.

Freidenvall, Lenita, and Mona Lena Krook. 2011. Discursive Strategies for Institutional Reform: Gender Quotas in Sweden and France. In *Gender, Politics, and Institutions: Towards a Feminist Institutionalism*, ed. Mona Lena Krook and Fiona Mackay, 42–57. New York: Palgrave Macmillan.

Hall, Peter A., and Rosemary C.R. Taylor. 1996. Political Science and the New Institutionalisms. *Political Studies* 44 (5): 936–957.

Hassett, Miranda K. 2007. *Anglican Communion in Crisis: How Episcopal Dissidents and Their African Allies Are Reshaping Anglicanism.* Princeton, NJ: Princeton University Press.

Hames, Mary. 2008. Lesbians and the Civil Union Act: A Critical Reflection. In *To Have and to Hold: The Making of Same-Sex Marriage in South Africa*, ed. Melanie Judge, Anthony Manion, and Shaun de Waal, 258–267. Auckland Park, South Africa: Fanele.

Heller, Patrick. 2009. Democratic Deepening in India and South Africa. *Journal of Asian and African Studies* 44 (1): 123–149.

Hoad, Neville. 2007. *African Intimacies: Race, Homosexuality, and Globalization.* Minneapolis: University of Minnesota Press.

Judge, Melanie, Anthony Manion, and Shaun de Waal. 2008. Introduction. In *To Have and to Hold: The Making of Same-Sex Marriage in South Africa*, ed. Melanie Judge, Anthony Manion, and Shaun de Waal, 1–14. Auckland Park, South Africa: Fanele.

Kamlomo, Gabriel. 2000. Gays, Lesbians Surface in Malawi. *Daily Times*, August 24: 2.
Kanyinji, Jeffrey. 2006. Big No to Homosexuality. *Daily Times*, January 1: 15.
Kasakura, Archibald. 2012. JB Won't Push MPs on Same Sex Law. *Malawi News*, May 26–June 1: 2.
Khunga, Suzgo. 2005. Legalise Homosexuality, Parliament Asked. *Sunday Times*, November 20: 3.
———. 2010. Gay Couple Pardoned. *Sunday Times*, May 30: 1, 3.
Krook, Mona Lena, and Fiona Mackay. 2011. Introduction: Gender, Politics, and Institutions. In *Gender, Politics, and Institutions: Towards a Feminist Institutionalism*, ed. Mona Lena Krook and Fiona Mackay, 1–20. New York: Palgrave Macmillan.
Mackay, Fiona, Meryl Kenny, and Louise Chappell. 2010. New Institutionalism through a Gender Lens: Towards a Feminist Institutionalism? *International Political Science Review* 31 (5): 573–588.
Mambulasa, Mandala. 2007. Should the Law Legalise Homosexuality? No, It's against Ordinances. *Daily Times*, February 4: 13.
Mapondera, Godfrey. 2005. Any Malawians Who Are Gays? *Sunday Times*, November 27: 24.
Massad, Joseph. 2002. Re-orienting Desire: The Gay International and the Arab World. *Public Culture* 14 (2): 361–385.
McKay, Tara, and Nicole Angotti. 2016. Ready Rhetorics: Political Homophobia and Activist Discourses in Malawi, Nigeria, and Uganda. *Qualitative Sociology* 39 (4): 397–420.
Michael, Dibi Ike. 2016. Malawians Demonstrate against Abortion, Same Sex Marriage. *Africa News*, December 7. http://www.africanews.com/2016/12/07/malawians-demonstrate-against-abortion-same-sex-marriage/
Mizere, Agnes. 2012. Review Anti-gay Laws. *Daily Times*, September 5: 2.
Mkhize, Nonhlanhla. 2008. (Not) in My Culture: Thoughts on Same-Sex Marriage and African Practices. In *To Have and to Hold: The Making of Same-Sex Marriage in South Africa*, ed. Melanie Judge, Anthony Manion, and Shaun de Waal, 97–106. Cape Town, South Africa: CPT Book Printers.
Mmana, Deogratias, and George Singini. 2012. Clerics Query Same Sex Laws. *Nation*, May 22: 3.
Moreau, Julie. 2017. 'Homophobia Hurts': Mourning as Resistance to Violence in South Africa. *Journal of Lesbian Studies* 21 (2): 204–218.
Mponda, Felix. 2012. Blues Will Eat Humble Pie. *Daily Times*, May 20. http://bnltimes.com/index.php/sunday-times/headlines/columns/326-letter-from-the-warm-heart-/6501-blues-will-eat-humble-pie
Msibi, Thabo. 2011. The Lies We Have Been Told: On (Homo)Sexuality in Africa. *Africa Today* 58 (1): 55–77.

Muholi, Zanele. 2004. Thinking Through Lesbian Rape. *Agenda* 18 (61): 116–125.
Munthali, Kondwani. 2011a. Gays Worse Than Dogs—Bingu. *Nation*, May 16: 2.
———. 2011b. Slow Down Mr. President—NGOs. *Nation*, May 6: 2.
Muwamba, Emmanuel. 2010. African NGOs Want Gay Suspects Released. *Nation*, February 1: 2.
Namangale, Frank. 2005. Churches, NGO Slum Homosexuality Proposal. *Daily Times*, February 3: 4.
Nassah, Idriss Ali. 2005. Things Stranger than Fiction. *Sunday Times*, November 20: 4.
Nhlane, Steven. 2010. Chileka 'Lovebirds' Are Sick. *Malawi News*, January 2–8: 15.
Nkhoma-Somba, Wezzie. 2010. Gays Get 14 Years. *Daily Times*, May 21: 1, 3.
Nyangulu, Deborah. 2006. The Constitutional Review Conference Unmasked. *Daily Times*, April 5: 5.
Nyirongo, Edwin. 2011. NGOs Selling Malawi for Money—Bingu. *Nation*, June 8: 4.
One in Nine Campaign. 2013. Introduction. In *What's in a Name? Language, Identity, and the Politics of Resistance*, 1–7. Johannesburg, South Africa: One in Nine Campaign.
Payton, Naith. 2015. Malawi's New Anti-LGBT Law Comes into Effect. *Pink News*, April 17. http://www.pinknews.co.uk/2015/04/17/malawi-anti-lgbt-law-signed-in/
Phiri, D. D. 2004. Human Rights and Morality. *Nation*, March 30: 8.
Plummer, Ken. 2004. The Sexual Spectacle: Making a Public Culture of Sexual Problems. In *Handbook of Social Problems: A Comparative International Perspective*, ed. George Ritzer, 521–541. Thousand Oaks, CA: Sage.
Posel, Deborah. 2005. Sex, Death, and the Fate of the Nation: Reflections on the Politicization of Sexuality in Post-apartheid South Africa. *Africa: Journal of the International African Institute* 75 (2): 125–153.
Reid, Graeme. 2010. The Canary of the Constitution: Same-Sex Equality in the Public Sphere. *Social Dynamics: A Journal of African Studies* 36 (1): 38–51.
Schmidt, Vivien A. 2008. Discursive Institutionalism: The Explanatory Power of Ideas and Discourse. *Annual Review of Political Science* 11: 303–326.
———. 2010. Taking Ideas and Discourse Seriously: Explaining Change through Discursive Institutionalism as the Fourth 'New Institutionalism'. *European Political Science Review* 2 (1): 1–25.
Sharra, Albert. 2012. We Have Not Yet Started Talking Same-Sex Marriages. *Weekend Nation*, June 2: 4.
Somanje, Caroline. 2009. Blantyre Gay Couple Arrested. *Nation*, December 29: 2.

Thoreson, Ryan Richard. 2008. Somewhere over the Rainbow Nation: Gay, Lesbian and Bisexual Activism in South Africa. *Journal of Southern African Studies* 34: 679–697.

Ashley Currier is an associate professor of women's, gender, and sexuality studies at the University of Cincinnati, USA. She is the author of *Out in Africa: LGBT Organizing in Namibia and South Africa* (2012). She is working on a book manuscript about the politicization of homosexuality in Malawi and another project examining mobilization around marriage equality in Kentucky (USA).

Julie Moreau is an assistant professor in the Department of Political Science and the Mark S. Bonham Centre for Sexual Diversity Studies at the University of Toronto, Canada. Her research interests include transnational queer studies, social movements, and citizenship. She is currently working on a book manuscript that explores the concept of queer citizenship and the construction of collective sexual identities in contexts of legal equality and another project that examines the diffusion of same-sex marriage norms in Latin America.

CHAPTER 6

Same-Sex Marriage in France and Spain: Comparing Resistance in a Centralized Secular Republic and the Dynamics of Change in a "Quasi-Federal" Constitutional Monarchy

Réjane Sénac

INTRODUCTION

By passing legislation giving same-sex couples the right to marry in 2005 (Law 13/2005 of July 1), Spain became the third country in the world—after the Netherlands (2001) and Belgium (2003)—to grant equal marriage rights at national level, regardless of sexual orientation. This was one of the groundbreaking policies that were putting Spain in the international spotlight, building what Ségolène Royal, the socialist candidate in the 2007 French presidential election, called the "Spanish model of equality"

I would like to thank Maxime Forest for his guidance and support as regards the Spanish case, particularly in connection with his participation in the Quality in Gender + Equality Policies (QUING) project, as well as Bronwyn Winter for her always meaningful advice.

R. Sénac (✉)
Centre de recherches politiques de Sciences Po, CNRS - Sciences Po, PRESAGE, Paris, France

made up of parity government, equality laws, and same-sex marriage (Cué, *El Pais,* June 17, 2016, 30) versus the longstanding "Scandinavian equality model" (Platero Mendez 2007, 37). The Spanish socialist government (Partido Socialista Obrero Español, PSOE) (2004–2011) was thus defined as a model to follow in terms of gender equality policies by the French socialist government (Parti Socialiste, PS) formed in 2012. The French government used Spanish gender equality policies as an inspiration, in particular as regards the Spanish framework law against gender violence (Organic Act 1/2004), the same-sex marriage law (Law 13/2005), and the law on effective equality between women and men (Constitutional Act 3/2007).

With the law of May 17, 2013, France became only the fourteenth country in the world to authorize same-sex marriage. Unlike in Spain, political and social opposition to the French law was huge, with mass demonstrations and a record number of amendments (the highest in 30 years). "La Manif pour tous" (Demonstration for all) is the main nongovernmental organization (NGO) coalition coordinating the (largely Catholic) opposition to the same-sex marriage law, known as Mariage pour tous (Marriage for all). "La Manif pour tous" has organized demonstrations or petitions unifying several hundred thousand people, or even millions if one adds demonstrations in Paris and the French provinces, since November 2012. These demonstrations—apart from those following the January 7, 2015 terrorist attacks—were the largest since 1984 when Catholic movements demonstrated in defense of private education. Indeed, opposition to same-sex marriage is linked with the mobilization of the Roman Catholic Church to defend "natural" gender differences (Rochefort 2014). The coalition against same-sex marriage promotes the "traditional family" against the alleged danger of psychological, social, and political chaos embodied, for them, by same-sex parenting (adoption, medically assisted procreation, parenting by surrogacy). It also rejects the questioning of gender roles, denouncing in particular an experiment called ABCD de l'égalité (ABCD of equality), set up as a pilot program with 600 primary school classes at the beginning of the 2013/2014 school year. The French opposition to these legislative developments in the name of the defense of the "traditional family" is revealing of the centrality of heteronormativity in its social and political order.

Comparison with reception of the Spanish law helps understand the singularity of both the Spanish and French cases. Even if the scale of the Spanish opposition was smaller than in France, ratification of the Spanish law was not exempt from conflict and confrontations, as evidenced by the demonstrations for and against and a court challenge by the opposition. The public protest on June 19, 2005 led by the right-wing party (PP) members, Spanish bishops, and the Spanish Family Forum (Foro Español de la Familia) rallied 1.5 million people for the protesters and 166,000 for the Government Delegation in Madrid. Two weeks later, the Spanish Lesbian, Gay, and Transgender Organization (Federación Estatal de Lesbianas, Gays, Transexuales, y Bisexuales, FELGT) estimated that two million people marched on Gay Pride Day in favor of the new law; police sources counted 97,000. The battle also took place on the legal terrain. In 2005, two judges, one from the city of Dénia (on July 21, 2005) and the other from Gran Canaria (in August 2005), refused to issue same-sex marriage licenses and filed a challenge against the same-sex marriage law before the Constitutional Court, based on Article 32 of the Constitution, which contains the phrase "Men and women have the right to contract marriage with full juridical equality." In December 2005, the Constitutional Court rejected both challenges on procedural grounds, because the judges did not have the appropriate standing to file them. This decision was confirmed on November 6, 2012, seven years after the September 30, 2005 separate constitutional challenge by the opposition party PP. Following the 2012 Constitutional Court decision to uphold the same-sex marriage law, with eight support votes and three against, the then PP government announced, through its Minister of Justice, that it would abide by the ruling and the law would not be repealed. The importance of respecting the law was also asserted by the King, Juan Carlos. When the media asked him, during the 2005 debate in the Cortes Generales (Spanish legislature), if he would sign the same-sex marriage law, he answered that he was the King of Spain, not of Belgium—a reference to King Baudouin of Belgium, devout Catholic, who refused in 1990 to sign the Belgian law legalizing abortion in the name of a "severe issue of conscience" ("grave problème de conscience"). The King encountered criticism by Carlist and other far right conservatives for signing the legislation on July 1, 2005.

This chapter, then, addresses the paradox of why France—a secular Republic—was so slow to grant same-sex marriage rights, while Spain—a "quasi-federal" constitutional monarchy—did so without delay. It will do this by comparing the institutional context in both countries.

The literature sheds light on the relationship between international influences (Paternotte and Kollman 2013; Ayoub and Paternotte 2014) and the importance of path dependency (Calvo 2007; Tremblay et al. 2011) in the national implementation of same-sex union laws.

In France, a longstanding Republic, the vote on the same-sex marriage law did not take place until 2013, more than two centuries after the Revolution (Lépinard 2007; Rosanvallon 2011) and 70 years after the end of the authoritarian Vichy regime, while in Spain such legislation was passed just 30 years after General Francisco Franco's death in November 1975. The Spanish case is characterized by the pace of the first reforms over a short period of time, from the beginning of the political transition at the end of the 1970s until 1986, when Spain joined the European Economic Community (today the EU) (Frotiée 2006; Frotiée and Rodriguez Garcia 2012). For the young Spanish democracy, the challenge was not only to build a democratic political system, based on the idea of reconciliation and consensus, but also to leave behind traditions, habits, mentalities, and inherited political culture from the former regime. In the French case, the longevity and centralism of the French Republic led the French socialist government to introduce same-sex marriage as the expression of continuity, in particular with regard to the principles of equality and secularism.

In order to test the hypothesis of a contrast between an assumed rupture with the political legacy for Spanish democracy and an attachment of the French Republic to an idealized inheritance, I will conduct an analysis of public discourse, in particular parliamentary debate. For the Spanish case, I use the findings of two projects funded by the European Commission—Policy Frames and Implementation Problems: the Case of Gender Mainstreaming (MAGEEQ), dealing with homosexual rights in Spain during the period 1995–2004, and Quality in Gender + Equality Policy (QUING)[1]—to analyze what they called "intimate citizenship," in particular the combination of policies on non-discrimination against lesbian, gay, bisexual, transgender, and intersex (LGBTQI) individuals and equal rights for same-sex couples, between 2006 and 2011.

I will begin with an analysis of the way in which the French law on same-sex marriage was presented as completing the historical evolution of marriage as a republican institution embodying equality and secularization, while the Spanish law was seen as a historic and political break with the past and the sign of a move toward modernity and democracy, as it came about 30 years after the early times of transition. I will next highlight the way in which controversies surrounding these laws address the role of the State with regard to the implementation of equality in a reformist (and not a transformative) approach for both Spain and France. I will then look at whether these laws can be described as an ambivalent reform, lying somewhere between revolution and compromise.

French and Spanish Sexual Rights in Context

A number of markers contextualize the French and Spanish debates surrounding the legalization of civil marriage and adoption for same-sex couples.

Although the French Revolution decriminalized homosexuality in 1791, the Vichy regime (Nazi-collaborationist regime ruled by Maréchal Pétain between 1940 and 1944) established a difference between the ages of sexual majority for homosexuals and heterosexuals in 1942. This discriminating legislation was in force until Article 331–2 of the penal code was repealed in 1982. Thus, in France, it is only since 1982 that a homosexual relationship with a person between 15 and 18 years of age is no longer considered an offence. Since 1985, discrimination in the workplace and in recruitment has become subject to penal sanctions. Finally, homosexuality was removed from the World Health Organization's list of mental illnesses only eight years later, in 1990. France became the first country in the world to declassify transsexualism as a mental illness through a 2010 Decree. This regulatory act from the Prime Minister (not stemming from a parliamentary vote) officially disqualified transsexualism as a psychiatric illness. In France as in Spain, the development of State Feminism (Mc Bride and Mazur 2012) toward the end of the 1970s and the beginning of the 1980s was a crucial time. France set up the first Secretariat of State for the Status of Women in 1974 and the first fully fledged Ministry for Women's Rights with Yvette Roudy's appointment in 1981.

In Spain, civil rights and women's and LGBTQI rights have undergone a large-scale transformation with key events like the democratization of the Spanish State and the Constitution of 1978. "Democracy brought about the beginning of formal equality; removing vestiges of discriminatory legislation, assuming new shapes inspired by a reflective incipient feminist movement which emerged clandestinely and flourished in the seventies and eighties as well as facilitating the legalization of left-wing political parties and the freedom of association (Larumbe 2001; Escario et al. 1996)" (Platero Mendez 2007, 34). As developed by the QUING project in its analysis of "intimate citizenship," in the first stage of Spanish democratization attention was focused mainly on reproductive rights. Spain decriminalized and legalized access to contraception in 1974, a few years after France, which passed the Neuwirth Law in 1967 and promulgated it in 1972. Concerning the legalization of abortion, in France, the demonstration on October 6, 1979, of about 50,000 women, to support the perpetuation of the Veil Law—allowing abortion to 12 weeks, promulgated in January 17, 1975 for a five-year term—embodied the role played by the feminist movement in the acquiring of this right. In Spain, the law on sexual and reproductive health and abortion was promulgated only in 2010, despite the fact that in 1937, during the second Republic and until its recriminalization from 1939 under the Franco dictatorship, Spain had been the fourth country—after Switzerland, the former Czechoslovakia, and Russia—to legalize abortion. Homosexual associations were legalized in 1980 and the law on "danger and social rehabilitation," explicitly punishing male homosexuality, was repealed in 1979. The law on public scandals remained operative until 1988, and the law against homophobia took effect with the Penal Code, also called the "Democracy Code," in 1995 (Platero Mendez 2008).

Given these two path dependencies, with the exclusion of the decriminalization of homosexuality during the French Revolution, France is not a more gender-equality and LGBTQI-friendly country than Spain. A survey by the Pew Research Center provides evidence that the pioneering role of France is far from being obvious (Pew Research Center 2013). This survey was conducted in 39 countries among 37,653 respondents from March 2 to May 1, 2013. It showed that Spain is in fact the dominant country in Europe and globally in terms of social acceptance of homosexuality: 88 percent of the interviewees considered that society should accept homosexuality (versus 60 percent for the USA and 77 percent for France). At first glance, the French and Spanish rankings may seem surprising with regard to the survey's general conclusion that there is greater acceptance of homosexuality in more secular and affluent countries. To complete this focus on public opinion, a Gallup Survey published on June 9, 2004 showed that most Spaniards agreed on legalizing same-sex marriage (61.2 percent for vs 20.8 percent against) and the right of homosexuals to adopt (54.1 percent vs 27 percent). Compare this with France, where in October 2012, a BVA Survey found that 58 percent of the French people surveyed agreed with same-sex marriage and 56 percent agreed with the right of homosexuals to adopt.

First, in order to understand the French position, despite the development of sexual orientation equality rights, French jurisprudence, which maintains a differential treatment in terms of family rights, must be taken into account. In 1997, the Court of Cassation (France's highest appellate court) recalled that "cohabitation results only from a stable and continuous relationship having the appearance of a marriage, thus between a man and a woman" (Third Civil Chamber, December 17, 1997). In 1999, the Civil Solidarity Pact known as PACS was adopted as "a contract entered into between two physical persons who have reached the age of majority, of different or the same sex, for the purposes of organizing their life in common" (Law 99/944 of November 15, 1999). Over the years, the PACS became more and more similar to civil marriage as regards mutual obligations between partners, although filiation and parental rights continue to be outside its remit. Thus, although it provides the couple with a legal status, it does not recognize other familial relations. In the years following the adoption of this new status, the left-wing parties fought for same-sex marriage. The socialist candidate, Ségolène Royal, showed her commitment to this issue during her 2007 presidential campaign, as did the Mayor of Montpellier, Hélène Mandroux, when she initiated a call for the legalization of same-sex marriage on November 14, 2009. Several bills on same-sex marriage were proposed but none were adopted. Examples include the bills proposed by the ecologists Martine Billard, Yves Cochet, Noël Mamère, and François de Rugy in 2010 and the socialist Patrick Bloche in 2011. In 2012, the socialist candidate in the presidential election, François Hollande, called for the legalization of marriage between same-sex couples in "Commitment 31" of his "60 Presidential Commitments." He has since delivered on his promise: same-sex marriage was legalized on April 23, 2013.

The extent of debate on the legitimacy of this law shows that despite consensual attachment to republican equality, its extension to sexual orientation remains profoundly polemical. These debates are part of controversies surrounding compatibility between attachment to the republican principle of equality, on the one hand, and to sexual complementarity on the other hand.

Indeed, in the 2012 French presidential election, every candidate without exception, from the far-right to the radical left, unanimously denounced the gender pay gap and gender-based violence, suggesting an end to the political divide over implementation of the constitutional principle of gender equality. However in 2013, debate surrounding both the same-sex marriage law and reforms in the school sector concerning gender equality education revitalized the issue of gender rights as a matter of political contention. Both reforms, in line with the governing left-wing coalition's program, faced fierce opposition, expressed through massive demonstrations and a widespread rejection of the so-called gender theory. This expression acted as a front to accuse the government of jeopardizing a heteronormative framing of sexual and family rights. The strength of this criticism involves the respect of both the "natural" order and the republican order. Indeed, for opponents of same-sex marriage and "gender theory education," heteronormativity is at the heart of the sexual contract (Pateman 1988). Through the reframing of the dichotomy between public and private spheres as a boundary between political and natural links, the non-application of democratic rules to the family is framed not as a contradiction, but as a political imperative inherent to the definition of the French *res publica*. By qualifying the analogy between the family and the State as "sophism" and "error" (Rousseau [1762]1964, 412), Rousseau—the author of *Du contrat social ou Principes du droit politique* (Of the Social Contract or Principles of Political Law) and of *Émile ou De l'éducation* (Emile, or On Education)—makes it impossible to apply to the family the democratic rule of the social pact. He presents the legitimacy of paternal authority on his subjects, who are his wife and his children, as sacrosanct because natural and vital (Rousseau [1762]1964, 300). In his treatise on education, *Émile ou De l'éducation*, Rousseau asserts that, in terms of the family sphere, "if you wish to remain on the right path, always follow the indications of nature. Everything that characterizes sex must be established by it." (1996 [1re éd. 1762] 473, my translation). By delegitimizing gender studies and gender policies as a threat to sexual differentiation, opponents of this "unnatural ideology," framed as ideologically driven social engineering, have joined the long-established club of those afraid of "an overly invasive type of democracy" (Fraisse 2010a). Taking into account this gendered and sexualized path dependency, the governmental withdrawal from bringing gender equality to schools through awareness-raising, and from gender as a concept relevant to policy making, can be interpreted as the difficulty for political representatives, even of the center-left, to deal with controversies over the sexism and heteronormativity of the republican legacy.

In Spain, between November 1975, when Franco died, and 1986, when Spain joined the European Economic Community (today the EU), the country transitioned from an extreme right-wing, closed dictatorship to a modern, Europe-oriented democracy. The establishment of the Instituto de la Mujer (Women's Institute, WI) in 1983 marks "the beginning of state feminism and gender equality public policies in Spain" (Gil 1996). "From this moment on, gender equality policies and the institutional frameworks around them, developed very rapidly.... Regional developments proved to be even more rapid and stronger than those at the national level (Bustelo 1998)" (Bustelo and Ortbals 2007, 202). Gender policies and state feminism were implemented by the socialist party PSOE (Valiente 1995), which governed Spain from 1982 until the mid-1990s and from 2004 until 2011. The PSOE government established equality as a priority, using in particular the Same-Sex Marriage Law (2005) and the Gender Equality Act (Ley Orgánica 3/2007, de 22 de marzo, para la igualdad efectiva de mujeres y hombres) as symbols of its equality ideology (Platero 2006, 103). Kerman Calvo addresses the paradoxical position of Spain as "a leading battlefield in the fight for the recognition of lesbian, gay (and also transgender) rights" (Calvo 2011, 167). He points to two main obstacles that created this paradox: LGBTQI movements were not as well funded and organized as those in countries with earlier LGBTQI rights, and "the seemingly strong influence of the Catholic Church on moral issues and policy" remained in place (Calvo 2011, 167). Analysis of a number of primary sources (press items, movement literature, and the written testimony of key activists) and secondary sources led him to identify shifts in attitudes and political structures that started in the early 1990s and created opportunities for change. These changes relate to significant transformations both in citizens' attitudes toward religion and the Catholic Church (Montero and Calvo 2000, 126–128), and in the agenda-setting processes of left-wing parties and LGBTQI movements. Indeed, " the larger political parties, including the 'Spanish Socialist Workers' Party (PSOE) opened up new arenas of electoral competition during the 1990s based on the so-called 'new' issues, most notably civil and minority rights and the environment (Almunia 2001, 441–444). ... [The] Spanish LG movement adjusted its demands and discourse to participate in agenda-setting processes" (Calvo 2011, 167–168). In contrast with the French quarrel on defining the coherent and faithful conception of the republican order, the Spanish defense of its same-sex marriage law is based on alliances between leftist parties and social movements in order to denounce and reshape the historical political order.

The Narratives of French Continuity and of Spanish Modernity

Based on a "double association between on the one hand, sexuality and the legal theory of equality and on the other hand, marriage and access to citizenship" (Paternotte 2011, 22), international discourse in favor of legalizing civil marriage between same-sex couples promotes a transformative conception of the law (Descoutures et al. 2008; Paternotte 2012; Tremblay 2014; Winter 2014), in particular with regard to the defense of human rights (Sanders 1994; Waites 2009). In this context, support for the Spanish July 2005 law and the French May 2013 law on same-sex marriage was motivated by a desire to remove "discrimination and subsequently, the violation of equal rights, leading to unequal citizenship" (Paternotte 2011, 22).

In the French case, Erwann Binet, a socialist MP in the Isère department and representative of the Law Commission, introduced the first discussion on the same-sex marriage law, asking the Prime Minister, Jean-Marc Ayrault, to "point out measures that the government is considering implementing to fight against intolerance and discrimination experienced by citizens on account of their sexual orientation." The Prime Minister answered by asserting that the law constitutes "new progress towards more equality and rights for all French citizens" (Assemblée nationale 2013, 459).

During the first public discussion of the law at the National Assembly on January 29, 2013, Justice Minister Christiane Taubira described the bill as being part of the historical evolution of civil marriage over two centuries and as a republican institution embodying the intertwining between the principles of equality and secularization. She specified: "This is what we have done today: we have reached the final stage of the movement of civil marriage towards equality ... a movement that was born with the secularization of society and marriage" (Assemblée nationale 2013, 470). The amendments tabled at the Law and Social Affairs Commissions by opponents to the law show that their answer to arguments based on historical secularization was designed to shift the debate. Their aim was to emphasize the role of men and women in procreation as the basis for the institution of marriage. Several (defeated) amendments proposed by the center-right Union for a Presidential Majority (Union pour la majorité présidentielle, UMP) members of parliament (MPs) use etymology to defend "the specific and unique dimension of marriage." Referring to the "latin words *matrimonium* and *maritare*, stemming respectively from *mater*, mother, and *mas*, husband, the male," the proposed Amendment CL478 defined marriage as "the legal form in which a woman prepares to become a mother by meeting with a man" (Commission des lois 2013, 41). In the Amendment, about 50 UMP MPs state that "the law can neither ignore nor abolish the difference between the sexes which is essential not only for the sustainability of a society but also for the child's identity, which can only be built in the context of a model of sexual otherness" (Commission des lois 2013, 42). The presence of both sexes in marriage thus becomes a "fundamental principle of the French constitution, recognized in numerous laws of our legislative corpus" (Commission des lois 2013, 42).

Six months after it was presented to the Council of Ministers on November 7, 2012, and after many hours of parliamentary debate, media controversies, and mass demonstrations, France promulgated the law legalizing civil marriage for same-sex couples through a ruling by the Constitutional Council on May 17, 2013. This means that the Rousseauist conceptualization of Republican marriage based on "natural" complementarity of the sexes is no more the legal French frame, but despite this legal change it is still the political and social norm. Equality for all, irrespective of sexual orientation, with regard to civil marriage was thus recognized in France twelve years after the Netherlands, eight years after Canada and Spain, seven years after South Africa, around the same time as Brazil, and two months before the UK. A month later, on June 25, 2013, Article 41 of the law introducing reforms to French school curricula was passed. It specifies that the purpose of teaching on moral and civic issues is that pupils might learn to have "respect for the person, for his/her origins and for his/her differences, for equality between women and men and for secularism." This reform is perceived by its opponents to be part of a system, together with the May 17, 2013 law, designed to deconstruct the centrality of sexual complementarity in the political, social, and familial order.

In contrast with the French republican narrative of political continuity, the Spanish political system is characterized by a path dependency of post-dictatorship. Political and civil society actors of the Spanish left wing claim so the rupture with a political inheritance which they openly denounce as sexist and homophobic.

Moreover, the federal nature of Spain's constitutional system, and not a centralized and centripetal one as in France, contributes to facilitating this break with historical legacy in that it challenges national politics, in particular in terms of discourse on equality and "de-familialization." Indeed, the impact of a "competitive federalism/regionalism" (Alonso and Forest 2012) led to institutional ismorphism, with regions copying groundbreaking legislative arrangements from other regions, notably on gender equality. So, going beyond the national debate on same-sex marriage, local and regional developments include gender and sexual orientation in their policies. "Not only have the regional parliaments legislated on partnerships and supported the global debate on same-sex marriage, they have also initiated a trend to consult civil society, including non-governmental organizations

(NGOs), and co-opted activists in the public administration" (Platero Mendez 2008, 173–74). As analyzed by the QUING project, while it can be assumed that in Spain, European Directives have greatly impacted sexual rights, Basque and Catalonian nationalist parties (PNV and ERC) have been the only ones to clearly refer to the EU legal order in the field of anti-discrimination policies. This is significant in terms of how subnational regionalist movements use the EU to affirm their own regional identities in contrast to a nation-state that is seen as holding them back (Crameri 2015). In terms of gender equality policies in the twenty-first century, Spain is thus characterized by the alliance of Europeanization and federalism. "The *differential fact/comparative grievance/mimesis effect* cycle was therefore consolidated (Moreno and Arriba 1999), creating what has been described as 'competitive federalism' (Colomer 1998) or 'competitive regionalism' (Börzel 2002)" (Alonso and Forest 2012, 198).

The promotion of gender equality as a tool to improve the quality of Spanish democracy is often referred to in the documents analyzed (law, policy plans, parliamentary debate, civil society texts). As part of the QUING project, analysis of the major documents produced by the major actors participating in the Spanish debates on same-sex marriage (1995–2007) points to the link between commitment to gender equality policies and quality of democracy. It "is especially relevant for supporting same-sex marriage, assuming Spain's vanguard position on the issue, in order to oppose any 'medium range' measures such as civil unions or registered partnerships" (Forest and Lopez 2009, 29). Regarding the Spanish opposition to same-sex marriage, the MAGEEQ project points out that if "in the constitution, the concept of family is wider and allows different interpretations, ... for some political actors, marriage should be limited to heterosexual couples: this idea is present in the Conservative Party's texts and debates analyzed (press article 1997; parliamentary debate 2000; electoral program 2004)" (MAGEEQ 2005, 8).

FRENCH AND SPANISH SAME-SEX MARRIAGE LAWS: AMBIVALENT REFORMS THAT LIE SOMEWHERE BETWEEN REVOLUTION AND COMPROMISE

How might French and Spanish legislators address the idea that sexual complementarity is central to the private and political sphere?

In France, opponents of same-sex marriage highlight the dangers that they believe a lack of sexual differentiation entails (Mossuz-Lavau 2009).

These detractors belong to a historical "ritornello" (Fraisse 1995, 2010a) reformulating "the fear of an intrusive type of democracy, which progresses according to the idea that all human beings are similar and abolishes the border between the sexes" (Fraisse 2010b, 12–13). French philosopher Geneviève Fraisse analyzes how resistance to egalitarian movements resulting from the supposed danger of confusing genders is a historical French obsession, which is not specific to twenty-first century reactionaries.

The fantasy of degeneration through mixophobia is a biopolitics similar to sexism and racism (Bauman 2003). It is, however, important to note that legal recognition of homosexuality can also be used as part of a nationalist and Islamophobic agenda (Hajjat and Mohammed 2014), strengthening the opposition between presumably sexist and homophobic Muslims and the supposed moral superiority of modern and open-minded Westerners (Delphy 2007; Eisenstein 2007; Puar 2007). This "homonationalist" strategy sheds light on the ambivalent position of Marine Le Pen, president of the extreme-right National Front (Jaunait et al. 2013; Fassin and Surkis 2012, 5–23). Her strategy is to avoid offending the defenders of the traditional family, while claiming to epitomize Western modernity.

How might legislators address this historical "ritornello" and radical right strategy? How do they stand in relation to the assertion that sexual complementarity is central to the definition of the social contract?

The adjournment of the family bill, which was to be presented to the Cabinet (Council of Ministers) in April, a few days after the municipal elections of March 23 and March 30, 2014, embodies the government's step backwards after the demonstration of the Manif pour tous. This demonstration, which took place on February 2, 2014, brought together more than half a million people, according to the organizers. Along with the institutional abandonment of the ABCD de l'égalité (Battaglia and Dupont 2014; Storti 2014) and of the word "gender," this backstep can be interpreted as a sign of the lack of governmental and presidential commitment to the ideological bases of the same-sex marriage law (Godard 2014).

The government presents its political choice as a compromise, but it can also be analyzed as the expression of an attachment to the traditional sexual order (Sénac 2009). Indeed, the backlash in terms of both family rights and educational policy illustrates that the law on same-sex marriage has not been enough to ensure that the essentialist ideology of sexual complementarity and the republican principle of equality are no longer linked together. Each human being in society is unique. However, certain differentiations, in particular sexual and racial, have an impact on whether or not one is considered to be a citizen like any other. Whether or not one is considered to be "different" in a political sense—that is, "non-brother" as regards the French republican connection "Liberty, Equality, Fraternity" (Sénac 2016)—is based on the founding myth of sexual and racial complementarity. By not questioning this founding myth explicitly and by distancing themselves from the academics who have analyzed it critically, political and institutional supporters of the law have transmitted an ambivalent "gender regime." They have failed to deconstruct discrimination based on gender or sexual orientation, thus contributing to a modern and insidious (Fraser 2009) form of "constituent racialized heterosexism" (Sénac 2017).

As Avishai Margalit (2010) argues, compromise does not solve the tension between peace and justice. In this context, the challenge is to express different positions in terms of pluralism and to accept that when positions are contradictory, compromise does not provide an adequate answer. The speech made by President Hollande at the 2012 annual meeting of the 36,000-member French Association of Mayors can be cited as an example of the French "rotten compromise" (to use Margalit's expression) in terms of LGBTQI policy. He suggested that the mayors could always invoke the "conscience clause" if they did not want to wed gay couples. This was an extraordinary statement from the very office that is supposed to be the guardian of the Constitution, especially because there is no such thing as a conscience clause in French law (Baruch 2013, 27).

When the family law was modified the day after the Manif pour tous demonstration on February 2, 2014, a collective of academics—sociologists, political analysts, and one historian—heavily criticized the government for caving in and for "the uniting of all right-wing parties, both moderate and radical, against gender studies" (Bargel et al. 2014).

Detractors of the so-called gender theory focus on the role of the State in the education of children. By taking initiatives such as the "ABCD de l'égalité" experiment (a pedagocial tool whose purpose is to fight sexism and gender stereotypes), the State is accused of going beyond its remit by situating itself on the side of morality rather than on the side of the law, by holding convictions about what is good, rather than by teaching civic principles. By defending the role of the traditional family (where the father remains the "head of the household") in the education of children, and in particular in the transmission of values and morality, opponents of "gender theory" are engaged in a battle over recognition of legitimate authority, a "clash of paternalisms" (Pélabay 2011). The main criticism consists of condemning the integration of gender equality and equality for all sexual orientations into the civics curriculum in schools. Such criticism expresses a gendered conception of the boundaries between the public and the private spheres in which the family is recognized as the only legitimate body to transmit ethical values such as what is good and what is fair. Should this separation between the good and the fair be understood as the expression of liberal neutrality?

In reality, what clearly distinguishes this argument from political liberalism is that limiting notions of what is good to the private sphere goes hand in hand with the presentation of heterosexuality as a condition for a good life in the moral sense. This position is in complete contradiction with the principles of equality and freedom of choice. Thus, it challenges the legitimacy of the State's involvement in the definition of what is fair and just. Furthermore, with regard to the liberal issue of the separation between private and public spheres, the position of opponents to "gender theory" is ambivalent. Although they call for the protection of the family as an intimate space that is outside politics, particularly with regard to the education of children, they take offence at the recognition of sexual orientation as a private choice. Thus, opposition to same-sex civil marriage expresses a French republican conservative position that is contradictory to political liberalism, in particular with respect to its attachment to normative neutrality.

In a post-civil war and post-dictatorship country such as Spain, the political is more explicitly understood, for the agents of change, as an ideological antagonism toward the political legacy (Mouffe 2014, 150). The adoption of same-sex marriage in Spain is linked both to a congruent coalition between left-wing political parties and LGBTQI movements (Chaques and Palau 2012; Lopez et al. 2007) and to a less cohesive coalition among opponents: the right-wing party PP, the moderate Catalan party Convergencia i Unio (CiU), and the Catholic Church. Moreover, the Federación Estatal de Lesbianas, Gays, Transexuales y Bisexuales - FELGTB's lobbying activity at the subnational level increases rights for same-sex couples on a regional level and fosters public mobilization. In contrast to the strong degree of congruence among the change coalition, the blocking coalition, "although the Catholic Church might have acted as a veto player with its strong mobilization capacity,[2] was not able to enforce its preference in the decision-making arena." (Schmitt et al. 2013, 436).

As regards the "quasi-federal" nature of Spanish political regime, Raquel Platero Mendez emphasizes the differences between the national-level focus on same-sex marriage (2002–2005) and previously, partnership rights (1995–2002), which obscures other LGBTQI issues, and regional and local levels that include emerging alternative frames surrounding the intersectionality of gender and sexual orientation. From this perspective, same-sex marriage is reformist and does not permit the gender contract to be reframed because it reinforces "the role of the state in regulating private life, giving privileges to some forms of families, making the values of monogamy or cohabitation stronger for instance" (Platero Mendez 2008, p. 188). The arguments for and against this law do not adopt an intersectional approach. In particular, "the center of resistance has used the gay stereotypes of child abuse, pedophilia, promiscuity, etc. that have little to do with lesbians, the needs of migrant LGBTQI individuals or the elderly" (Platero Mendez 2007, 42).

Conclusion: Spanish Modern Democracy Versus the French Mythicized Republic

The philosopher Jean-Marc Ferry sets out a distinction between the three pillars of the democratic rule of law (2014): the principles express the universality of fundamental rights; the norms arise from the commonality of popular sovereignty; and the values reflect the plurality of the identity-building process, in particular as regards spiritual legacy and community-based interests. Using this typology, opposition to same-sex marriage must be analyzed not as an expression of communitarian values, but as a quarrel over the meaning of fundamental rights, in particular the equality and liberty principles, but also of secularization and its implementation.

By expressing the tensions between legitimacy and legality, comparative analysis of Spanish and French rhetorical and policy agendas surrounding same-sex marriage laws shows that "it is not so much society that questions homosexuality as homosexuality that challenges society" (Fassin 2008), and emphasizes the importance of political legacies as regards sexism and heteronormativity.

While in France, the stake was for same-sex marriage proponents and opponents to present themselves as sole guarantors of republican continuity, in Spain, the socialist majority undertook a historic break with a past denounced as unfair, in a path dependency of democratic transition. Tainted with the laggard syndrome, the process of expanding rights in Spain can be analyzed as belonging to a political reframing of modernization and

Europeanness. More precisely, under Zapatero's governments, expanding gender rights was seen as a way to connect Spain to North-European (social) democracies. In contrast to the Spanish use of gender and sexual policies as a marker of modern democracy, the importance of the French controversies on the legalization of same-sex marriage have to be analyzed in relation to the vitality of the myth of an egalitarian republic.

Notes

1. For a detailed theoretical and methodological framework of the MAGEEQ project (FP5), see www.mageeq.net; for the QUING project (FP6), see www.quing.eu
2. As late as the mid-1990s, during the Episcopal Conference, the Catholic Church's campaign against homosexuals argued that homosexuality is the result of bad habits, bad company, and negative early experiences. It intensified its activity from the 2000s onward (i.e. published several official press statements, presenting a pastoral directory for the family in 2003).

References

Almunia, Joaquim. 2001. *Memorias Politicas.* Madrid: Punto de lectura.
Alonso, Alba, and Maxime Forest. 2012. Is Gender Equality Soluble into Self-Governance? Regionalizing and Europeanizing Gender Policies in Spain. In *The Europeanizaion of Gender Equality Policies: A Discursive-Sociological Approach*, ed. Emanuela Lombardo and Maxime Forest, 192–213. Basingstoke: Palgrave Macmillan.
Assemblée nationale. 2013. *Journal officiel de la République française.* Second Session, January 29.
Ayoub, Phillip M., and David Paternotte, eds. 2014. *LGBT Activism and the Making of Europe: A Rainbow Europe* ? Basingstoke: Palgrave Macmillan.
Bargel, Lucie, Laure Bereni, Michel Bozon, Delphine Dulong, Éric Fassin, Rose-Marie Lagrave, Sandrine Lévêque, Frédérique Matonti, and Florence Rochefort. 2014. Désolante capitulation gouvernementale. Le genre ne concerne pas que les bobos. *Le Monde*, February 7.
Baruch, Marc Olivier. 2013. Gay Marriage and the Limits of French Liberalism. *Dissent* 60: 24–28.
Battaglia, Mattea, and Gaëlle Dupont. 2014. Égalité garçon-fille: le 'plan d'action' qui cache un recul du gouvernement. *Le Monde*, June 30.
Bauman, Zygmunt. 2003. *La Vie en miettes. Expérience postmoderne et moralité.* Paris: Hachette.

Börzel, Tanja. 2002. *States and Regions in the European Union: Institutional Adaptation in Germany and Spain*. Cambridge: Cambridge University Press.
Bustelo, Maria. 1998. Regional Public Policies for Gender Equality in Spain: Analysis and Evaluation. Paper presented at the conference of the European Consortium for Political Research, Warwick, 23–28 March.
Bustelo, Maria, and Candice D. Ortbals. 2007. The Evolution of Spanish State Feminism: A Fragmented Landscape. In *Changing State Feminism*, ed. Joyce Outshoorn and Johanna Kantola, 201–223. Basingstoke: Palgrave Macmillan.
Calvo, Kerman. 2007. Sacrifices that Pay: Polity Membership, Political Opportunities and the Recognition of Same-Sex Marriage in Spain. *South European Society & Politics* 12 (3): 295–314.
———. 2011. Spain: Building Reciprocal Relations between Lesbian and Gay Organizations and the State. In *The Lesbian and Gay Movement and the State*, ed. Manon Tremblay, David Paternotte, and Carol Johnson, 177–180. Farnham: Ashgate.
Chaqués-Bonafont, Laura, and Anna Palau. 2012. From Prohibition to Permissiveness: A Two Wave Change on Morality Issues in Spain. In *Morality Politics in Western Europe; Parties, Agendas and Policy Choices*, ed. Isabelle Engeli, Christoffer Green-Pedersen, and Lars Thorup Larsen, 62–87. Basingstoke: Palgrave Macmillan.
Colomer, Jordi. 1998. *La transición de la democracia: el modelo español*. Barcelona: Anagrama.
Commission des lois. 2013. Projet de loi ouvrant le mariage aux couples de personnes de même sexe, Amendements soumis à la commission, 13 janvier. http://www.assemblee-nationale.fr/14/pdf/amendements_commissions/cloi/0344-01.pdf
Crameri, Kathryn. 2015. Political Power and Civil Counterpower: The Complex Dynamics of the Catalan Independence Movement. *Nationalism and Ethnic Politics* 21 (1): 104–120.
Delphy, Christine. 2002. A War for Afghan Women. In *September 11, 2011: Feminist Perspectives*, ed. Susan Hawthorne and Bronwyn Winter, 302–315. Melbourne: Spinifex.
Delphy, Christine. 2007. A War for Afghan Women. In *September 11, 2001: Feminist Perspectives*, ed. Susan Hawthrone and Bronwyn Winter, 302–315. Melbourne: Spinifex.
Descoutures, Virginie, Marie Digoix, Éric Fassin, and Wilfried Rault, eds. 2008. *Mariages et homosexualités dans le monde. L'arrangement des normes familiales*. Paris: Autrement.
Eisenstein, Zillah. 2007. *Sexual Decoys: Gender, Race and War in Imperial Democracy*. Melbourne: Spinifex Press.
Escario, Pilar, et al. 1996. *Lo personal es politico. El movimiento feminista en la Transicion, Ministerio de Asuntos Sociales*. Madrid: Instituto de la Mujer.

Fassin, Éric. 2008. *L'Inversion de la question homosexuelle*. Paris: Amsterdam.
Fassin, Eric, and Judith Surkis. 2012. Sexual Boundaries, European Identities, and Transnational Migrations in Europe. *Public Culture* 22 (3): 5–23.
Ferry, Jean-Marc. 2014. *Les Voies de la relance européenne*. Lausanne: Fondation Jean-Monnet pour l'Europe.
Forest, Maxime, and Silvia Lopez. 2009. *QUING LARG Comparative Country Studies Spain*.
Fraisse, Geneviève. 1995. *Muse de la raison. Démocratie et exclusion des femmes en France*. Paris: Gallimard.
———. 2010a. Sur l'incompatibilité supposée entre l'amour et le féminisme. In *À côté du genre. Sexe et philosophie de l'égalité*. Paris: Le bord de l'eau.
———. 2010b. *Les Femmes et leur histoire*. Paris: Gallimard.
Fraser, Nancy. 2009. Feminism, Capitalism and the Cunning of History. *New Left Review* 56, March–April.
Frotiée, Brigitte. 2006. L'égalité des sexes en Espagne comme enjeu politique dans le processus de démocratisation. *Politique européenne* 20: 75–98.
Frotiée, Brigitte, and Maria Jesus Rodriguez Garcia. 2012. La prise en charge des questions d'égalité femmes-hommes en Espagne (1975–2012). *Revue française des affaires sociales* 2–3: 112–129.
Gil, Juana. 1996. *Las politicas de igualdad en Espana*. Granada: Universidad de Granda.
Godard, Thomas. 2014. Peillon dans le piège de la "théorie du genre": une maladresse linguistique et politique. LePlus.NouvelObs.com, January 30. http://leplus.nouvelobs.com/contribution/1138212-peillon-dans-le-piege-de-la-theorie-du-genre-une-maladresse-linguistique-et-politique.html
Hajjat, Abdellali, and Marwan Mohammed, eds. 2014. Sociologie de l'islamophobie. *Sociologie* 5 (1): 120.
Jaunait, Alexandre, Amélie Le Renard, and Élisabeth Marteu, eds. 2013. Nationalismes sexuels. *Raisons politiques* 49: 171.
Larumbe, Maria Angeles. 2001. El feminism en la Transición Española. In *Una immensa minoria influencia y feminismo en la transición*, 139–196. Segardiana: Prensas Universitarias de Zaragoza.
Lépinard, Éléonore. 2007. *L'Égalité introuvable. La parité, les féministes et la République*. Paris: Presses de Sciences Po.
Lopez, Silvia, Elin Peterson, and Raquel Platero. 2007. *Issue Histories Spain: Series of Timelines of Policy Debates*. Quality in Gender + Equality Policies – QUING Project, Vienna, Institute for Human Sciences. Accessed 15 April 2017. http://www.quing.eu/files/results/ih_spain.pdf
MAGEEQ. 2005. *Framing Homosexual Rights in Spain: Findings of the MAGEEQ Project*. Paper presented at the MAGEEQ Conference in Brussels.
Margalit, Avishai. 2010. *On Compromise and Rotten Compromises*. Princeton, NJ: Princeton University Press.

Mc Bride, Dorothy E., and Amy Mazur, eds. 2012. *The Politics of State Feminism: Innovation in Comparative Research*. Philadelphia, PA: Temple University Press.
Montero, José Ramon, and Kerman Calvo. 2000. Religiosity and Party Choice in Spain: An Elusive Cleavage? In *Religion and Mass Electoral Behavior in Europe*, ed. David Broughton and Hans Martien ten Napel, 118–139. London: Routledge.
Moreno, Luis, and Ana Arriba. 1999. *Welfare and Decentralization in Spain*. Florencia: EUI (European Forum, WP 99/8).
Mossuz-Lavau, Janine. 2009. *Guerre des sexes, stop!* Paris: Flammarion.
Mouffe, Chantal. 2014. By Way of a Postscript. *Parallax* 20 (2): 149–157.
Pateman, Carole. 1988. *The Sexual Contract*. Stanford, CA: Stanford University Press.
Paternotte, David. 2011. *Revendiquer le « mariage gay »*. Bruxelles: Editions de l'Université de Bruxelles.
———. 2012. La juridification du droit comme matrice de l'action collective: la revendication du droit au mariage entre personnes du même sexe. *Politique et Sociétés* 31 (2): 93–112.
Paternotte, David, and Kelly Kollman. 2013. Regulating Intimate Relationships in the European Polity: Same-sex Unions and Policy Convergence. *Social Politics* 20 (4): 510–533.
Pélabay, Janie. 2011. Former le "bon citoyen" libéral. L'éducation morale et civique aux prises avec le pluralisme. *Raisons politiques* 44: 117–138.
Pew Research Center. 2013. The Global Divide on Homosexuality and Greater Acceptance in More Secular and Affluent Countries, June 4. http://www.pew-global.org/2013/06/04/the-global-divide-on-homosexuality/
Platero Mendez, Raquel. 2006. Invisibiliza el matrimonio homosexual a las lesbianas? In *Orientaciones*, vol. 10, 103–120. Madrid: Fundacion Triangulo.
———. 2007. The Limits of Equality. The Intersectionality of Gender and Sexuality in Spanish Policy Making. *Kvinder, Køn & Forskning* 1: 33–49.
———. 2008. Intersecting Gender and Sexual Orientation: An Analysis of Sexuality and Citizenship in Gender Equality Policies in Spain. In *Contesting Citizenship*, ed. Birte Siim and Judith Squires. London: Routledge.
Puar, Jasbir K. 2007. *Terrorist Assemblages: Homonationalism in Queer Times*. Durham: Duke University Press.
Rochefort, Florence. 2014. 'Mariage pour tous': genre, religions et sécularisation. In *Qu'est-ce-que le genre?* ed. Laurie Laufer and Florence Rochefort, 213–230. Paris: Payot.
Rosanvallon, Pierre. 2011. *La Société des égaux*. Paris: Seuil.
Rousseau, Jean-Jacques. 1964 [1762]. *Du contrat social*. In *Œuvres complètes*, vol. vol. 3. Paris: Gallimard, Bibliothèque de la Pléiade.
———. 1996 [1762]. *Émile, ou De l'éducation*. Paris: Gallimard.

Sanders, Douglas. 1994. Constructing Lesbian and Gay Rights. *Revue canadienne droit et société* 9 (2): 99–111.
Schmitt, Sophie, Eva-Maria Euchner, and Caroline Preidel. 2013. Regulating Prostitution and Same-sex Marriage in Italy and Spain: The Interplay of Political and Societal veto Players in Two Catholic Societies. *Journal of European Public Policy* 20 (3): 425–441.
Sénac, Réjane. 2016. The Contemporary Conversation about the French Connection 'Liberté, Egalité, Fraternité': Neoliberal Equality and 'Non-brothers'. *Revue Française de Civilisation Britannique* XXI-1.
———. 2017. *Les non-frères au pays de l'égalité*. Paris: Presses de Sciences Po.
Sénac-Slawinski, Réjane. 2009. Parity and the Sexual Order. In *Women, Feminism, and Femininity in the 21st Century: American and French Perspectives*, ed. Béatrice Mousli and Eve-Alice Roustang-Stoller, 133–154. Basingstoke: Palgrave Macmillan.
Storti, Martine. 2014. L'abandon des ABCD de l'égalité, symbole de l'abdication idéologique de la gauche. *Le Monde*, July 2.
Tremblay, Manon. 2014. Secular Humanism vs. Social Conservatism: Analyzing Canadian House of Commons Debates on Same-Sex Mariage. *Scholars World* 2 (1): 7–22.
Tremblay, Manon, David Paternotte, and Carol Johnson, eds. 2011. *The Lesbian and Gay Movement and the State*. Farnham: Ashgate.
Valiente, Celia. 1995. The Power of Persuasion: The Instituto de la Mujer in Spain. In *Comparative State Feminism*, ed. D. Stetson and Amy G. Mazur, 221–236. Thousand Oaks, CA: Sage.
Waites, Matthew. 2009. Critique of 'Sexual Orientation' and 'Gender Identity' in Human Discourses: Global Queer Politics beyond the Yogyakarta Principles. *Contemporary Politics* 15 (1): 137–156.
Winter, Bronwyn. 2014. 'The Ties that Bind Us': The Hidden Knots of Gay Marriage. *Portal: Journal of Multidisciplinary International Studies*, 11 (1). ePress.lib.uts.edu.au

Réjane Sénac is a French National Centre for Scientific Research (CNRS) tenured researcher/lecturer at the Centre for Political Research at Sciences Po Paris, France (CEVIPOF). She is a member of the steering committee for Sciences Po's Gender Studies program, PRESAGE. Her research focuses on public justifications of equality policies (such as parity, diversity, same-sex marriage). Publications include *L'ordre sexué: la percepton des inégalités femmes-hommes* (PUF, 2007); *L'égalité sous conditions: genre, parité, diversité* (Presses de Sciences Po, 2015); and *Les non-frères au pays de l'égalité* (Presses de Sciences Po, 2017).

CHAPTER 7

Europeanizing vs. Nationalizing the Issue of Same-Sex Marriage in Central Europe: A Comparative Analysis of Framing Processes in Croatia, Hungary, Slovakia, and Slovenia

Maxime Forest

INTRODUCTION

Issues such as the politicization of reproductive rights, the masculinization of politics, or the impact of market transition have been thoroughly addressed by the literature on post-socialist transformations (see, among others: Kaplan et al. 1997; Gal and Kligman 2000a, b; Matland and Montgomery 2003, Forest 2011). Initially building upon the categories, sequences, and actors identified for precedent waves of democratization in Latin America and Southern Europe, this literature progressively developed a finer-grained picture, taking into account the different paths of extrica-

---

Although comparisons and analyses of the role of the EU variable developed in this paper are my own, I wish to acknowledge the work and inputs from QUING teams at the Central European University Budapest and the Peace Institute, Ljubljana.

M. Forest (✉)
Sciences Po Paris, Paris, France

tion from state socialism experienced in Central and Eastern European Countries (CEECs) and their long-lasting impact on features such as institutional legacies or social structures (Gal and Kligman 2000a, b).

More recently, the process of accession to the European Union (EU) has been described as a window of opportunity for challenging the gendered dimension of the post-socialist transformation. Yet the interest for the impact of this process on gender equality and lesbian, gay, bisexual, transgender, queer/questioning, and intersex (LGBTQI) rights has been mainly formulated in terms of implementation of and convergence with EU legal provisions on gender equality and non-discrimination, due to the unprecedented conditionality of the EU Eastern enlargement compared to previous EU enlargement waves. This conditionality led to analysis of the legislative and policy instruments consecutively adopted by the candidate countries as elements of convergence, assuming that they would necessarily contribute to greater integration. Yet, studies (such as Roth 2004; Forest 2006a) have shown instead the differentiating effect of Europeanization, with vastly different impacts across countries and issues, thus suggesting, with Claudio Radaelli (2004), that "Europeanization is *not* convergence."

As they moved from neo-functionalist approaches to neo-institutionalism, with a greater emphasis placed on how actors and discourses contribute to shaping institutions (Schimmelfennig and Sedelmeier 2004; Schmidt 2010; Woll and Jacquot 2010; Lombardo and Forest 2012), European integration studies have also made salient the need for a more comprehensive definition of Europeanization, that goes far beyond implementation and includes social learning, norm diffusion, and a broad definition of policy transfers (Dolowitz and Marsh 1996). Simultaneously, the making of gender equality and anti-discrimination policies, both at the EU and the national levels, has become a rich area of investigation in the 28 countries of the enlarged EU (EU-28), as shown by large, international comparative projects which also covered CEECs.

Reshaping "intimate citizenship," a broad category developed within the context of the EU-funded QUING project, has long been addressed in the CEECs mainly through the sub-issue of reproductive rights. Abortion rights, in particular, have since 1990 triggered discourses in favor of traditional family values and a restriction of women's participation in the public sphere, pointing out the pervasiveness of rhetorical arguments linking LGBTQI rights with the preservation of traditional marriage and the demographic future of the nation. The rights of LGBTQI minorities, and the recognition of non-heterosexual forms of partnerships and families, also reveal the discursive linkage between the politics of population growth and the redefinition of LGBTQI rights (Buzogány 2008; Forest 2008). Two opposite trends have attracted scholars' attention. On the one hand, the recognition of same-sex couples has been publicly debated in most of the CEECs since the mid-1990s, with a positive but limited outcome in Croatia, the Czech Republic, Hungary, and more recently, Estonia, in the forms of registered civil partnerships open to same-sex couples. Simultaneously, EU accession made the approval of better designed anti-discrimination provisions compulsory, supposedly including discriminations on the grounds of sexual orientation in a number of areas, as listed in two EU directives (2000/78 EC and 2000/43 EC). On the other hand, debates related to the recognition of same-sex partnerships and the approval of anti-discrimination laws have been highly controversial, and backlashes were reported in the post-accession period (Buzogány 2008; Slootmaeckers and Sircar 2014; Kahlina 2014), including steps to ban same-sex marriage in constitutions.

In this chapter, I will, first, briefly discuss how and why demands for the recognition of same-sex couples did emerge in some countries, while they were silenced in others. The indirect influence of external variables will be included. Second, I will examine the domestic impact of the EU on the recognition of same-sex couples, as well as the contentious dimension of this recognition for domestic actors, framed as "Europeanization vs. nationalization" in four country cases: Hungary, Slovenia, Slovakia, and Croatia. These countries are chosen because they are the CEECs where the recognition of same-sex couples has triggered the most legal and policy changes. This chapter draws primarily on three bodies of research: the comparative critical frame analysis carried out by the team of the EU-funded QUING project, to which I contributed from 2007 to 2011; my own legislative tracking of debates on this issue between 2012 and 2017; and my earlier work on the gendering of democratic transition and Europeanization in CEECs. Policy frames are understood here, according to Mieke Verloo's definition (2005), as an organizing principle that turns an issue incidentally and inconsistently addressed in the public space into a meaningful problem, articulating a diagnosis and a prognosis in the form of recommended or actual policy solutions.

Regulating Sexual Orientation in Central and Eastern Europe

From State Socialism to Democracy

In this section, I will sketch the political and institutional contexts in which demands regarding LGBTQI rights in general, and the recognition of same-sex couples in particular, have emerged in CEECs. Those contexts were heavily marked by transnational variables such as the blueprint that the Sovietization process initiated after World War II imposed on the regulation of intimate citizenship, or the transition to liberal (market) democracy initiated from 1989 onward. Yet, neither the Soviet model nor the pathway to democracy imposed themselves uniformly. During the early phase of the Sovietization of States, legal orders, economies, and societies in Central and Eastern Europe (CEE) (1945–1956), the Soviet model regarding gender rights was going through a process of aggiornamento in the USSR itself, leading popular democracies in Eastern Europe to adopt legislations that combined far-reaching sexual and reproductive rights with a relatively conservative definition of the family. Differences remained noticeable among CEECs' gender regimes, also reflecting path-dependent features toward former institutional and legal settings. Four decades later, the transition to liberal democracy followed different pathways, which notably was reflected in the nature of the early debates over the legal recognition of homosexuality, and the development of LGBTQI organizations. Through a brief account of these different contexts, I will highlight a few features that help make sense of further developments in the context of EU accession, and support the choice of four country cases.

With the notable exception of Poland, which had banished homosexuality from its penal code as early as 1932 (Dąbrowska 2007), the first wave of depenalization occurred in the early 1960s in CEE, at the end of the Stalinist era. Previously, discriminatory provisions explicitly mentioning sexual orientation had been introduced or reinforced, largely influenced by the family doctrine expounded in the Soviet Law of 1944, which made abortion a criminal offense and made divorce practically impossible. Adopted in the context of the huge human losses of World War II, the Soviet Law subordinated the regulation of intimacy to a strictly pro-birth policy. After Stalin's death and before the Twentieth Congress of the Soviet Communist Party in 1956, critical articles were published in Soviet *Literaturnaia Gazeta*, calling for the most severe restrictions to be abolished (Nakachi 2006). Abortion was re-legalized in 1957 and in popular CEE democracies this process of *aggiornamento* made it possible to enact more liberal legislation as early as 1953, granting reproductive rights to Czech, and later to Hungarian women (1956). As another consequence of the liberalization of pro-birth policies (following the post-war relative increase in birth rates), the penalization of homosexual relationships, understood as sexual relationships, was removed from the penal codes in Czechoslovakia and Hungary (1961), and in the German Democratic Republic (1968), except residual provisions concerning the age of consent.

However, the hygienist discourse of public authorities on intimacy and sexuality, with a strong condemnation of "antisocial" behaviors, prevented any public expression of homosexuality, which remained a criminal offence in the Soviet Union, Yugoslavia, Bulgaria, and Romania. The first public debate on the regulation of sexual orientation was held in the latter half of the 1970s in Yugoslavia, and homosexuality was decriminalized in 1977. The first gay and lesbian organizations were officially registered over the 1980s in Slovenia and Hungary (Kuhar and Takacs 2007; Kuhar 2008a). In both cases, these early developments are to be linked to the specific pathways that Yugoslavia (and more specifically its wealthiest republic, Slovenia) and Hungary had undertaken during the late period of state socialism: in Yugoslavia, a unique system of self-management in workers-owned companies developed from the 1970s onward, which paved the way for a certain degree of autonomy of civil society organizations (Jancar 1985), whereas in Hungary ever greater portions of society were progressively taken out from a strict state control as a specific path of "market socialism" during the 1980s. As illustrated by Table 7.1, the first post-1989 debates on the regulation of sexual minorities' rights thus emerged in highly differentiated contexts, ranging from prohibition to incipient visibility. It is therefore not surprising that these debates focused on different issues (depenalization, equalization of the age of consent, recognition of same-sex partnerships, or judicial protection against homophobia).

With transition to democracy and freedom of assembly, civil society organizations have blossomed across the region. Yet, LGBTQI organizations developed at different speeds, due to different degrees of opposition from their respective societies and different windows of opportunity for bringing their demands in the public debate (Flam 2001). In Poland or Lithuania, for instance, incipient LGBTQI communities first had to deal with the strength of traditional, heteronormative values and were mainly

Table 7.1. Recognition of LGBTQI rights in CEEC: an overview

	Decriminalization of homosexual consented intercourses	Age of consent equal as for heterosexual partners	Legal recognition of same-sex couples (debated)	Gay marriage (debated)
Bulgaria	2002	2002	–	–
Croatia	1977	1997	(2001) **2003**	(2013)
Czech Rep.	1961	1990	(1992, 1997–99) **2006**	–
Estonia	1992	1992	**2016**	(2005)
Hungary	1961	2002	1996* (2006) **2009**	(2011)
Latvia	1992	2004	(1999, 2006)	–
Lithuania	1992	1992	(2004, 2006)	–
Poland	1932	1932	(2004)	–
Romania	2001	2001	(2002)	–
Slovakia	1961	1990	(2002)	(2015)
Slovenia	1977	1977	(2003) **2005**	(2009, 2015)

Source: QUING deliverable n°19 + updated by the author
*Non-registered partnership

engaged in a politics of anti-discrimination, in order to prevent the most brutal assaults against gay and lesbian individuals. They found a resolute opponent in the Catholic Church, with strong lobbying and social mobilization capacities, as they did in Slovakia, although to a lesser extent due to a higher degree of secularization achieved under Czechoslovakia. Similarly, in Latvia, LGBTQI communities have faced strong political opposition and limited civil society support, in a context where the politics of identity are fully determined by the question of the citizenship status of the large Russian-speaking community (which amounts to 40 percent of the population) and the tense relations with the Russian neighbor. As in Poland, the right to assembly has been repeatedly denied to these organizations, and both countries repeatedly rank as the most homo-negative in the Rainbow Europe Index issued by ILGA-Europe, the Europe-wide gay rights umbrella organization. In Estonia, the demands of LGBTQI organizations have long been ignored, rather than receiving consistent or articulated opposition. In Romania and Bulgaria, sexual minorities' rights did not emerge as a public matter until the early 2000s. Far more distant to EU gross domestic product (GDP) average than all other CEE candidate countries that joined the Union in 2004, both countries went through an even more conditional process of accession that was eventually delayed to 2007. This built up a context which drastically limited the opposition to EU-driven developments in the field of anti-discrimination, with decriminalizing homosexuality as a first step. In Croatia, the latest of the CEECs to have joined the EU bloc, in 2013, LGBTQI organizations emerged well after the end of the War of Independence in 1995, and the movement's breakthrough did not come before 2002. Until the country formally opened EU accession negotiations, domestic anti-discrimination claims had been silenced by the religious and nationalistic references that shaped post-1991 Croatian political culture (Kuhar 2008a; Kuhar and Čeplak 2016). While acknowledging their differences, it can be said that in all those countries, it is the process of EU accession, rather than endogenous variables, which opened some limited opportunities to bring LGBTQI rights forward, by erasing discriminatory provisions from penal codes and transposing EU anti-discrimination directives in domestic legal orders.

The cases of the Czech Republic, Hungary, and Slovenia contrast somewhat with these abovementioned developments. Following earlier developments in the 1980s, Hungary or Slovenia have seen the emergence of relatively active LGBTQI scenes from the early years of their democratic transitions. In Hungary, gay pride marches were held undisturbed from 1996 up to 2006 (Dombos and Kriszán 2008), and Budapest even marketed itself as a gay-friendly "party" destination, following the model set by reunited Berlin in the 1990s. On the legal ground, a decision of the Constitutional Court prescribed the legal recognition of same-sex couples as early as 1995. Czechoslovakia of the 1980s, still strongly impacted by the "normalization" process inaugurated after the Soviet invasion of 1968, had presented a more adverse context for the development of such organizations. Hence, those which emerged after 1989, although not confronted with strong societal resistance, did not have the organizational capacities to influence policy making at a time when crucial reforms were being carried out. In absence of such pressures, when the Czech cabinet drafted a set of amendments to the Civil Code in 1992, proposed articles on same-sex relations were all rejected (Nedbálková 2006; Röder 2007a). The cases of the Czech Republic, Hungary, and Slovenia illustrate situations in which endogenous developments have taken place prior to the context of EU accession negotiations, launched by the late 1990s in most of CEE.

Making Sense of Diversity

Along with path-dependent features mentioned earlier, such as the role of the Catholic Church, the war in the Balkans, or the politics of identity generated by the presence of large Russian communities, these latter cases invite us to address the "domestic impact of Europe," as Thomas Risse and Tanja Börzel (2003) put it. This impact includes, for example, the differentiating pulse given to the debates over the recognition of same-sex couples by the Europeanization process in which CEECs engaged from the late 1990s onward. Simultaneously, addressing domestic vs. EU-driven variables suggests a selection from the above-listed cases of the most characteristic of these two categories of variables, and those where this question has triggered the most legal and institutional developments, namely Croatia, Hungary, Slovakia, and Slovenia.

External influences in general have played a role throughout the debates on same-sex partnerships that have developed in the CEECs. This variable covers knowledge about institutional arrangements and ways of doing things in other political contexts (Dolowitz and Marsh 1996). Moreover, the first changes in regulating homosexuality were introduced as a necessary effort to meet international standards in the preservation of human rights, as defined in international conventions or in the best practices promoted by the United Nations and other transnational actors, including non-governmental organizations (NGOs). Due to its conditionality and to the wide range of processes it covers, Europeanization must nonetheless be distinguished from other sources of influence. Besides, although Europeanization, through the politics of anti-discrimination, had an impact on these debates in *every* new member state, this impact must be differentiated. In some cases it has been the main impetus for putting these issues on the agenda in the first place, while in others it provided a new window of opportunity for the advocacy of LGBTQI rights in general, thus regenerating former discussions.

The development of gender equality and anti-discrimination policies at EU level, including not only hard law but also paradigms, models of governance, and good practices, does not produce similar—or even comparable—effects in the member states (Forest 2006a; Röder 2007b). Comparative projects carried out in country samples that integrate different generations of member states, from the founders to the latecomers, highlight different patterns (Liebert 2003). These differences depend not only on time (the later the accession, the broader the scope and content of these policies areas at the EU level), but also of the policy and institutional legacy at the domestic level in the affected area (Caporaso and Jupille 2001). Paying attention to the *domestic* impact of Europeanization, this approach can be extended from the level of legislative and institutional instruments to the level of soft mechanisms and practices. This latter level of analysis is adopted in sociological approaches to Europeanization (Woll and Jacquot 2010), which stress the impact of EU accession on the actors involved in these policy areas at the national and subnational levels, and, conversely, the *uses* made of "Europe" by those same actors. These uses include: Europe as a historical reference disconnected from the EU as a set of institutions; and the EU as an instance of legitimization, as a political and social trendsetter, or as a threat to national values and interests (Neumayer 2006).

The highly differentiating effect of Europeanization thus affects these different levels of analysis and, understandably, its impact varies greatly from one policy area to another. Intimate citizenship accounts for only a small part of the considerable amount of gender equality and anti-discrimination policies of the EU, and there are formally—in the form of directives—few EU-level legal grounds for the regulation of LGBTQI rights. Yet, along with existing provisions, the case law of the European Court of Justice (ECJ) "deftly managed to slide into place as an autonomous norm-setter, expanding the entitlements of LGBT individuals, and even awarding them more rights and benefits than their national governments were willing to grant them" (De Waele and Van der Vleuten 2011). Additionally, in this area, Europeanization also consists of soft instruments and norm diffusion, including through the transformation of patterns of collective action. With the introduction of EU policies, funding procedures, and call for expertise, feminist and LGBTQI organizations have thus been led to bring substantial changes to their agendas, methods of action, or strategic framings (Forest 2006a, b). If we consider such a broad definition of Europeanization, there is no doubt that the politics of recognition of same-sex relationships and partnerships in CEECs have been impacted in a number of ways. Yet, this impact has been of variable intensity, alternately constituting a variable or a consistent framing of the issues at stake. Although their comprehensive assessment falls out of the scope of this chapter, these differentiating patterns, and the way domestic variables interplay with Europeanization patterns, can be illustrated through the specific debates in the countries discussed in this chapter.

Framing Recognition of Same-Sex Couples: Between Nationalization and Europeanization

Domestic Framing of the Issue of Gay Marriage? Hungary and Slovenia

Hungary
To comply with a decision of the Constitutional Court in 1995, the then left-wing government opened *unregistered* cohabitation[1] to same-sex couples and initiated the complete recodification of civil law (including the Civil Code and the Family Code). The framing of the short debates that resulted in the 1996 civil law reforms was characterized by emphasis on human rights and non-discrimination, and the need, assumed by the Constitutional Court, to make ordinary law conform to the principles stated in the 1949 Constitution and to ratified international treaties and conventions. If the whole process started soon after the Socialist Party (Magyar Szocialista Párt, MSZP) won an absolute majority (1994), governing in coalition with liberal Free Democrats' Alliance (Szabad Demokraták Szövetsége, SZDSZ), the then centrist opposition from the Hungarian Civic Alliance (Magyar Polgári Szövetség, FIDESZ) did not attempt to make the reform a *casus belli* and even proved to be rather supportive (Dombos and Kriszán 2008). Much more controversial, however, were the long processes that ended with the equalization of the age of consent and the adoption of more comprehensive anti-discrimination legislation. Fierce disputes also occurred in relation to the discussion of a *registered* partnership open to both same-sex and heterosexual couples. This polemic occurred in a context of growing ideological polarization in the aftermath of the contested victory of the Socialist Party, in 2006 (Buzogány 2008).

These violent debates, which spread well beyond the walls of Parliament, with unprecedented assaults against sexual minorities, evidenced a discursive framing that linked the recognition of same-sex couples with the politics of population growth. Fueled by non-parliamentary right-wing organizations, public concern over demographic issues was explicitly linked to the preservation of national virtues and to the condemnation of deviant behaviors undermining the "reproductive health" of the nation. As a collateral effect of the "second political culture" developed by the FIDESZ once in the opposition, this frame became dominant in one of the main parliamentary forces in Hungary. Vehement opposition among conservatives to the granting of new rights to LGBTQI people made center-left parties, which had been so far mostly passive, more determined in advocating liberal values.

The debate on the Registered Partnership Act, which was adopted in December 2007 and came into force in early 2009, took place in the aftermath of the battles over the equalization of the age of consent and the approval of an Anti-Discrimination Act covering discriminations based on sexual orientation. This debate has therefore also been shaped by the references to the EU policy framework. However, it mainly stressed country—or even more meaningfully—nation-specific arguments. Grounded in an ethnic- and religious-based understanding of nationhood and citizenship, opposition to the new laws was reinforced by a discourse on the demographic decline of the nation, and the threat posed by domestic ethnic and sexual minorities. Within the broader context of the polarization of Hungarian party politics, the preservation of the nation against threats such as same-sex marriage has become commonplace for the FIDESZ and for far-right parties such as Jobbik. As a result of this politicization of an issue that initially triggered little political contestation, same-sex marriage was explicitly prohibited by the new Constitution adopted in 2011 by FIDESZ's two-third majority. The law came into force in January 2012, and does not contain any sort of protection against discrimination on the grounds of sexual orientation. Since that time, the refugee crisis that placed Hungary on migration routes to the EU has largely obliterated this discussion, with Viktor Orban's anti-migrant diatribes dominating, although fighting Islamization, multiculturalism, and homosexuality occasionally coincide in public debate.

Slovenia
During the 1990s, LGBTQI collectives repeatedly brought the issues of same-sex partnerships and gay marriage into the public discussion, arguing that article 14 of the Constitution prohibits discrimination based on any personal circumstances and that article 141 of the Penal Code explicitly prohibits discrimination on the basis of sexual orientation. An expert group on the issue was established within the Ministry of Labor and Social Affairs, including representatives of LGBTQI organizations. However, the first draft was never transmitted to the Slovene Council. Another expert group was established in 2001, but it was explicitly requested not to include the sub-issues of adoption and legal protection of same-sex families (Jalušič et al. 2007).

Nevertheless, the first bill on the recognition of same-sex couples, submitted in 2003 on behalf of the post-communist Union of Social Democrats (Združena lista socialnih demokratov, ZLSD), with the lip-service support of the then ruling center-left Liberal Democrats of Slovenia (LDS), granted them substantial rights, despite opposition from the right-wing People's Party. During the first parliamentary debate, the main argument of its most resolute opponents was that "The law cannot equate something that cannot be equated. (...) Due to the physical survival of the society (...) public authority has to stand (...) to ensure families to be prolific. (...) The homosexual unions do not and cannot by far fulfil these tasks" (New Slovenia MP, right wing conservative, quoted in Kuhar 2008, 60–63). This demographic argument was also discursively linked to promoting "natural" reproduction over adoption or medically assisted reproduction, allegedly in order to preserve the ethnic homogeneity of the Slovenian nation. As noted by Roman Kuhar (2008a), despite this demographic framing, lesbians remained invisible during the legislative process.

An agreement was reached between coalition partners in March 2004, but final approval was suspended to upcoming elections. Following the victory of the right-wing Slovenian Democratic Party (Slovenska Demokratska Stranka, SDS), the initial bill was rejected and the SDS drafted its own bill, reducing the rights of same-sex couples to a minimum without consulting LGBTQI organizations. The Same-Sex Partnership Act (Zakon o registraciji istospolne partnerske skupnosti, ZRIPS) adopted on June 2005, thus contained a limited number of rights, such as limited inheritance rights or shared medical insurance. Leaving aside the issue of parental rights, no social and pension rights were granted and the Act came into force in June 2006.

Barely three years later, the Constitutional Court found that preventing registered partners from inheriting each other's properties and treating them differently from married couples was constitutive of discrimination on the ground of sexual orientation, thus breaching Article 14 of the Constitution. In response, the government had six months to provide a new regulation. The then ruling center-left LDS intended to legalize same-sex marriage through a reform to the Family Code. This reform was first presented in September 2009 and brought before Parliament in December. After being adopted at first reading in March 2010, the bill was nonetheless modified by the government to address the strong resistance that it had sparked among the public. The new version maintained marriage as an institution reserved for heterosexual couples, but same-sex couples were granted similar rights to married couples, except for joint adoption. This bill was passed in June 2011, but was immediately challenged by The Civil Initiative for the Family and Rights of Children, which eventually managed to gather sufficient support to hold a referendum, drawing upon resources and support from the Catholic Church (Kuhar 2015). Authorized by the Constitutional Court, this referendum ended up rejecting the bill.

In 2014, the government prepared a new bill, equalizing rights among different partnership regimes, except for medically assisted procreation and adoption. Suspended pending the result of early elections, this bill was soon challenged by a parliamentary bill on same-sex marriage. Coming from the left-wing opposition, it intended to grant same-sex couples rights equal to those of heterosexual married couples. It received the support of two of the parties represented in the majority coalition and was passed in March 2015. Again, The Civil Initiative for the Family and Rights of Children managed to collect signatures with a view to demanding a popular-initiative referendum. While the government seemed reluctant to oppose the referendum, a group of MPs called an extraordinary session of the House, which voted to declare that the referendum would violate the Constitution in the areas of human rights and constitutional freedoms. The Civil Initiative appealed to the Constitutional Court in March 2015. The judgement rendered on October 22 contested the legitimacy of the National Assembly to decide on the constitutionality of the referendum, which was held in December 2015. The bill was rejected by 63.5 percent of voters, and although turnout only reached 36.4 percent, it was sufficient to validate the result and to prevent Slovenia from becoming the first CEEC to legalize same-sex marriage.

Although references to Western democracies and the ECJ's rulings in matters of LGBTQI rights were occasionally brought into the debates on registered partnership recognition, Roman Kuhar and Metka Mencin Čeplak (2016) insist that policy transfers and Europeanization processes have played a relatively marginal role in Slovenia. Instead, debates appeared to be tightly framed by domestic institutions and (coalition) party politics. Whereas references to Article 13 of the Amsterdam Treaty, which prohibits discrimination including on the ground of sexual orientation, could have supported the decision made by the Constitutional Court in 2009, only similar provisions held in the national fundamental law were mentioned. Therefore, while it can be assumed that Europeanization mattered for the broader context of the recognition of equal rights with respect to citizenship and nationality, it only remotely affected the discursive framing that eventually led to the rejection of gay marriage.

Contentious Europeanization Versus the Nation: Croatia and Slovakia

Croatia

In Croatia, the long reign of nationalist and conservative Franjo Tudjman's Croatian Democratic Party (Hrvatska demokratska zajednica, HDZ) from 1991 to 2000 and above all, the war in which the country was involved from 1991 to 1995, have long thwarted any attempt to put same-sex marriage on the agenda (Dedic 2007). However, taking advantage of the announced reform of the Family Law, so far unregistered LGBTQI organizations came out in the early 2000s, pushing for the legal recognition of same-sex couples. With wide media coverage and the support of the Minister of Social and Labor affairs, most of the amendments suggested by these recent organizations were taken into account in the first draft of the bill, renamed Family, Marriage, and Common Law Marriage Act, approved at its first reading. In order to ensure the bill would pass through further readings, LGBTQI organizations and the Ministry strategically agreed, as they had in Slovenia, to address families and same-sex partnerships in two separate laws. Pragmatism proved to be successful, as the Same-Sex Civil Union Act was adopted in July 2003, despite fierce opposition from the conservative parties, relaying the positions of the Catholic Church and non-parliamentary nationalist organizations (Kuhar 2015). While maintaining most of the legal privileges of heterosexual marriage by including a very limited number of rights (mutual support and common property), it constituted a first step for LGBTIQ advocates.

This fast-track adoption process did not hinder different framings from being articulated during the debates. An equality and anti-discrimination frame was opposed by a frame combining references to "Natural Law" with Catholic and nationalist values, as expressed by the words of a female HDZ MP: "Here we are not talking about Human rights. This bill is a project of destruction of the foundations of Croatian families and the Croatian State. It is a surgery against the values of the Patriotic war and the values of the Christian family" (Kuhar 2008b). Ironically, while the "Patriotic war" was the main cause of the decrease in population and fertility rates that occurred in the early 1990s, this articulation attempted to present demographic trends as a result of imported social diseases such as homosexuality, as evidenced in parliamentary debates quoted in Kuhar (2008b, 2011). Meanwhile, the "equality and anti-discrimination" frame revealed itself to be ambiguous and inconsistent, as it was used to support the approval of a law that remained largely discriminatory, alongside an argument that LGBTQI people were too few to constitute a demographic threat to the nation.

A next round of debate on same-sex partnership took place in 2005, when a bill was drafted by LGBTQI organizations, as a step further in the recognition of same-sex partnerships. The document largely drew upon the Slovenian bill discussed at roughly the same time, thus granting social, health, tax, inheritance, and pension rights equal to those of heterosexual married couples. The HDZ blocked the discussion at an early stage, and the bill was finally rejected in 2006 by a right-wing coalition. These debates, which largely referred to the Catholic values ascribed to Croatian society, reinforced the conservative framing of the issue (Dedic 2007), with the growing implication of the Catholic Church (Kuhar 2015). Simultaneously, as the debate over EU membership was gaining relevance, this conservative stance on the family was increasingly framed as a limit to be imposed on the expected consequences of EU membership on issues related to intimate citizenship. This trend eventually materialized in two consecutive referendums, held successively in January 2012 on EU accession, as required by the Croatian Constitution, and in December 2013 with a view to reforming the Constitution in order to explicitly prohibit same-sex marriage. While 66 percent of voters cast their ballot in favor of EU accession, barely two years later a similar proportion voted to modify the Constitution in order to make marriage the union of a man and a woman, against the position of both the prime minister and the president. Called by U ime obitelji (In the Name of the Family), a civic initiative supported by the Catholic Church, the referendum proposal had first secured 700,000 signatures (Slootmaeckers and Sircar 2014).

Slovakia

In 1997, echoing the first parliamentary debate on same-sex partnership in the Czech Republic, a Draft of the Act on a Registered Partnership of Homosexual Couples was published in *Aspekt*, a feminist journal with a limited impact among politicians. In 2000, an informal platform of NGOs, Iniciatíva Inakosť (Initiative Otherness) was established, the main objective of which was to pursue the adoption of a law on registered partnerships. Moreover, four NGOs representing gay and lesbian minorities initiated the draft of the Act on Same-Sex Partnership (Očenášová 2007).

According to NGOs, the draft drew upon Articles 1 and 12 of the Constitution, while a counter-proposal from Christian Democrats (Krest'anskodemokratické Hnutie, KDH) tried to subsume the situation of same-sex couples under existing sections of the Civil Code. The draft of the Act was not included to the parliamentary agenda. As a third attempt, Iniciatíva Inakosť collaborated with a cluster of MP from different parties on a draft making homosexual partnership equal to heterosexual marriage in all matters except adoption and medically assisted procreation. Submitted in October 2001, it did not proceed to the second reading.

Much more impressive is the record of the *anti*-agenda of same-sex partnership. In 2000, Slovakia signed a bilateral treaty with the Holy See, where it pledged (Article 11) to support and protect only heterosexual marriage and the family that comes from such a marriage. In 2002, at the instigation of one of the then ruling coalition parties (Christian Democratic Movement), the Parliament approved a Declaration of the National Council of the Slovak Republic about the EU Member States' Sovereignty in Cultural and Ethical Issues. In the Declaration, respect for the sovereignty of the EU member states is required regarding the protection of family and marriage as a founding institution. In 2004, a provision was introduced into the Law on Elementary and Secondary Schools, according to which "it is not permitted to influence sexual orientation, which is contradicting human dignity and traditional values of European culture (...)."

Public debate in Slovakia has long been dominated by a conservative frame based on the preservation of marriage and the principle that other forms of unions contradict (Catholic) European values. This frame has been articulated mainly by Christian Democrats, who barely account for 10 percent of the vote, but who proved a key actor in coalition-building from 1999 to 2012 and enjoyed a larger audience on social and morality issues. Besides, populist and nationalist discourse cultivated among prominent members of the Slovak National Party (Slovenska Narodna Strana, SNS) provide some clear occurrences of a framing of LGBTQI rights issues grounded on the assumption that *homosexuality is a disease*, an allegedly imported "plague" that needs to be eradicated. However, a human rights and anti-discrimination frame has been emerging since the victory of SMER (social democrats) in 2006 and despite the presence of SNS members in governmental functions during the term 2006–2010. With the support of LGBTQI organizations and some prominent politicians, this frame tended to go beyond the limited references to sexual orientation introduced in the 2004 Anti-Discrimination Act adopted under the pressure of the European Commission. In addition, the Christian-Democratic movement lost its key position in the majority in 2012.

However, opposition to the legal recognition of LGBTQI rights in general and same-sex couples in particular has not faded in Slovakia. In June 2014, an overwhelming majority of the left-dominated Parliament voted an amendment to the Constitution that anchors the definition of marriage as the "legally recognized union between a man and a woman," raising new concerns for LGBTQI advocates. This amendment did not end with the claims of the Alliance for Family, an umbrella organization supported by the Catholic Church, which called for a referendum. After gathering 400,000 signatures to hold the referendum in a country of five million inhabitants, the vote took place in February 2015 on three questions: framing marriage as the union of a man and a woman; prohibiting adoption for same-sex couples; and opposing sexual education in public schools. Although opponents to the referendum did not effectively join forces, the referendum did not pass the required 50 percent threshold, as only 21 percent of voters cast their ballot.

Slovakia, which claimed its sovereignty in cultural and ethical issues in 2002, prior to joining the EU, thus embodies an ambivalent use of the references to Europeanness. Christian Democrats have now lost their momentum in Slovak politics, but the Catholic Church, with the support of right-wing civil society organizations, has shown the same willingness to protect "European values." And under the current red-brown coalition,[2] outspoken nationalism is mobilized both against the threats brought by refugees from the Middle East and in defense of traditional family values.

Conclusion

The legal recognition of same-sex partnerships and its highly differential treatment in the enlarged EU account for the huge diversity of the politics of intimate citizenship in post-socialist Europe. However, such diversity cannot only be framed as the consequence of differences in social or cultural values that Europeanization, among other historical trends, might contribute to bridging. These debates mostly originate in the very conditions of the post-socialist transformation. If four decades of Soviet domination and/or socialist regimes had produced some common patterns in the politics of family, bodily integrity, and gender, this period did not shape a sole "gender regime" (Jancar 1978; Heitlinger 1979; Gal and Kligman 2000a, b). Instead, as documented by the issue of sexual minorities, various social and legislative arrangements have remained that distinguish the respective situations of Central Europe, South-Eastern Europe, and former Soviet Republics such as the Baltic States. Moreover, while it is true that the transition to democracy provided a window of opportunity for new social actors to place new issues on the political agenda, most initial changes registered in the field of intimate citizenship were fostered by governments, whether to meet international standards or—often with opposite outcomes—to promote social values that had been stigmatized or proscribed under Communist regimes. The institutional and political paths of extrication from state socialism thus contributed to shaping the politics of gender after socialism (Gal and Kligman 2000a, b). This process partly explains, for example, the diverging features of the debates on the recognition of sexual minorities. Mobilized actors and issues at stake (decriminalization of homosexuality, equalization of the age of consent, anti-discrimination policies, same-sex partnership, and gay marriage) have been different according to domestic contexts, as have been the timelines, milestones, and policy outcomes of these debates. A comparative analysis of the different frames that have been developed around these issues might help to systematize the findings of case studies. Such an endeavor suggests the need to pay attention to the cognitive understandings of a same issue that are competing in the public space, and to the voices articulating them. In the case of LGBTQI rights in CEECs, such a perspective invites a differential assessment of the roles of domestic and EU-driven variables.

Among domestic variables, falls the role of the Catholic church, which has gained strength over the 2010s to ground heterosexual marriage in Constitutions, either through parliamentary vote (Slovakia) or referendum (Croatia, Slovakia, Slovenia), with different outcomes. These attempts have faced some resistance in highly secularized Slovenia and have met contradictory results in Catholic Slovakia, where a referendum brought about by Catholic forces failed to meet the participation threshold in 2015, while in Croatia, another referendum prospered in the presence of a much lower threshold. Yet, altogether, they appear to have triggered a backlash in the recognition of same-sex partnerships. Another domestic variable is the imbrication of same-sex couple recognition with the demographic fate of the nation. A consistent frame in Hungary, it also appears as an important framing element in Croatia and Slovenia.

Certainly, Europeanization, understood as a set of processes at the levels of policy making and institutionalization, along with practices of advocacy and political or social mobilization, is playing an important role in bringing these issues to the light in CEECs. Yet, its impact depends on institutional arrangements inherited from state socialism and the transition to democracy, on the nature of the social actors mobilized around these issues, on the level of pressure exerted by European institutions, and on the more general policy discussion to which these debates are related (anti-discrimination policies, family or welfare policies, civil code reforms). The country cases discussed in this chapter illustrate these differentiated domestic impacts of Europeanization, notably as concerns the tension between nationalizing and Europeanizing frames in debates on the regulation of same-sex couples' recognition in post-socialist Europe.

NOTES

1. Unregistered cohabitation, opened to both heterosexual and homosexual couples, entails automatic accrual of cohabitation rights upon the parties moving in together, without requiring registration before a notary.
2. The ruling coalition led by the Social Democrats includes the far-right Slovak National Party.

REFERENCES

Börzel, Tanja A., and Thomas Risse. 2003. Conceptualizing the Domestic Impact of Europe. In *The Politics of Europeanization*, ed. Kevin Featherstone and Claudio Radaelli, 57–80. New York: Oxford University Press.
Buzogány, Aron. 2008. *Joining Europe, Not Sodom. LGBTQI Rights and the Limits of Europeanization in Hungary and Romania*. Paper Given at the 40th AAASS Annual Conference, Philadelphia, November.
Caporaso, James A., and Joseph Jupille. 2001. The Europeanization of Gender Equality Policy and Domestic Structural Change. In *Transforming Europe: Europeanization and Domestic Change*, ed. Cowles M. Green, James A. Caporaso, and Thomas Risse, 21–43. Ithaca, NY: Cornell University Press.
Dąbrowska, Magdalena. 2007. *Series of Timelines of Policy Debates in Selected Topics, Poland*. Vienna: Institute of Human Sciences.
De Waele, Henri, and Anna van der Vleuten. 2011. Judicial Activism in the European Court of Justice: The Case of LGBT Rights. *Michigan State Journal of International Law* 19 (3): 639–666.

Dedic, Jasminka. 2007. *Series of Timelines of Policy Debates: Croatia.* QUING Deliverable No. 19, IWM, Vienna.
Dolowitz, David, and David Marsh. 1996. Who Learns What From Whom? A Review of the Policy Transfer Literature. *Political studies* 14 (2): 343–357.
Dombos, Tomos, and Andrea Krizsán. 2008. *Series of LARG Country Reports: Hungary.* QUING Deliverable No. 40, IWM, Vienna.
Flam, Helena. 2001. *Pink, Purple, Green: Women's Religious, Environmental and Gay/Lesbian Movements in Central Europe today.* Boulder, CO: East European Monographs.
Forest, Maxime. 2006a. Emerging Gender Interest Groups in the New Member States: The Case of the Czech Republic. *Perspectives on European Politics and Society* 7 (2): 170–185.
———. 2006b. Les transferts institutionnels à l'usage des politiques du genre en Europe centrale. *Revue internationale de politique comparée* 13 (2): 259–278.
———. 2008. *The Politics of Intimate Citizenship and Anti-discrimination in Central and Eastern Europe. From Country-Specific Debates to Contentious Europeanization?* Paper Presented at the 40th AAASS Annual Conference, Philadelphia, November 20–23.
———. 2011. Women in Executives in Central and Eastern Europe. In *Women in Executives: A Global Overview*, ed. Gretchen Bauer and Manon Tremblay, 65–84. New York: Routledge.
Gal, Susan, and Gal Kligman. 2000a. *The Politics of Gender after Socialism.* Princeton, NJ: Princeton University Press.
———, eds. 2000b. *Reproducing Gender: Politics, Publics and Everyday Life After Socialism.* Princeton, NJ: Princeton University Press.
Heitlinger, Alena. 1979. *Women and State Socialism: Sex Inequality in the Soviet Union and Czechoslovakia.* Montreal: McGill-Queen's University Press.
Woll, Cornelia and Sophie Jacquot. 2010. Using Europe: Strategic Action in Multi-level Politics. *Comparative European Politics* 8: 110–126.
Jalušič, Vlasta, Roman Kuhar, et al. 2007. *Series of Timelines of Policy Debates: Slovenia.* QUING Deliverable No. 19, IWM, Vienna.
Jancar, Barbara. 1978. *Women under Communism.* Baltimore, MD: John Hopkins University Press.
———. 1985. The New Feminism in Yugoslavia. In *Yugoslavia in the 1980s*, ed. Pedro Ramet. Boulder, CO: Westview Press.
Kahlina, Katja. 2014. Local Histories, European LGBTQI Designs: Sexual Citizenship, Nationalism, and 'Europeanisation' in Post-Yugoslav Croatia and Serbia. *Women's Studies International Forum.* https://doi.org/10.1016/j.wsif.2014.07.006.
Kaplan, Cora, Joan W. Scott, and Debra Keats, eds. 1997. *Transitions Environments Translations: Feminisms in International Politics.* New York: Routledge.

Kuhar, Roman. 2008a. *Series of LARG Country Report: Slovenia.* QUING Deliverable No. 40, IWM, Vienna.
———. 2008b. *Series of LARG Country Report: Croatia.* QUING Deliverable No. 40, IWM, Vienna.
———. 2011. Resisting Change. Same-Sex Partnership Policy Debates in Croatia and Slovenia. *Südost Europa* 59: 25–49.
———. 2015. Playing with Science: Sexual Citizenship and the Roman Catholic Church Counter-narratives in Slovenia and Croatia. *Women's Studies International Forum* 49: 84–92.
Kuhar, Roman, and Metka Mencin Čeplak. 2016. Same-Sex Partnership Debate in Slovenia: Between Declarative Support and Lack of Political Will. In *The EU Enlargement and Gay Politics*, ed. K. Slootmaeckers, H. Touquet, and P. Vermeersch. Basingstoke: Palgrave Macmillan.
Kuhar, Roman, and Judith Takacs. 2007. *Beyond the Pink Curtain. Everyday Life of LGBTQI People in Eastern Europe.* Ljubljana: Peace Institut.
Liebert, Ulrike. 2003. *Europeanisation and Gender Equality: Reframing Public Policy in EU member States.* Brussels: Peter Lang.
———, eds. 2012. *The Europeanization of Gender Equality Policies: A Discursive Sociological Approach.* Basingtoke: Palgrave Macmillan.
Matland, Robert, and Kathleen A. Montgomery, eds. 2003. *Women's Access to Political Power in Post-Communist Europe.* Oxford: Oxford University Press.
Nakachi, Mie. 2006. N.S. Krushschev and the 1944 Soviet Family Law: Politics, Reproduction and Language. *East European Politics & Societies* 20 (1): 40–68.
Neumayer, Laure. 2006. *L'enjeu européen dans les transformations postcommunistes.* Paris: Belin.
Očenášová, Zuzana. 2007. *Series of Timelines of Policy Debates: Slovakia.* QUING Deliverable No. 19, IWM, Vienna.
Radaelli, Claudio. 2004. Europeanisation: Solution or Problem. *European Integration Online Papers* 8 (16). http://eiop.or.at/eiop/texte/2004-016a.html
Röder, Ingrid. 2007a. *Series of Timelines of Policy Debates: The Czech Rep.* QUING Deliverable No. 19, IWM, Vienna.
———. 2007b. *Gender Equality, Pre-accession Assistance and Europeanisation: Two Post-Socialist Countries on Their Way to the European Union.* Berlin: Logos-Verlag.
Roth, Silke. 2004. One Step Forwards, One Step Backwards, One Step Forwards: The Impact of EU Policy on Gender Relations in Central and Eastern Europe. *Transitions* XLIV (1): 15–27.
Schimmelfennig, Frank, and Ulrike Sedelmeier. 2004. Governance by Conditionality. EU Rule Tranfer to the Candidate Countries of Central and Eastern Europe. *Journal of European Public Policy* 11: 661–679.

Schmidt, Vivien. 2010. On Putting Ideas into Perspective: Schmidt on Kessler, Martin and Hudson, and Smith. In *The Role of Ideas in Political Analysis: A Portrait of Contemporary Debates*, ed. Andreas Gofas and Colin Hay. London: Routledge.

Slootmaeckers, Koen and Indraneel Sircar. 2014. *Croatia, the EU, and the Marriage Referendum: The Symbolic Case of LGBTQI Rights*. Paper Presented at the ECPR General Conference. Glasgow, September 3–6.

Verloo, Mieke. 2005. Mainstreaming Gender Equality in Europe. A Critical Frame Analysis. *The Greek Review of Social Research* 117: 11–35.

Maxime Forest is research associate at Sciences Po Paris, France (OFCE). Previously, as a postdoctoral researcher at University Complutense, Madrid, he participated in the Quality in Gender + Equality Policies (QUING) project, an EU-wide comparative analysis including the politics of intimate citizenship. His research interests cover the Europeanization of gender and anti-discrimination policies and neo-institutionalist approaches to the politics of gender in Central and Southern Europe. His recent publications include *The Politics of Feminist Knowledge Transfer* (Palgrave, 2016), coedited with Maria Bustelo and Lucy Ferguson, and *The Europeanization of Gender Equality Policies: A Discursive-Sociological Approach* (Palgrave, 2012), coedited with Emanuela Lombardo.

CHAPTER 8

Preserving the Social Fabric: Debating Family, Equality and Polity in the UK, the Republic of Ireland and Australia

Bronwyn Winter

INTRODUCTION

The UK, the Republic of Ireland and Australia have a long shared history, shaped, particularly through colonization/occupation and associated migrations, by shared language, culture, worldviews and even political and legal systems. These commonalities hold, notwithstanding some significant differences, many of which are *also* due to the legacy of occupation and colonization. However, in the process of institutionalization of same-sex marriage, it is the differences, much more than the commonalities, that would appear, at first view, to have suggested specific institutional path-dependencies and thus quite different outcomes. Yet, all three countries have largely defied such institutionally logical expectations and gone in the opposite direction from what one might have predicted at the beginning of this millennium, when the Netherlands became the first country in the world to legalize same-sex marriage, in December 2000. This chapter investigates these expectation-defying pathways, and will rely largely on discursive institutional (DI) analysis to do so.

B. Winter (✉)
The University of Sydney, Sydney, NSW, Australia

© The Author(s) 2018
B. Winter et al. (eds.), *Global Perspectives on Same-Sex Marriage*, Global Queer Politics, https://doi.org/10.1007/978-3-319-62764-9_8

Discussions of same-sex marriage also point to transnational factors, seen as largely exogenous: the globalization of lesbian, gay, bisexual, and transgender (LGBT) rights discourse and its adoption within institutions such as the United Nations (UN), the Council of Europe and the European Union (EU). This globalized and (semi-)institutionalized discourse translates into a tendency towards policy convergence (perhaps most marked in Western Europe), and in particular, the tying of same-sex marriage to concepts cherished by capitalist democracies: equality, human rights and justice. Although these factors play a role in the British, Irish and Australian cases, what is fascinating about a comparison between these three national contexts is the importance played by endogenous factors, and indeed endogenous *discursive* factors. Moreover, these three cases highlight the dialectic between constraint and enablement that Schmidt (2010) discusses: how existing institutions can appear alternately as roadblocks or as the foundation on which change can be built, depending on the political will and various *rapports de force* (relationships of power or influence) between the different actors at the time. Moreover, this comparison will show that political and legal institutional actors are not simply *respondents* to the discursive climate produced by national and transnational civil society actors, but can also contribute, through anticipatory counter-action, to creating it, as Michael Dorf and Sidney Tarrow (2014) have observed in relation to social counter-movements in the USA. In other words, institutional actors can pre-empt and even provoke social movement action, through their discourses, decisions and laws—in short, through the concrete expressions they give to their political will (Johnson and Tremblay 2016). In some cases, such as those of the UK and the Republic of Ireland, governments can use a conservative discursive framework to change some aspects of the content of "marriage," "without compromising its ideational and conceptual integrity" (Grube and van Acker 2016, 184). In others (perhaps most notoriously the US Defense of Marriage Act of 1996 and the Australian Marriage Amendment Act of 2004, the latter discussed in this chapter), pre-emptive actions by states have wrested the discursive leadership role from civil society actors, rendering rhetorically and indeed legally explicit a narrower, passéist conceptualization of "marriage," and, by extension, "family."

National debates over same-sex marriage have invariably been imbricated, alongside debates over national-cultural values, with debates over the family and its meaning in modern societies. This is to some extent unsurprising, as family is foregrounded in international and European human rights treaties as the fundamental unit of society and primary vehicle for legal recognition of private life, affective relationships and the care of children (Winter 2017). All national laws regulating relationships, the care of children and welfare regimes contain explicit references to the family. Moreover, differing views of the family are explicitly or implicitly embedded within the values frames used by both advocates and opponents of same-sex marriage, even if those "values" are often the cloak in which political expediency is disguised. These frames are, for both sides of the debate, alternately inscribed as universalist aspirations (human rights, equality, justice, sexual citizenship) or particularist ones (the Republic; religion; "African" or "Asian" values; preservation, reinforcement or perfectioning of the national fabric).

In 2012, the Network of European LGBTIQ* Families Associations (NELFA) reinforced the "family" frame when it launched the International Family Equality Day (IFED). According to NELFA's 2017 press release, IFED is now celebrated by lesbian, gay, bisexual, transgender, intersex and queer/questioning (LGBTIQ) organizations in some 80 countries, and is recognized by the Council of Europe as "an important tool to combat homophobia and transphobia and to promote a tolerant and cohesive society" (NELFA 2017). The timing of IFED on May 7 is organized to lead up to the International Day Against Homophobia and Transphobia (IDAHOT), which was launched in 2004 and takes place every year on May 17. In 2017 IDAHOT joined with NELFA to focus on families (NELFA 2017, IDAHOT website).[1]

In keeping with this international trend, the idea of *family* and its national, cultural and indeed religious role has been, if not the only element of the national conversation in the UK, Ireland and Australia over same-sex marriage, certainly one of the key ones.

Some Institutional Background

The UK, Ireland and Australia are all bicameral Westminster-system regimes. Although Ireland is a republic and elects its head of state by universal suffrage, the president's powers are, like those of the Queen in the UK and the Governor-General in Australia, largely ceremonial. (The role of the president in Ireland became more politicized during Mary Robinson's term [1990–1997]; she was more interventionist than the norm, notably in sexual liberalization and human rights matters. I will return presently to the historical and symbolic importance of Robinson's presidency.) In all three countries, the government is chosen from among the elected ministers in the legislature, usually all members of the majority party or, in the case of ruling coalitions, the coalition parties. There is thus not the same strong separation between the legislative and executive branches as that which exists in a number of other countries discussed in this book, such as the USA, France or Argentina, where ministers are appointed from outside the legislative branch (although in Argentina they are not technically part of the executive either). This intermingling of the roles of the ruling party or coalition and parliamentary party politics has some bearing on the conduct of debates and enacting of legislation on same-sex marriage.

As concerns regional powers, in the UK, Wales, Scotland and Northern Ireland all have devolved unicameral governments that deal with locally specific matters, but national and parliamentary sovereignty remains with Westminster. In Ireland, power is centralized although the 26 county governments have responsibility for locally relevant infrastructural matters. By contrast, Australia is a federal system: individual states have a reasonable amount of autonomy, albeit far less than in the US. We will see that state versus commonwealth, or federal (national), jurisdictions and powers have been an important factor in the development of the same-sex marriage debate in Australia. In all three countries, however, the regulation of marriage is a national matter, covered by statutory legislation in the UK and Australia and by the Constitution in Ireland, which is why legalization of same-sex marriage required a referendum there. The UK, unlike Ireland and Australia, has no single formal Constitution: its "constitution" is considered to be the sum of formal laws and principles by which the nation is ruled. As there is no Constitution as such, no referendum held in the UK is legally binding on the government, unlike the Irish and Australian cases—a matter much discussed in the wake of the "Brexit" "referendum" of 23 June 2016. None of the three countries have a Charter or Bill of Rights—although the adoption of one has been long debated in the UK and Australia—but many fundamental rights are covered within either the Constitution or statutory legislation. It is thus not certain that the absence of a Charter of Rights has been a significant factor in any of the countries, even if its presence *was* a factor in Canada (see Johnson and Tremblay 2016 for a comparison of the Canadian and Australian cases).

However, all three countries do have human rights agencies, which have played various discursive roles in the same-sex marriage debate. The Irish Human Rights Commission was set up concurrently with that of Northern Ireland under the terms of the 1998 Good Friday agreement; in

2014 it merged with the Equality Authority to create the Irish Human Rights and Equality Commission (IHREC). Its role is limited to the promotion of human rights, including policy recommendations to parliament, and legal advice in human rights cases. The former Equality Authority produced an early report, in 2001, on the rights of same-sex couples (IHREC 2015). The Australian Human Rights Commission (AHRC), on the other hand, has the power to investigate, and resolve through conciliation, cases brought under relevant statutory legislation and to conduct enquiries into human rights issues, but no power to adjudicate or to change laws. In recent decades the AHRC has often found itself at odds with the government, notably in matters such as refugee rights and the recent debate over proposed amendments to the Race Discrimination Act. (A government proposal to replace the words "offend," "insult" and "humiliate" with "harass" in Section 18C was defeated by the Senate in March 2017.) The AHRC has conducted a number of enquiries on LGBT rights, and in 2012 it produced a position paper in support of same-sex marriage as a human rights and equality issue (AHRC 2012). In contrast, the UK Equality and Human Rights Commission (EHRC, formed in 2007 out of the merger of a number of other bodies) has intervened mainly after the fact to comment on the government's 2013 same-sex marriage bill, which subsequently became law, and on aspects of its application since that time. Of the three bodies, the AHRC could thus be seen as the most structurally and discursively proactive, although this latter proactivity is also in part a response to entrenched hostility to certain human rights and equality matters by a number of conservative Australian governments since John Howard first became prime Minister in 1996.

Two other institutional factors are important to consider here: the role of the courts and the role and status of the Christian religion. In all three countries, the same-sex marriage issue has come before the courts at various stages of the process. In the UK and Ireland, juridical activism by civil society actors has been part of the path towards legalization, while in Australia juridical activism has been used both by civil society actors to push for legalization and by the Federal government to block it.

The religious factor has been most in evidence in Ireland, where Article 44(1) of the Constitution stipulates that the state shall "respect and honour religion"; Article 40(6) also prohibits blasphemy (although a referendum on repealing this article is under discussion at the time of writing). Yet religion has not been absent from the UK and particularly the

Australian conversations. Although both states are essentially secular, and Article 116 of the Australian Constitution protects freedom of religion and prohibits the State from formally imposing any religious observance, religion intervenes in public life in various ways. Examples include the formal designation of the British monarch as Head of the Church of England (for fairly obvious historical reasons) and the reciting of the Lord's Prayer (Psalm 23) at the opening of sittings of the Australian Federal parliament. In both the UK and Australia, there are formally constituted, non-partisan groups of Christians in parliament (Christians in Parliament in the UK and Parliamentary Christian Fellowship in Australia). These groups do not have a stated political position on same-sex marriage, but some religious lobbies have outspokenly opposed it. At the same time, in all three countries, high-profile Christians have also been advocates for same-sex marriage; in Ireland, the role of Catholic advocates was instrumental in the success of the 2015 referendum.

THE UK: JURIDICAL AND DISCURSIVE ACTIVISM

In the Introduction to this book, we noted that legal incrementalism has worked in Western European countries in a way that it has not across the Atlantic, going from civil partnership recognition towards same-sex marriage over a period of some 10 to 15 years. The UK certainly follows this pattern. Its Civil Partnership Act, which was passed in 2004, legalized civil unions between same-sex couples and followed a number of similar decisions in other European countries (e.g. France 1999; Germany 2001). As such, it can be seen as the result of a combination of Western European policy transfer/convergence (Paternotte and Kollman 2013) and civil society activism. There has long been a highly visible and active gay movement in the UK; for example, the International Lesbian, Gay, bisexual, transgender and intersex Association (ILGA) was founded as the International Gay Association in Manchester, at the 1978 conference of the UK organization Campaign for Homosexual Equality. The Civil Partnership Act was also the result of the political opportunity presented by the second Blair government, a Labour government committed to the then popular centre-left "Third Way," which combined economic neoliberalism with a progressive stance on non-economic social justice issues, and which has continued to characterize most of mainstream centre-left and centrist politics in the Western world. (For more on the Third Way, see Giddens 1998, 2001.)

When Legal Incrementalism Becomes Also a Roadblock

At the same time, civil partnership recognition did act as a partial roadblock in the UK, through a High Court interpretation of European human rights law and case law, with reference to UK case law and the existing civil partnership law, in a judgment handed down in 2006. Well-known feminist academics and lesbian activists Celia Kitzinger and Sue Wilkinson petitioned the British High Court for UK recognition of their August 2003 marriage, conducted in British Columbia (the second Canadian province, after Ontario, to legalize same-sex marriage through a Court of Appeal ruling on 8 July of that year). As a transnational test of marriage recognition, it was the first such case to be brought in Europe (Wilkinson and Kitzinger 2007).

Wilkinson and Kitzinger claimed that the British refusal to recognize their marriage was a violation of their human rights under Articles 12 (the right to marry) and 14 (on non-discrimination, read in conjunction with Articles 12 and 8, the latter concerning respect for private and family life) of the European Convention on Human Rights. In her arguments as Petitioner, Wilkinson reinforced legal and political framings of marriage as "society's fundamental social institution for recognising couple relationships." Kitzinger, as first respondent, further argued that in depriving her and Wilkinson of marriage recognition, the UK was denying them "full citizenship" (both cited in Potter 2006). These statements are telling in their association of marital status with full institutional recognition of individual rights and citizenship.

In dismissing Wilkinson's petition, the presiding judge, Sir Mark Potter, explicitly referenced UK case law, which has since 1866 reaffirmed that marriage in the UK is between a man and a woman (Potter 2006, para. 11 ff). In referencing the European Convention on Human Rights, and related European Court of Human Rights case law on same-sex partnerships and partnership entitlements, which deferred to national law in most cases, Justice Potter rejected the petitioner's claim that the right to marry and respect for family life could be reinterpreted outside the bounds of existing British law. He noted, with reference to Article 12 on the right of "men and women" to marry, that "this cannot be said to be an area where there is a Europe-wide consensus on the subject, by reason or reference to which the Convention should be treated as having evolved and expanded its scope to encompass same-sex relationships within the concept of marriage" (Potter 2006, para. 62). (The full text of Article 12 is: "Men and women of marriageable age have the right to marry and to found a family, *according to the national laws governing the exercise of this right*" [emphasis added].) On the contrary, Potter saw the European consensus as being rather that marriage was a strictly heterosexual institution, bound to the purpose of procreation and nurturing of children "in which both paternal and maternal influences are available" (Potter 2006, para. 118). As such, "the belief that this form of relationship is the one which best encourages stability in a well regulated society" did not constitute discrimination against homosexuals (para. 119). Moreover, he stated, the 2004 Civil Partnership law already afforded to Wilkinson and Kitzinger precisely the British recognition of their overseas marriage that they sought; it was not a "lesser" status, but a "parallel and equalising institution" which differed from marriage only in the name and in its exclusion from religious ceremony (Potter 2006, para. 50). Wilkinson and Kitzinger, in their commentary on the case, were "deeply disappointed," not only for themselves but "for LGBT *families* nationwide" (Wilkinson and Kitzinger 2007, 5: emphasis added).

Wilkinson and Kitzinger did not take their case further (UK Court of Appeal, then European Court of Human Rights) because the cost of doing so was prohibitive, all the more because the High Court dismissal was accompanied by an order to pay £25,000 court costs.

Indirect Juridical Activism Meets Liberal-Conservative Convergence
However, the case did resonate strongly with social movements, and as such can be seen as a political if not a legal success. Marriage equality campaigns were founded in Scotland in 2008 (Marriage Equality, part of the Equality Network) and in England and Wales in 2010 (Equal Love UK, the name being adopted from the campaign launched in Victoria, Australia, in 2004). It was also in 2010 that 13 years of Labour rule ended, following a general election which first delivered a hung parliament, then a new Conservative-Liberal coalition government following the resignation of Gordon Brown (Labour) as prime minister and the appointment of David Cameron (Conservative) as his replacement. The marriage equality movement thus had a new, and ostensibly more conservative, interlocutor to deal with.

Peter Tatchell, founder and leader of Equal Love UK, immediately set to work lobbying the coalition government and in doing so, framed same-sex marriage as fitting with conservative values. In an article published in autumn, 2011, Tatchell wrote, "Conservatives rightly encourage and approve loving, stable relationships because enduring care and commitment are good for individuals, families and for the well-being of society as a whole" and that "gay marriage doesn't undermine marriage, it strengthens it" (Tatchell 2011a). In writing these words, he cited public opinion (two thirds in favour of legalizing same-sex marriage at that time). Importantly, the Equal Love campaign generalized its equality demand to include heterosexuals, to whom civil partnerships were not available at that time; the campaign thus demanded the extension of civil partnership rights to heterosexuals at the same time as the extension of marriage rights to lesbians and gay men. Tatchell's framing was highly successful, to the point that Tatchell claimed credit for the framing used by David Cameron at the 2011 Conservative Party conference held on 5 October (Tatchell 2011b). In his speech, Cameron elaborated on his 2006 commitment to supporting gay marriage—expressed in the same year that Wilkinson's and Kitzinger's petition was dismissed—and his recently announced consultation process on the best way towards legalization. He famously stated:

> Conservatives believe in the ties that bind us; that society is stronger when we make vows to each other and support each other. So I don't support gay marriage despite being a Conservative. I support gay marriage because I'm a Conservative. (Cameron 2011)

For perhaps the first time anywhere, same-sex marriage was reframed as a *conservative* value, consistent with the status of marriage and family (regulated by marriage) as society's fundamental institution.

At the same time, Cameron's explicit support for same-sex marriage built on an existing liberal consensus, formerly articulated through Blairism, and the above-cited statement was made during the period of the historic Liberal-Conservative coalition which enabled the formation of a majority government following the 2010 election. (The coalition government was the first since the Churchill war ministry of World War II [1940–45] and lasted until the Conservative Party, still led by Cameron, won an outright majority in 2015.) Cameron could, then, be said to represent the liberal wing of the Conservative Party, and between 2010 and 2016—when Cameron resigned following the "Yes" vote in the "Brexit" referendum—the British daily press, from tabloid to so-called broadsheet, regularly characterized Cameron as a "progressive Conservative," "really a liberal" and even "Britain's most progressive Prime Minister."

In the UK, then, a combination of juridical activism and strategically framed campaigns that exploited a political opportunity to tap into already existing support among powerful Conservatives (Cameron, Boris Johnson) won the day for same-sex marriage. Throughout the campaign, both activists and their supporters in the political class foregrounded marriage and the family as *fundamental institution and value* and same-sex marriage as reinforcing rather than undermining that institution, by bringing more of the population into it.

Ireland: Catholic/catholic Inclusion

The situation of the Irish Republic as regards the institutionalization of same-sex marriage is unique in the world as it is the only country to have formally adopted same-sex marriage by popular vote, because its Constitution required it. The cultural, political and legal influence of the Catholic religion has been a major obstacle to progress for both women's rights and gay rights, and two major elements in such progress—the legalization of divorce (Fifteenth Amendment, 1995) and of same-sex marriage (Thirty-Fourth Amendment, 2015)—have required constitutional amendments. Not all amendments have been progressive, however; the Eighth Amendment, giving the unborn a right to life and thus prohibiting abortion, obtained 66.9 percent of the referendum vote in 1983 (as opposed to a narrow win of 50.3 percent in the case of divorce 12 years later). At the time of writing, a possible referendum to allow abortion up to 12 weeks of pregnancy is under discussion, following a majority vote to amend, but not completely repeal, the Eighth Amendment in a Citizen's Assembly held on 22 April 2017. Unsurprisingly, opposition to abortion and opposition to same-sex marriage has come from the same conservative Catholic sources, such as the lobby group Family & Life.

It is thus extraordinary that such a deeply Catholic country, which has been historically so resistant to granting women greater rights in public, private and reproductive life, should legalize same-sex marriage; comparisons with Latin America and indeed Latin Europe come readily to mind, at least on a superficial level. The 2016 Irish Census showed that 78.31 percent of Irish citizens continue to identify as Catholic, and although regular Mass attendance has been declining for the last three decades, 41.3 percent of Irish respondents to the 2010 European Social Survey stated that they attended Mass at least once per week.[2]

Endogenous and Exogenous Factors

How then, did Ireland move from such social conservatism to embracing same-sex marriage in the space of a generation? In answering this question, the role of the Robinson presidency must be acknowledged, without overstating its importance. Elected in 1990, Robinson was the first female president in the history of the Republic, and the first non-Fianna Fáil president since 1945 (Fianna Fáil being the mainstream conservative party). She came to the presidency with a strong record of advocacy for women's and minority rights, in particular during her term as an independent member of the Irish Senate during the 1970s. Robinson had also been, prior to her presidency, a legal adviser for the Campaign for Homosexual Law Reform (CHLF), which was founded by David Norris to campaign for the decriminalization of (male) homosexuality (legislated in 1993). Central to that campaign, once again, was the European Convention on Human Rights; it was a 1988 ruling on the case taken by Senator Norris to the European Court of Human Rights, which found that Ireland had violated Article 8 of the Convention on the right to privacy, that finally led to Irish decriminalization of male homosexuality.

As president, Robinson transformed the role from what had been jokingly called a retirement option for Fianna Fáil party elders to a proactive one, that of statesperson and advocate for the rights of all. Clearly, she would not have been elected, and her work would not have had as much impact, were it not for the strong presence of civil society activism: trade unions, women's rights, gay rights, Traveler rights and so on. It is arguable that the political history of Ireland long ago sowed the seeds of such activism; many feminists, for example, were part of, or associated with, the Irish independence movement, and for many those associations continue through North-South interactions. At the same time, the strongly Catholic underpinnings of nation-formation have resulted in waves of backlash against feminism (and gay rights). Yet it was partly a response to precisely such a conservative backlash in the 1980s that led to such widespread support for Robinson. Her presidency, which she left two months before term to take up her appointment as UN Human Rights Commissioner, certainly put human rights and equality issues at the centre of Ireland's political map.

The factors in Ireland's adoption of same-sex marriage are not, however, simply endogenous. For one thing, Ireland embraced Europeanization with fervour, and both EU treaties and the non-EU European Convention on Human Rights are key reference points in Ireland for both economic neoliberalism (from Celtic tigerhood to EU-driven austerity adjustments) and human rights and equality rhetoric. Just as important, however, if not even more so, is the Irish diaspora. Both the "yes" and "no" campaigns around same-sex marriage in Ireland were in great part politically supported and even bankrolled from the USA, of which, according to the US Census Bureau, some 10 percent of the citizenry claim Irish ancestry.[3] The USA also has the world's second largest Irish-born emigrant population after the UK; Australia comes third (Kenny 2015). Apart from transAtlantic connections of such groups as Family & Life, the "no" side was supported by the wealthy and influential US National Organization for Marriage (NOM), although NOM claims it did not donate directly to the campaign (which would have been illegal in Ireland in the leadup to a referendum) (McDonald 2015). On the "yes" side, Chuck Feeney's Atlantic Philanthropies organization was similarly accused of bankrolling the campaign but flatly denied doing so. The organization did, however, donate some US$4.7 million, according to its own published figures, to the Irish organization Gay and Lesbian Equality Network between 2005 and 2011,[4] and published a number of articles in support of the Irish "yes" vote on its website (see also Kelly 2015).

Catholic Catholics

As concerns the influence of religion, under both global and local pressures to evolve in the face of a declining Church membership, the Catholic Church in Ireland, like the Conservative Party in the UK, no longer presented a united front in its defence of traditionalist values. Just as David Cameron had framed his support for same-sex marriage in the very name of conservative family values, a number of prominent Catholics in Ireland defended same-sex marriage in the very name of their religion. Admittedly, many of them are perceived as dissident by the Catholic establishment, such as Tony Flannery, suspended by the Vatican in 2012 for supporting homosexual rights and advocating the ordination of women. In the weeks preceding the 22 May 2015 referendum, Fr Flannery advocated a "yes" vote as consistent with Catholic values of love, acceptance and equality before God (Flannery 2015). Another prominent example is former Irish president Mary McAleese (Mary Robinson's successor). Speaking at an event organized by LGBT rights group BeLonG To, in the days preceding the referendum, McAleese said that as a practising Catholic who had been in a happy heterosexual marriage for 40 years, she knew that happy marriages were good for individuals and society, and that as a mother of a gay son, "the only children affected by this referendum [would] be Ireland's gay children," whose future was in the hands of all Irish people (cited in Minihan 2015).

Even a number of Irish clergy who opposed same-sex marriage chose to be nuanced in their views. Archbishop of Dublin Diarmuid Martin, who strongly supported the "no" vote, also stated publicly that he had "no wish to stuff [his] religious views down other people's throats." He aimed rather to convince others not by dogmatism but by reasoned argument (Martin 2015). In fact, according to Mark Silk, writing for the Religion News Service, a body affiliated with the School of Journalism at the University of Missouri, the very success of the Irish referendum depended on the Catholic Church being very "catholic," in the small-c sense of the term ("universal, all-inclusive"). That is, Silk sees the Catholic Church as inclusive, broad-ranging, accommodating of diversity, unlike the Protestant Church dominant in the USA, which values the heterosexual nuclear family as "the church in miniature" (Silk 2015). Silk went on to suggest that there was also more support for same-sex marriage among US Catholics than among US Protestants, although he did not offer figures to back up this claim. Finally, he argued, the Irish Catholic Church is closely identified with the Irish people "in an integral, even tribal way, so that it must be where the Irish people are" (Silk 2015). Silk was of course writing from within the USA, where organized Protestantism, especially in its evangelist forms, has been hugely influential in opposing same-sex marriage. I would also suggest that once again, this "tribal" integration of "Church" and "people" in Ireland is rooted in the sociopolitical history of the country; the Catholic Church, for all its considerable institutional power today, is also historically and culturally associated with Irish resistance against colonial (and Protestant) domination.

Thus, in Ireland, the same-sex marriage debate did not at all play out as "the Church" versus "the People" or indeed "the State," as it had, for example, in France two years earlier (and indeed in relation to many other issues before that), at least in the case of Church versus State. Although the Irish Church was divided over the issue, many key figures among its hierarchy and its faithful chose inclusiveness—and indeed pragmatism in the face of popular support for same-sex marriage—over dogma. They preferred to welcome gay men and lesbians into the Catholic/catholic family, thus reinforcing that family, rather than expel them from it, with possible deleterious impacts on its overall size and health.

Australia: Pre-emptive Interventionism

Australia is the most surprising of the three cases studied in this chapter. As a liberal democracy with a history of egalitarianism, Australia might have been expected to be a world leader on such a matter as same-sex marriage. After all, it was the first country in the world to recognize same-sex couple relationships for immigration purposes; the first (and successful) test case, in 1982, was based on an interpretation of the "compassionate and humanitarian grounds" section of the Migration Act, and a gay-specific "interdependency" provision was added to the Act in 1992. This addition preceded by two years the national Human Rights (Sexual Conduct) Act, which overruled the continued outlawing of male homosexuality in the state of Tasmania (the first decriminalization had been in the state of South Australia in 1975). Moreover, gay culture is quite mainstream in Australia. The Sydney Gay and Lesbian Mardi Gras, for example, is one of the world's best known LGBT festivals, and a major tourist dollar earner both for the City of Sydney and the state of New South Wales (NSW), and gay and lesbian themes feature almost routinely in popular television and radio. Individual states had successively brought in some form of same-sex relationship recognition following the Australian Capital Territory's (ACT's) lead in 1994, although the degree and form of recognition varied from one state to another (Bernstein and Naples 2015, 1237–8). In 2008, the then Rudd government (Australian Labor Party, ALP) introduced a range of measures at Federal level that removed discrimination against same-sex couples in matters of tax, inheritance, health and employment. Two thirds of Australians support legalization of same-sex marriage and Australia is one of the world's most secularized countries. All would thus seem to converge to set the stage for legalization of same-sex marriage.

Why, then, has Australia, the supposed gay haven of the Southern Hemisphere, gone so resolutely against the international liberal-democratic grain in refusing to legalize same-sex marriage?

Mary Bernstein and Nancy Naples (2015) have suggested that marriage has much less sociocultural importance in Australia than in the USA, and thus that non-marital relationship recognition was more important than marriage to gay rights movements in Australia—at least, it was prior to 2004. Their point about the relative importance of marriage is debatable, but it is true that Australian gay and lesbian activists seeking recognition of their relationships were not particularly interested in marriage prior to

2004. Bernstein and Naples have also argued that the lack of an Australian Bill of Rights has closed off juridical activism as a form of campaigning for marriage rights, as has been the case in the USA. Carol Johnson has further suggested that non-legalization in Australia is due to a lack of political will among successive Australian governments, including Labor ones (in Johnson and Tremblay 2016). Yet the Australian story is more than the sum of these parts. Moreover, there *was* in fact juridical activism in Australia, which was a factor in pushing an already masculinist and heterosexist government to enact the 2004 Marriage Amendment Act, spelling out that marriage could only be between a man and a woman.

The Marriage Amendment Act

Just as Sue Wilkinson and Celia Kitzinger were to do in the UK two years later, in 2004 Jason McCheyne and Adrian Tuazon (subsequently Jason and Adrian Tuazon-McCheyne) petitioned an Australian court to have their overseas marriage recognized in Australia. They had married in Toronto in January 2004, and in February they petitioned the Australian Family Court, which has Federal jurisdiction in all matters of marriage, divorce and child custody, to have the marriage validated in Australia. The Family Court invited the Federal government to give its opinion; the government's response was a law, passed in August of that year. The Marriage Amendment Act (2004) amended the 1961 Marriage Act to read that "*marriage* means the union of a man and a woman to the exclusion of all others, voluntarily entered into for life" (Subsection 5[1], emphasis in original), and that "a union solemnised in a foreign country between (a) a man and another man; or (b) a woman and another woman; must not be recognised as a marriage in Australia" (Section 88EA). The Family Court thus had no legal choice but to throw the Tuazon-McCheynes' case out.

The Marriage Amendment Act was brought in by a Liberal-National coalition government (the Coalition) headed by Prime Minister John Howard. The Liberal Party in Australia is the equivalent of the Republican Party in the USA or the Conservative Party in the UK, hence the entry into Australian vernacular of "small-l liberal" to describe a more progressive conceptualization of liberalism, such as that commonly understood in the USA. The National Party (formerly the Country Party), which always governs in coalition with the Liberals, has a strong rural base and is similarly conservative. First elected in 1996 and re-elected three times, to remain in power for almost 12 years, the Howard governments were characterized by neoliberalism on the economic front accompanied by an extreme social conservatism and, particularly after 9/11, a muscular "security" and anti-refugee discourse. Howard tapped into a (white Anglo male) anti-elitism that has been part of the Australian national psyche since the first penal settlements in the late eighteenth century. Similarly to George W. Bush (or indeed Donald Trump) in the USA, Howard defended what he called "mainstream" values against "special interest groups"—which included pretty much anyone who was not a white heterosexual man (Winter 2007), and reintroduced Christian rhetoric into Australian politics (Maddox 2005).

By 2004, then, the dominant political climate was one of conservatism and meanness; the Marriage Amendment Act fitted neatly into that pattern. That pre-emptive piece of legislation, however, provoked an equal and opposite LGBT reaction. Almost overnight, "marriage equality" became the mantra of a movement that hitherto had not shown massive interest in the issue. Equal Love, founded in the state of Victoria in 2004, and Australian Marriage Equality, founded nationally the same year, were both responses to the Marriage Amendment Act (although planning for the former had begun after the Netherlands legalization in 2001).

Yet successive Howard governments were not the only ones to oppose same-sex marriage. Famously, Australia's first and to date only female Prime Minister, Julia Gillard (ALP, 2010–2013), did not support it when in power (although her position subsequently changed), because "the 1970s feminist" in her "saw much to be concerned with from a gender perspective with traditional marriage." She thus "thought the better approach was not to change the old but to create something new through civil unions" (Gillard 2015). Although marriage equality activists deplored her position, many feminists, and indeed a number of gay men, agreed with it. (In fact, the increasing mainstreaming of same-sex marriage throughout the liberal democratic capitalist world has tended to obscure the fact that lesbians and gay men do not all speak with one voice on this issue.) During Gillard's time, however, her personal position did not represent a party line, the issue being left to an individual conscience vote. In 2012, a private member's bill to legalize same-sex marriage, put to parliament by Labor backbencher Stephen Jones, was defeated by 98 votes to 42 in the lower house. The Labor conscience vote was instrumental in its defeat, as it had been on previous occasions when Greens Members of Parliament had presented same-sex marriage bills.

Same-sex marriage, then, met with opposition among both the left and right of the Australian political class, albeit for quite different reasons, and when the Coalition was re-elected in 2013 and again in 2016, that opposition seemed set to continue.

Out in Politics

However, a few developments—both endogenous and exogenous—between 2011 and 2015 gradually caused a discursive if not legislative shift among both the political class and the wider population.

The first of these developments is the role of visible gay parliamentarians. This visibility is not recent: the first high-profile gay politician was the founding leader of the Greens, Bob Brown, who first came out to the media in 1976 (the Greens Party was founded in 1992). However, a key figure in pushing the acceptable (and multicultural) family face of same-sex marriage has been Senator Penny Wong, who is, at the time of writing, Labor leader in the Senate and shadow Minister for Foreign Affairs (previously Climate Change Minister, 2007–2010, and Finance Minister, 2010–2013). Wong, who was born in Malaysia and is a practising member of the Uniting Church (Protestant), is probably Australia's highest-profile lesbian, and a strong advocate for same-sex marriage. In 2011, the media made much of the birth of her first daughter to partner Sophie Allouache; a repeat media exposure occurred in 2014, with the birth of their second daughter, also to Allouache. Although Wong is neither the first nor currently the only openly gay Federal politician, she is the first high-profile lesbian one, and although her non-whiteness may not please all, her Christian family-ness makes the Wong-Allouache couple and their daughters the poster family for same-sex marriage.

The second development came in 2013, the year after the Australian Human Rights Commission's position paper favouring same-sex marriage. On 22 October, the unicameral parliament of the tiny Australian Capital Territory (ACT) narrowly passed the Marriage Equality (Same-Sex) Act 2013 by nine votes to eight. Then Prime Minister Tony Abbott (Liberal), a former protégé of Howard, immediately took a case against the Act to Australia's High Court. Marriage being a matter of Federal jurisdiction in Australia, the High Court had no choice but to strike down the ACT law on 12 December 2013, because it contravened the provisions of the Marriage Amendment Act 2004. The 31 gay and lesbian couples who had married in Canberra on 7 December 2013 thus remained legally married for only five days.

It is then that global influences returned to the forefront, through the Irish referendum of 2015, which triggered a new discursive shift in Australia. Calls abounded at first for an Australian referendum on the issue, but both the political class and political and legal commentators were quick to point out that with marriage not being a constitutional matter in Australia, a referendum was not applicable. However, in 2016, new Coalition Prime Minister Malcolm Turnbull, who had ousted Abbott in a leadership spill in September 2015, followed the mood of demands for a referendum—and attempted to calm the right flank of his own party—by proposing a national plebiscite when elected in 2016. This proposal met with ferocious opposition from the ALP (which now had a party line in favour of same-sex marriage) and the Greens, who considered it a waste of public money and a waste of time, given that two thirds of public opinion already favoured legalization. The plebiscite bill was defeated in the Senate in November 2016, and at the time of writing the issue is stalemated, even though moderate Liberals have now joined Labor and the Greens in calling for a parliamentary vote. The corporate sector has also begun to play a significant role, notably in collaboration with Australian Marriage Equality, in lobbying politicians on the issue (AME n.d., *Weekend Australian* 2017). It could be that the "business case" for same-sex marriage will sway the Coalition government where rights and family and marriage equality arguments have not.

Conclusion

The UK, Ireland and Australia all present in some ways cases against type, going in the opposite direction from what might logically have been expected, given the institutional and political constraints or possibilities within the countries in question. In the UK, it was the Conservative Party, and notably then Prime Minister David Cameron, that became determinant in legalizing same-sex marriage there, in the very name of conservative values. In Ireland, Catholic priests and practising Catholics became advocates for marriage equality in the name of religious inclusivity and equality before God. In Australia, both the right and sections of the left have held up legalization on more than one occasion, when one might have expected Australia to be one of the world's leaders on the issue.

In all three cases, the discursive role of social and political actors who have used the very institutions within which they operate to advocate or oppose same-sex marriage has been decisive. In all three cases, framings and reframings of the family as the fundamental value of society, and the role of marriage in preserving it, have been foregrounded: by activists, by politicians, and by the media.

Yet, the deep irony of the legalization of same-sex marriage is that gay men and lesbians may be jumping on a sinking ship, as heterosexuals abandon the institution in increasing numbers. In the first 15 months following the UK legislation coming into force (in March 2014), the Office for National Statistics (ONS) reported that 7366 same-sex marriages had been conducted in England and Wales (of which 55 percent were between women), and 7732 couples chose to convert their civil partnerships into marriages. Conversely, the ONS observed a falling off in the numbers of same-sex civil partnerships from February 2014, in relation to numbers for the previous year.[5] Yet, as gay marriages were coming onto the statistical map, the heterosexual marriage rate was falling, resulting in a net 6 percent drop between 2012 and 2014. In fact, only 20 women and men per thousand were marrying (each other) in 2014 as opposed to seventy per thousand 30 years previously (ONS 2017). In Ireland, figures released by the Central Statistics Office (CSO) in April 2017 showed that 1056 same-sex couples had married in 2016 (of which some 57 percent were male), while heterosexual marriages had declined by 4.6 percent relative to 2015. Similarly, in Australia, the (heterosexual) marriage rate decreased by 6.3 percent from 2014 to 2015, while the divorce rate went up by 4.3 percent (ABS 2016).

Seen in the light of such statistics, as well as Irish concerns about the population abandoning the Church, same-sex marriage can be seen as a political manoeuvre to shore up what seems to be a failing institution. It will be interesting to see how the same-sex divorce figures stack up in coming years.

Notes

1. http://dayagainsthomophobia.org/idahot-2017-will-focus-on-families/. Accessed May 6, 2017.
2. Irish census results available at: http://cso.ie/en/csolatestnews/press-pages/2017/census2016summaryresults-part1/. Accessed 28 April 2017. Social Survey results cited by Faith Survey UK, available at: https://faithsurvey.co.uk/irish-census.html. Accessed 28 April 2017.
3. https://www.census.gov/newsroom/facts-for-features/2017/cb17-ff05.html. Accessed 28 April 2017.

4. Atlantic Philanthropies website: http://www.atlanticphilanthropies.org/grantees/gay-and-lesbian-equality-network. Accessed 3 May 2017.
5. ONSarchive:http://webarchive.nationalarchives.gov.uk/20160105160709/http:/www.ons.gov.uk/ons/rel/vsob1/marriages-in-england-and-wales--provisional-/for-same-sex-couples--2014/sty-for-same-sex-couples-2014.html

References

AHRC (Australian Human Rights Commission). 2012. *Marriage Equality in a Changing World: Position Paper on Marriage Equality*. Sydney: AHRC. Accessed 28 April 2017. http://www.humanrights.gov.au/lesbian-gay-bisexual-trans-and-intersex-equality-0

AME (Australian Marriage Equality). n.d. Join Corporations that Support Marriage Equality. Accessed 2 May 2017. http://www.australianmarriage-equality.org/open-letter-of-support/

Bernstein, Mary, and Nancy Naples. 2015. Altared States: Legal Structuring and Relationship Recognition in the United States, Canada, and Australia. *American Sociological Review* 80 (6): 1226–1249.

Cameron, David. 2011. Keynote Speech, Conservative Party Conference. Manchester, October 5. Accessed 13 March 2014. https://www.theguardian.com/politics/2011/oct/05/david-cameron-conservative-party-speech

Dorf, Michael C., and Sidney Tarrow. 2014. Strange Bedfellows: How an Anticipatory Countermovement Brought Same-Sex Marriage into the Public Arena. *Law and Social Inquiry* 39 (2): 449–473. https://doi.org/10.1111/lsi.12069.

Flannery, Fr Tony. 2015. God's Love Is Not Diminished by One's Sexual Orientation. *The Independent Ireland*, May 3. Accessed 28 April 2017. http://www.independent.ie/opinion/comment/gods-love-is-not-diminished-by-ones-sexual-orientation-31191224.html

Giddens, Anthony. 1998. *The Third Way: The Renewal of Social Democracy*. Oxford: Polity Press.

———, ed. 2001. *The Global Third Way Debate*. Oxford: Polity Press.

Gillard, Julia. 2015. Annual Michael Kirby Lecture, Victoria University College of Law and Justice, Melbourne, August 26. Accessed 5 May 2017. https://www.scribd.com/doc/276139019/Hon-Julia-Gillard-Michael-Kirby-Lecture-26AUG2015

Grube, Dennis, and Elizabeth van Acker. 2016. Rhetorically Defining a Social Institution: How Leaders Have Framed Same-Sex Marriage. *Australian Journal of Political Science* 52 (2): 183–198. https://doi.org/10.1080/10361146.2016.1260683.

IHREC (Irish Human Rights and Equality Commission). 2015. *Equality Authority Report 2001*. Dublin: IHREC. Accessed 28 April 2017. https://www.ihrec.ie/documents/equality-authority-annual-report-2001/

Johnson, Carol, and Manon Tremblay. 2016. Comparing Same-Sex Marriage in Australia and Canada: Institutions and Political Will. *Government and Opposition* 36. https://doi.org/10.1017/gov.2016.36.

Kelly, Michael. 2015. How Same-Sex Marriage Won Out in Ireland. *The Catholic World Report*, May 26. Accessed April 28, 2017. http://www.catholicworldreport.com/Item/3902/how_samesex_marriage_won_out_in_ireland.aspx

Kenny, Clara. 2015. The Global Irish: Where Do They Live. *The Irish Times*, February 4. Accessed 28 April 2017. http://www.irishtimes.com/life-and-style/generation-emigration/the-global-irish-where-do-they-live-1.2089347

Maddox, Marion. 2005. *God Under Howard*. Sydney: Allen & Unwin.

Martin, Archbishop Diarmuid. 2015. I Encourage Everyone to Vote and to Reflect Carefully. *The Irish Times*, May 19. Accessed 29 April 2017. http://www.irishtimes.com/opinion/archbishop-diarmuid-martin-i-encourage-everyone-to-vote-and-to-reflect-carefully-1.2217278

McDonald, Henry. 2015. US Christians 'Bankrolling' No Campaign in Ireland's Gay Marriage Referendum. *The Guardian*, May 17. Accessed 28 April 2017. https://www.theguardian.com/world/2015/may/16/us-christians-no-campaign-ireland-gay-marriage-referendum

Minihan, Mary. 2015. Mary McAleese: No Vote Would 'Cost Our Gay Children Everything'. *The Irish Times*, May 19. Accessed 29 April 2017. http://www.irishtimes.com/news/politics/mary-mcaleese-no-vote-would-cost-our-gay-children-everything-1.2218061

NELFA (Network of European LGBTIQ* Families Associations). 2017. Press Release: "Love Makes a Family," May 5. Brussels: NELFA. Accessed 5 May 2017. http://nelfa.org/media/

Paternotte, David, and Kelly Kollman. 2013. Regulating Intimate Relationships in the European Polity: Same-Sex Unions and Policy Convergence. *Social Politics* 20 (4): 510–533. https://doi.org/10.1093/sp/jxs024.

Potter, Sir Mark. 2006. Judgement in the Case of Wilkinson v Kitzinger [2006] EWHC 2022 (Fam). Accessed 22 April 2017. http://www.familylawweek.co.uk/site.aspx?i=ed2118

Schmidt, Vivien A. 2010. Taking Ideas and Discourse Seriously: Explaining Change Through Discursive Institutionalism as the Fourth 'New Institutionalism'. *European Political Science Review* 2 (1): 1–25. https://doi.org/10.1017/S175577390999021X.

Silk, Mark. 2015. Irish Catholicism Supports Same-Sex Marriage!. *Religion News Service*, May 23. Accessed 30 April 2017. http://religionnews.com/2015/05/23/irish-catholicism-supports-same-sex-marriage/

Tatchell, Peter. 2011a. Two Wrongs Don't Make a Right. *The Progressive Conscience*, Autumn. Accessed 26 April 2017. http://www.petertatchell.net/lgbt_rights/partnerships/how-the-tories-were-won-to-marriage-equality.htm

———. 2011b. How the Tories Were Won to Marriage Equality. Self-published Online, October 13. Accessed 26 April 2017. http://www.petertatchell.net/lgbt_rights/partnerships/how-the-tories-were-won-to-marriage-equality.htm

Weekend Australian, The. 2017. Corporate Same-Sex Marriage Campaign Months in the Making, March 28. Accessed 4 May 2017. http://www.theaustralian.com.au/business/companies/corporate-samesex-marriage-campaign-was-months-in-the-making/news-story/a720c5ae4a7063f1fd93f0c6df9d7641

Wilkinson, Sue, and Celia Kitzinger. 2007. Editorial. *Lesbian & Gay Psychology Review* 8 (1): 3–11.

Winter, Bronwyn. 2007. Pre-emptive Fridge Magnets and Other Weapons of Masculinist Destruction: The Rhetoric and Reality of 'Safeguarding Australia'. *Signs: A Journal of Women, Culture and Society* 33 (1): 25–52.

———. 2017. Tampering with Society's DNA' or 'Making Society Stronger': Family, Religion and Gay Rights in the Construction of the Nation. In *Gendering Nationalism: Intersections of Nation, Gender and Sexuality in the 21st Century*, ed. J. Mulholland et al. Basingstoke: Palgrave Macmillan.

Bronwyn Winter is Deputy Director of the European Studies Program at the University of Sydney, Australia. Her research addresses a range of global theoretical and political issues that lie at the intersections of gender, sexuality, ethnicity, religion, globalization, militarization and the state. Publications include *Hijab and the Republic: Uncovering the French Headscarf Debate* (2008) and *Women, Insecurity and Violence in a Post-9/11 World* (2017). She is currently working on a monograph on the political economy of same-sex marriage. She holds the French title of *Chevalier dans l'Ordre des Palmes Académiques*.

CHAPTER 9

The Globalization of LGBT Identity and Same-Sex Marriage as a Catalyst of Neo-institutional Values: Singapore and Indonesia in Focus

Hendri Yulius, Shawna Tang, and Baden Offord

INTRODUCTION

The globalization of lesbian, gay, bisexual, and transgender (LGBT)[1] rights discourse—including the institutionalization of same-sex marriage—has encouraged new thinking about the connections between gender, sexuality, and sociopolitical transformations in Western countries. Many recent studies demonstrate the interplays between LGBT rights and migration, counter-terrorism, nationalism, and neo-liberal policies and politics (Duggan 2002; Puar 2007; Perez 2015; Stella et al. 2016). Nevertheless, the transnational impacts of such institutionalization of sexual and/or gender identity and marriage equality have been

H. Yulius (✉)
University of Sydney, Sydney, NSW, Australia

S. Tang
Western Sydney University, Sydney, NSW, Australia

B. Offord
Curtin University, Perth, WA, Australia

© The Author(s) 2018
B. Winter et al. (eds.), *Global Perspectives on Same-Sex Marriage*, Global Queer Politics, https://doi.org/10.1007/978-3-319-62764-9_9

under-examined in the context of Southeast Asia, where in most countries homosexuality is still deemed irreconcilable with local cultures. A large portion of existing literature on sexual citizenship in the region, particularly Indonesia and Singapore, still primarily revolves around LGBT movements, political homophobia, popular cultures, and constructions of identities (Bennett and Davies 2015; Boellstorff 2007; Chua 2014; Murtagh 2013; Offord 2011; Tang 2017; Yue and Zubillaga-Pow 2012).

Southeast Asia is nonetheless a critical region in which to explore how the impact of same-sex marriage and LGBT rights discourse at the international level is being negotiated and responded to through state and civil institutions. The countries across this region are highly diverse in terms of their cultures, histories, and politics. A Buddhist kingdom (Thailand) sits next to a socialist polity (Vietnam). The region includes the largest Muslim nation in the world (Indonesia) and other majority Muslim states (Malaysia and Brunei), a majority Christian country (the Philippines), as well as one of the most successful global and multicultural city-states (Singapore). A recent study of the peak inter-regional organization, the Association of South East Asian Nations (ASEAN) in terms of its explicit *ASEAN 2015* promotion of 'human rights for all its peoples' has been strongly critiqued by ASEAN civil society organizations for not adequately including LGBT people and communities. As Langlois et al. (2017, 14) comment:

> While the Philippines seems to be reversing course on its previous preparedness to support SOGIE [sexual orientation, gender identity and gender expression] rights, and Indonesia is gripped by an LGBTQ moral panic that has tacit governmental support, in other parts of ASEAN political and legislative moves are well advanced for the recognition of same-sex relationships (including through marriage equality) and significant advances have been made on other SOGIE issues. Thailand and Vietnam are the leadings states in this regard (UNDP, USAID 2016).

The focus of this chapter is on the institutional and state responses and reactions to issues of same-sex marriage and analytics of the relationship between state, civil society institutions, and international humanitarian organizations in two neighboring countries in Southeast Asia: Singapore and Indonesia. Each country has specific colonial histories, ethnic, religious, social, and cultural conditions, and explicitly shows the negotiations of the social-cultural boundaries formed around non-normative genders and sexualities, particularly after the institutionalization of same-sex marriage.

Since the US Supreme Court's ruling on marriage equality in 2015, Indonesia has increasingly become a very hostile place for LGBT communities, with fundamentalist Muslim as well as political pressures and legal attempts to criminalize homosexuality becoming extant. Those anti-LGBT groups and discourses mainstream and promote the term LGBT to wider public audience, which have subsequently led state agencies to begin using the term in public statements and announcements (Yulius 2016a). However, through a closer examination in the next section, the anti-LGBT reactions should also be positioned as a form of counter-movements by conservative groups in relation to the expanding visibilities of LGBT Indonesians and support from international humanitarian organizations for LGBT rights issues.

The increasing province of same-sex marriage internationally has also had a significant impact on Singapore's governing of sexuality and gender. Although Singapore has a thriving gay culture and an abundance of creative spaces for LGBT people and communities to express themselves, laws that criminalize homosexuality exist, a remnant of British colonialism. Such laws have contributed to a numbing effect on how Singaporean society ultimately considers LGBT claims to full citizenship. The discursive institutionalization of sexuality in Singapore has been sharply hewn through explicit state support and maintenance of sexual borders that reify the heteronormative ideal of the nuclear family. Same-sex marriage has also been a significant pivot for anti-LGBT Christian Evangelists, who see the threat to heterosexual marriage as an attack upon the Singaporean state and its culture. The conservative Christian opposition to same-sex marriage has itself extended into other religious alliances, such as homophobia among Singapore's significant Muslim minorities, based on similar fears and rhetoric. Against these reactions, claims for recognition of Singaporean LGBT people and communities have become intrinsic to its public culture through events such as the very popular LGBT annual Pink Dot gathering.

In the next sections we discuss Indonesia and Singapore as two distinct Southeast Asian societies that are worth discussing and analyzing very carefully in relation to the effects of Western sociopolitical transformations of gender and sexuality, particularly same-sex marriage. The struggles for and against LGBT visibility and recognition in these nations has become galvanized by how same-sex marriage across the world, and even closer, in their region (e.g., in Australia, New Zealand, Vietnam, Taiwan), has made an impact on both state and civil society debates, conversations, and actions.

Indonesia

Institutionalizing Sex: The Birth of LGBT Subjects

Although Indonesia has diverse terms to delineate non-normative genders and sexualities, the evolution of modern homosexual subjects has taken place through three distinctive periods. Each shares a coincidence with the shifts in the country's sociopolitical landscapes and carries different means of institutionalizing sex. To understand the extent to which (and how) the institutionalization of sex operates in each timeframe, it is necessary to understand a set of theoretical protocols on discursive institutionalization. As the Introduction of this book points out, discursive neo-institutionalism is of specific relevance for interrogating deeply embedded norms and discourses on genders and sexualities, and their impacts on policies and institutions. On the other hand, drawing from Louis Althusser's interpellation (1971) and Foucault's contribution on historicizing sexuality (1987), such discursive institutional practices require discursive technologies to channel particular intimate desires and practices into distinct sexual identities, making gender/sexuality a concrete aspect of one's self. In this sense, the incitement to tell the truth about one's self has become central in designing and ascribing identity and subjectivity to individuals, which in turn renders them visible and legitimate (Fassin 2012; Foucault 1987; Nguyen 2010).

The first stage of the evolution of Indonesian modern homosexual subjects appeared to take place in the late 1970s and early 1980s (Boellstorff 2005). During the repressive New Order era (1966–1998), while homosexuality was not perceived as a direct threat, the state constantly deployed traditional heteronormative family values and endorsed it as a criterion of adulthood and successful citizenship. Indonesian homosexual subjects began to learn of the possibility to name one self as gay or *lesbi* (Indonesian term for lesbian) through fragmented messages from mass media that started to discuss homosexuality issues. Yet this self-recognition did not translate Indonesian gay and *lesbi* subjectivities into positive selfhood. The homosexual subjects saw their desires as abnormal and hence their response was to marry in a heterosexual relationship to gain recognition as a successful adult citizen (Boellstorff 2005; Howard 1996).

The first *waria* (inadequately translated as transgender woman) organization, Himpunan Wadam Djakarta (Hiwad) was formed in the late 1960s to deliver government support for its community. The first gay and lesbian movements in Indonesia began in 1982, through the formation of the gay organization Lambda Indonesia in Solo (Offord 2011). The striking difference between the two groups is that while the former was dominated by poor *waria* from the lower social classes, the latter was led by upper-middle-class gay men. Further, Lambda Indonesia could be understood as a 'transnational' form of activism, in which the US-generated homosexual symbology and Western discourses of sexuality were adopted and deployed at the local levels.

There was a very specific production of modern gay subjects through the activists' efforts. Through its publications, counseling, and networking services, Lambda Indonesia encouraged male homosexuals to confidently embrace gay identity, connected those living in non-urban areas with the urban ones, and increased societal acceptance. The last was articulated through imagining and emphasizing the continuity of same-sex practices in some local ethno-linguistic groups with modern homosexuality (G 1982). This strategy also aimed to remove the stigma of Westernization attached to homosexuality. Despite their lesser visibility, lesbian organizations were also dispersedly blossoming in the 1980s. Almost similar with their gay counterparts, SAPHO and the Association of Indonesian Lesbians (Persatuan Lesbian Indonesia, Perlesin) initially strived to develop self-esteem among lesbian Indonesians (Agustine 2008; Offord 2003). Such dissemination of Western sexual knowledge and 'interpellation' processes signified the rise of modern homosexual identity in the country. As such, homosexual subjects then increasingly treated their sexuality as an innate feature that should be embraced and accepted.

This early phase of sexual citizenship, however, made a remarkable turn throughout the 1990s. Indonesian gay and lesbian activists began to receive material and non-material assistance from Western activists, academics, and international organizations (Blackwood 2010; Oetomo 2003; UNDP, USAID 2014). Besides the circulation of the term LGBT among limited gay and lesbian networks, the influx of foreign funding for HIV/AIDS prevention—which mainly targeted gay men, men having sex with men (MSM), and *waria*—also contributed to the increasing globalization and institutionalization of those sexual identities (Altman 2001; Blackwood 2010). Positioning those groups as key affected populations, gay and HIV/AIDS activists disseminated sexuality knowledge and increasingly placed a greater emphasis on sexual identities through multiple forms of encounters, from training to outreach efforts. At this historical juncture, there were convivial relations between gay identity and an individual's wellbeing (Oetomo 2003). Due to the difficulties with identification and outreach, closeted gay men were considered more vulnerable to HIV infection. Training on HIV/AIDS then often included and distributed Western sexuality knowledge that channeled and labeled individuals' desires with particular sexual/gender identities.

While the HIV/AIDS intervention was rendered significant in the production of gay, MSM, and transgender subjects, the third stage of the development of homosexual identity in Indonesia corresponded with Indonesia's democratization (Davies and Yulius 2018). The collapse of President Soeharto's authoritarian regime in 1998 brought new hopes for the fulfillment of human rights protections. Civil society and human rights movements, including LGBT organizations, proliferated. Interventions and support from international humanitarian and/or human rights organizations for mainstreaming human rights in the post-authoritarian state were significant in imbuing gender and sexual identity with human rights perspectives, rendering them as the basis of citizenship rights-claiming (Alicias-Garen and Jahja 2015). Since 2004, for example, the Dutch humanitarian organization Hivos has channeled its support to 25 local LGBT organizations in 18 provinces to 'create a safe, vibrant, strong and sustainable LGBT movement in the region' (Alicias-Garen and Jahja 2015, 2). As such, the term LGBT also became increasingly popular among activists at this juncture.

The enactment of the Yogyakarta Principles in 2006 has become a solid ground for LGBT activists to articulate and demand sexual citizenship rights (Altman and Symons 2016). Through support from international organizations both for LGBT rights and HIV/AIDS causes, activists were able to have direct contact with movements overseas, from which they gained emotional, technical, and material resources. Nevertheless, despite the adoption of LGBT terms and transnational influences, the movements differ significantly from the North-American model. The LGBT organizations carry out their activisms by avoiding liberal human rights discourse. For instance, rather than demanding same-sex marriage, the activists have been more focused on sustaining public campaign and education to eradicate negative stigma on homosexuality, addressing violence against LGBT people, and advocating the government to give equal public service access (e.g., health and education) to LGBT people. The main aim of these efforts is to increase social acceptance and to advocate for basic citizenship rights for LGBT people, such as access to health, education, and employment.

As Indonesian LGBT organizations have increasingly used the term LGBT, activists have also learned to deploy the Sexual Orientation, Gender Identity, Expression, and Sex Charateristics (SOGIESC) model. Such circuits of sexuality/gender knowledge are obtained through encounters with transnational sexuality discourse and LGBT movements. This technology is strategically taken up by activists to sensitize and fashion individuals with non-normative sexuality/gender into a particular sexualized/gendered identity. There is a widely accepted belief among activists that a lack of such sexuality/gender knowledge impedes an individual's self-acceptance. Through these mechanisms, activists become nodes to transfer transnational sexual identity, which in turn perpetuate sexual subjectivities at the local levels.

Such deployment has unsurprisingly produced the new truth of sexuality leading to the proliferation of sexual and gender identities, from *transmen*, *pansexual*, or *intersex* to *queer* (Agustine et al. 2014). Both HIV/AIDS and sexual/reproductive health and rights organizations have also begun to use the SOGIESC model and integrate it into their comprehensive sexuality education model. International humanitarian and/or human rights organizations have increasingly used and institutionalized this sexual category in their practices as well.

The contemporary interpellation and institutionalization of homosexual identity has therefore occurred through different sociopolitical environments in Indonesia, which in turn has produced evolving sexualized subjects. Through discursive technologies, sexual practices/desires are fashioned and channeled into solidified identities. Lack of recognition and understanding of such sexual identity is then treated as a fundamental axis of basic citizenship rights-claiming that would help to increase access to public service and protection toward LGBT people. Yet as explored in the next section, the institutionalization of LGBT identity and the globalization of such discursive identity have produced detrimental effects for LGBT Indonesians.

The (Further) Institutionalization of the Institutionalized

LGBT as a social category in Indonesia is a phenomenon inseparable from the interpellation and institutionalization process to construct LGBT people as legitimate subjects for rights-claiming. As a consequence, the increasing visibilities and representations of LGBT Indonesians have also inadvertently invited multiple counter-attacks from conservative groups and government bodies. This process further leads to multiple efforts to discursively define and institutionalize these subjects into specific policies and practices. The legalization of same-sex marriage in the US, followed by public exposure of international humanitarian organizations' support to local LGBT movements, has tightened and exacerbated surveillance and repressions that were relatively dispersed and sporadic in the previous few decades. Examining these counter-attacks and reactionary responses is hence necessary in order to understand the dynamics at play in this globalization of LGBT identity.

During the New Order era, homosexuality was not perceived as a direct threat to the state (Boellstorff 2005). Negative stigmas and representations of homosexuality occupying print media nevertheless remained prevalent (Blackwood 2007). Such portrayals strongly corresponded with the state's strategy to control sexuality through its deployment of normative traditional gender and familial norms (Robinson 2015). In response to the intensifying same-sex marriage discussions in international spaces during the 1990s, the state felt the need to emphasize its commitment to heterosexual family principles (Offord 2011). At the 1994 International Conference on Population and Development in Cairo, the Minister of Population declared that Indonesia would not support same-sex marriage, while that same year the Ministry of Women's Affairs publicly said that lesbianism was not part of Indonesian culture (Blackwood 2010). Such denouncement interestingly did not translate into systematic prosecution by the state. It was—rather paradoxically—after the fall of this authoritarian regime that non-normative sexualities have consistently become a new conduit for control and regulation.

While democratization has led to various efforts to mainstream protection of human rights, it has also been accompanied by the rise of Islamic conservative groups that have acquired more political power and visibility. Although Soeharto's regime previously repressed those groups, his attitudes toward Islamic groups gradually shifted and loosened in the last years of the regime due to deteriorating relationships with powerful military commanders (Wichelen 2010). These initial moves subsequently allowed political Islam to become a significant political force, through expansion of Islamic television programs, increased support for Islamic schools, and the repeal of prohibitions on veiling (Wichelen 2010).

In addition, decentralization of authority to district-level government has offered fertile ground for attempts to regulate women's bodies and non-normative sexualities through local regulations inspired by Islamic values

(Robinson 2015). Some provincial ordinances conflated male homosexual acts with immoral behavior and abnormality, positioning them equally with prostitution, adultery, and consumption of alcoholic beverages (UNDP, USAID 2014). The special autonomy granted to Aceh as a political solution to the conflicts in the province has also led to legislation based on the Shariah criminal code. This legislation explicitly polices and outlaws male homosexual acts, through a frivolous conflation of homosexuality with anal intercourse between men (Yulius 2015). These policies, although problematic and confusing as to whether they are policing homosexual identity, sexual practices between men, or both, signify the beginning of discursive institutionalization of homosexual subjects in local policies.

In the realignment of political Islam with the fledgling democratic climate, religious vigilante groups have also increasingly championed raids and protests against LGBT-related events (Davies 2015; Robinson 2015). Nevertheless, at national level, homosexuality began to be explicitly incorporated into the controversial Pornography Law that has been effectively enforced since 2008. Pornographic content also includes and covers 'deviant sexual intercourse, including necrophilia, bestiality, oral sex, anal sex, and lesbian, and homosexuals [*sic*]' (Yulius 2016a).

Contestations around non-normative sexualities and genders continue dispersedly across different state institutions and often produce contradictory effects among them. While homosexuality is policed through those local ordinances and the national Pornography Law, in 2008 the Department of Social Affairs issued a guidebook of social services for *waria*, which identified the groups as parts of diversity that have the potential to contribute to the country's development. However, this position shifted shortly afterward (Yulius 2016b).

In 2012, the Ministry of Social Affairs, formerly known as the Department of Social Affairs, treated and included gay men, lesbians, and *waria* as minority groups with social problems, alongside street children, the homeless, and people with disability. This formulation associates their sexual identities with social problems, which justified ministerial interventions to provide social rehabilitation, protection, and empowerment. Quite contrary to the activists' arguments that the Ministry would convert their identities through its rehabilitative programs, anonymous and off-the-record discussion with an officer-in-charge from the Ministry's minority groups section revealed that the primary aim of the Ministerial programs is practically to integrate these marginalized groups within their families and societies. Such social integration is vaguely predicated upon how they could function in and contribute to society (*hidup bermasyarakat*), regardless of their personal sexual orientation and expressions. Equally intriguing, since 2007 the Indonesian government started to receive funding from the Global Fund against AIDS, Tuberculosis, and Malaria (GFATM), which targeted MSM and transgender women, as well as gay men (Alicias-Garen and Jahja 2015). This international support has in turn forged relationships between civil society organizations—including gay/*waria*/MSM organizations working for HIV/AIDS—and the Ministry of Health.

While the absence of the term LGBT might mark the unfamiliarity of policymakers with the terminology, the inclusion of homosexual and transgender subjects in the aforementioned policies signals the gradual awareness of some state bodies of non-normative genders and sexualities, and their efforts to capture, define, and regulate. Moreover, it also surprisingly demonstrates inherent frictions and contradictions of the discursive institutionalization process of homosexual subjects across state bodies and operations. In some policies, homosexuality was overtly condemned; in some others, homosexual subjects become part of ministerial programs.

The year 2016 was pivotal for the landscape of non-normative sexualities in Indonesia. Only a few months after the US legalization of same-sex marriage, reports about the 'rapidly' increasing number of gay men in some cities broke headlines in a number of local and national media outlets. The basis of such claims came from data from the National Commission of AIDS, HIV/AIDS organizations, and the District Health Office (*Dinas Kesehatan*), whose programs have tackled and targeted homosexual subjects to reduce HIV transmissions (Tempo 2015, 2016). The classification and institutionalization of sexual identities in HIV/AIDS programs have enabled not only visibility of homosexual subjects, but also conversion of non-normative sexual subjects into quantifiable measurements, as explained in the above section. On the other hand, the increasing deployment of the SOGIESC model has also contributed to the proliferation of new sexualized/gendered subjects that subsequently feeds into the nation's recent anti-LGBT hysteria.

The year 2016, according to activists, was the culmination of the dispersed attacks against homosexuality that were previously generated by vigilante groups. These multiple elements—the US marriage equality decision, moral panic over the allegedly expeditious increase of LGBT people, public exposure of international organizations' involvement for domestic LGBT rights, and the rise of religious conservatism—have produced a powerful backlash against LGBT Indonesians. Public officials, politicians, civil society and professional organizations all made public denouncements concerning LGBT people, associating them with proxy war, Western intervention, abnormality, mental illness, and threats to the moral fiber of Indonesia's youth (Yulius 2016c). Moreover, anti-LGBT groups have oversimplified and conflated local LGBT activism with efforts to legalize same-sex marriage, although that is not the aim (Yulius 2016d).

The overemphasis on same-sex marriage emerged because of a strange coincidence between global marriage equality and a local gay marriage that was made public by the media. A few months after the US same-sex marriage equality became legal, photos and information of a marriage between Indonesian and Caucasian gay men in Bali became viral in social media (*Rappler* 2015). This then led to national controversies and anti-homosexual attitudes that strongly contributed to moral panics, creating an alarm to the possibility of same-sex marriage in the country. Drawing on this incident, anti-LGBT groups begin to associate LGBT activisms with same-sex marriage.

Conservative groups have made a great deal of effort to further institutionalize and criminalize LGBT subjects. Aliansi Cinta Keluarga (Family Love Alliance) has taken consistent legal steps to revise the existing Criminal Code to designate consensual same-sex relationships/homosexual practices as a crime (Yulius 2017a). In the Court hearing to revise this policy, through deploying ambiguous information, this organization argued that the US marriage equality decision has led to the outbreaks of Kaposi Sarcoma, a form of cancer commonly found in patients with AIDS (Yulius 2016f). Further, they moved forward to conflating HIV/AIDS patients with unproductivity that in turn would become the state's burden. While same-sex marriage has been regularly used to attack LGBT activism, it is intriguing to see how various logics are molded behind such claims, in which frivolous associations and entanglements between same-sex marriage, HIV/AIDS, and productivity are created. This makes the same-sex marriage issue not only about sexuality per se but threatens the heterosexual family's status as foundational to the state.

Moreover, the ongoing debates and controversies on LGBT have led to further institutionalization of LGBT. Lawmakers have planned to include a ban on LGBT-related content in the amendment to the 2002 Broadcasting Law (*Jakarta Post* 2017). In a similar vein, the Ministry of Youth and Sports also began to use the term LGBT to prohibit LGBT Indonesians from joining the 2016 Creative Youth Ambassador Selection (Yulius 2016e). The term LGBT, previously circulated among activists and community networks, has suddenly erupted in public and entered the common parlance since 2016. Nowadays it is no longer an acronym describing a variety of gender and sexual identities, but instead has been used as a single category to address an individual with non-normative gender and sexuality, particularly the ones who have non-normative gender expressions, for example, men with feminine mannerisms (Yulius 2017b). The recent developments of anti-LGBT attitudes have manifested through the arrests of gay men involved in the alleged sex parties and the caning of two gay men in Aceh after the neighbor witnessed and reported their intimacy (Yulius 2017c). This new development reveals the consistent attack against homosexuality and/or non-normative sexual practices, which further collapses the boundaries between public and private and mostly positions male homosexuals as the target.

Singapore and Same-Sex Marriage?

The institutionalization of same-sex marriage around the world is both a near and distant affair for Singaporeans. Citizens of the highly connected global city, should, in theory, be well attuned to transnational LGBT developments. But even with the increasing legislation and proximity of international same-sex marriages in recent years—New Zealand in 2013, all of the US and Ireland in 2015, and Taiwan most recently in 2017, for instance—Singaporeans are, by and large, detached from these LGBT developments. Only two small segments of Singaporean society, broadly identifiable as religious conservatives and liberal progressives, and the ruling People's Action Party (PAP) government caught up in the oppositional politics, have been vociferously participating in same-sex equality debates.

This section examines how various institutionalisms—historical, sociological, and discursive—shape both Singaporean indifference to, and desire for, same-sex equality in the postcolonial city-state. It pays attention to how historical institutions in Singapore create pathways to the sedimentation of particular sexuality and gender understandings; how policy agents and political players, including LGBT activists and their opponents, participate in and shape homosexual contentions; and the discourses on same-sex equality in Singapore. These domestic dynamics in turn shape and co-constitute transnational LGBT discourses and developments. Although there are three distinct dimensions of analysis, each form of neo-institutionalism is not to be taken as discrete and coherent but as co-constitutive and complex.

British Colonialism and Postcolonial Institutional Legacies

An ineluctable fact of life for Singaporean LGBTs is that being gay remains illegal. Statute Section 377A of the Penal Code prohibits any act, or abetment, of gross indecency between men in public or in private. Punishment amounts to two years' imprisonment. A British colonial legacy, the sodomy law was formulated in the Empire and then exported to all British colonies in Asia. Although the British Empire and most former colonies have decriminalized homosexuality, Singapore, along with Malaysia, Brunei, and Myanmar, has held on to the sodomy law.

The artifact of colonial rule has had multiple effects on the lives of local gay men. Anti-homosexuality enforcements took the form of police entrapments. Figures from public records released by the state, calibrated with independent research, reveal that convictions under Section 377A have been carried out almost every year between 1988 and 2007 (*Yawning Bread* 2007; Chua 2003; Gopalan 2007). In a study of local newspaper reports, Leong notes a period of heightened policing in the early 1990s, when almost every month there were news reports about men being convicted for indecency (Leong 2005).

This intense period of persecutions coincided with Singapore's participation at the 1993 World Conference on Human Rights in Vienna. Ironically, rather than being taken to task for the contravention of human rights in its persecution of sexual minorities, the occasion of the Human Rights convention provided the PAP government an opportunity to articulate postcolonial difference by stating that Singapore needed to forge its own pathway. 'Identifying the core rights which are truly universal will not always be easy ... every country must find its own way,' said the foreign minister: 'We have intervened to change individual social behavior in ways other countries consider intrusive ... deployed laws that others may find harsh... We do not think that our arrangements will suit everybody. But they suit ourselves' (Wong Kang Seng, cited in Offord 1999, 303). The minister then proceeded to use homosexuality as a trope of difference 'to consolidate the imagined border' between Singapore and the West, declaring that 'homosexual rights are a Western issue' (Offord 1999, 305). The self-Orientalizing East/West binary the postcolonial state invokes for its self-definition would be repeatedly used to interpellate sexual minorities so as to construct same-sex equality and rights as a neo-colonial imposition of the West on so-called Asian values in Singapore.

Although Section 377A convictions declined over the years, with the government conceding in 2007 that it would in fact not proactively enforce the law, the existence of this piece of colonial legislation has set forth a series of effects. First, it institutionalizes unequal rights and lack of protection for gay men. Second, it allows discriminatory practices by government and private agencies to go unaddressed because standing up is tantamount to admitting to a crime. A prime example of state discriminatory practice would be the Media Development Authority's (MDA) censoring of all positive portrayals of LGBT issues through stringent guidelines on its free-to-air television and radio codes, stating that 'music associated with drugs, alternative lifestyles (e.g. homosexuality) or the worship of the occult or the devil should not be broadcast,' or that 'themes or subplots on lifestyles such as homosexuality, lesbianism, bisexualism, transsexualism, transvestism, paedophilia and incest should be treated with utmost caution.' The code explicitly states that the media's treatment of homosexuality 'should not in any way promote, justify or glamorise such lifestyles,' and 'dialogue or information concerning the above topics should not be broadcast.' Past instances of homosexuality appearing on local mainstream television have included a lewd figure bent on seducing an innocent handsome man, an effeminate man unable to keep a job down, and colorful cross-dressing slapstick characters. Third, it creates social stigma affecting all LGBTs. Fourth, it justifies withholding public protections and benefits, such as equal access to pension, health, immigration, housing, and family support for LGBT individuals, among other things. The effects of the law, even when not enforced, are far reaching. Effectively, it disenfranchises and erases LGBT lives in Singapore. In Singaporean public consciousness, therefore, issues of LGBT rights and equality are far removed and of little concern for most people.

Heteronormativity in Singapore privileges heterosexual lives and concerns, and the married, monogamous, procreative couple is valorized by the state as the foundation of Singaporean society. National policies have been designed and put in service of this specific model of the Singaporean family, including housing subsidies, generous tax rebates, baby bonuses, and a host of other benefits too many to enumerate. In institutionalizing these norms of gender and sexuality, heterosexuality is naturalized and taken for granted at the level of everyday life, making non-normative genders and sexualities strange and alien to the Singaporean. What it means to be Singaporean is thus understood in heteronormative terms. Indeed, the heterosexual nuclear family is constantly invoked by the state as a bulwark against calls for lesbian and gay enfranchisement. In refusing the repeal of Section 377A, for instance, the prime minister stated that 'by "family" in Singapore, we mean one man one woman, marrying, having children and bringing up children within that framework of a stable family unit' (Lee 2007).

The institutionalization of norms of gender and sexuality around the family is an anti-homosexual stance, but it is more than about the exclusion of homosexuality. The state's constant valorization of the heteronormative family as the 'basic building block of society' has a longer provenance. Specifically, this narrow definition of the family was put in place and used by the British colonial administration of households in Singapore as early as the 1940s, which the postcolonial administrators modeled after and mobilized for their own socioeconomic development policies. One evidence for this is how the postcolonial PAP government has used the nuclear family form as the qualification criteria for its public housing program, a key development policy. Why would the postcolonial masters and their colonial predecessors have vested interest in the heterosexual nuclear family? Compelling research has shown that it has to do with colonial orientalist definitions of 'modern' subjects in the 'backward' colonies, and postcolonial anxieties over national survival and development (Oswin 2010, 2014). Indeed, it has been the belief of the postcolonial PAP government that the social regeneration of the Singaporean population was of utmost importance for a small nation lacking in land and resources. Furthermore, a 'quality' population is what is needed; thus, at various points, the state has been pro-natalist and anti-natalist, applying eugenicist ideas to encourage those it deems desirable to procreate for the nation, and discourage those it deems undesirable from doing so (see Heng and Devan 1992). Not only have these heteronormative impulses entirely subsumed LGBT issues and existence, the foregrounding of the heterosexual nuclear family form has been redeployed by conservatives and other opponents of same-sex equality as an essential 'truth' and core 'tradition' that should not be shaken by same-sex imaginings.

LGBT Contestations and Constitutional Challenges

The first time in Singapore's independent history that the presence of homosexuals was openly acknowledged in parliament took place in 2007, when LGBT activists petitioned to repeal Section 377A of the Penal Code. Siew Kum Hong, a nominated member of parliament who submitted the petition on behalf of the community of activists, put forth several arguments about LGBT equality not often heard in the nation's parliamentary chambers: it was unconstitutional for gay men to be treated unequally; laws were meant to protect against harm, not legislate against consensual activity; keeping Section 377A to signpost the values of Singapore's conservative majority is a form of tyranny that would undermine the nation's democratic principles. Each of these arguments was met with a series of quizzical objections from Thio Li Ann, the conservative nominated member of parliament, who argued that the law equally affects heterosexual males experimenting with sodomy, and thus applies equally; demonstrable harm is evident in 'anal-penetrative sex' being 'inherently damaging to the body' which she, in a fit of barely disguised contempt, likened to 'shoving a straw up your nose to drink.' Although the arguments were more rhetorical than reasonable, all but a few of the country's highest officials thumped their seats in approval of Thio's parliamentary speech. In the end, it was decided that the law would be kept but not enforced because Singapore is a conservative society; when public opinions shifted, the law would be removed. In a country where parliamentary proceedings are typically 'monologues by the single party government' (Chua 2007, 60) and abstracted from public culture, the debates did little to shift or inform sociopolitical attitudes toward same-sex equality.

The PAP's ambivalence, uncharacteristic of a typically resolute state, did, however, create discursive space for LGBT supporters and their opponents. LGBT advocates brought into the public sphere a series of arguments concerning the status of 'modern' Singapore in the international arena. Retaining the law would mean that Singapore would remain one of the last few countries in Southeast Asia to preserve a British colonial relic; this is not in keeping with how Singapore prides itself as being at the forefront of modernization in the region. Furthermore, keeping an unenforceable law risks bringing the nation's legal system into disrepute. Simultaneously, opponents of LGBT equality latched onto postcolonial developmentalist anxieties, arguing that legalizing homosexuality would lower the nation's already precariously low birth rates, erode the 'Asian values' of Singaporean society through the acceptance of Western liberal values, and lead it down a slippery slope of moral degradation of same-sex marriage and LGBT families, which would ultimately weaken religious authority and indeed all of society. These arguments put forth by conservatives are those drawn from US Christian Right anti-gay movements, but the irony seems lost to them. Significantly, conflicts between the two oppositional groups—LGBT activists on the one hand, and the Christian counter-movement on the other hand—provide discursive prisms through which the open borders of the nation, and the lack of state omnipotence in reshaping transnational sexuality and gender ideologies that flow through the nation, become evident. Catalyzed by transnational values and norms, political activism on both sides took off.

In 2009, a group of Christian conservatives gained control of Singapore's most established women's rights group, the Association of Women for Action and Research (AWARE), by voting church representatives into AWARE's executive committee. The impetus for the steeplejacking, it seems, is AWARE's 'promotion of lesbianism' (*New Paper* 2009). The new religious leaders have been increasingly concerned with AWARE's LGBT-supportive events and its sexuality program, in which homosexuality is presented to students in neutral and not negative terms. Thus, they sought to return AWARE 'back to the original purpose' (*New Paper* 2009). Outraged by the seizure of power, liberal members of AWARE canvassed support from all Singaporean women for no-confidence votes in the new Christian team, ousting the group successfully through mobilizing the public sphere.

In 2014, religious conservatives and LGBT supporters were to clash again very publicly, through a series of incidents. The first controversy arose over the Health Promotion Board's (HPB) publication of LGBT-specific healthcare information on its webpage. LGBT leaders lauded the HPB for being inclusive and for applying professional guidelines from international bodies, such as UNESCO and UNAIDS, in the provision of the information. Religious conservatives, however, took offense, alleging that HPB was promoting homosexuality through identifying LGBT counseling services and that moreover, HPB's acknowledgement that 'homosexuals can have long-lasting relationships' promoted homosexuality (cited from Loh 2014). Subsequently, HPB removed all links to LGBT websites. The second incident relates to the withdrawal of gay-themed children's books by the National Library Board (NLB) after a library user wrote to express concern about the books' content; *And Tango Makes Three* (Parnell and Richardson 2005) features a pair of gay penguins while *The White Swan Express* (Okimoto et al. 2002) mentions a lesbian couple. When the NLB declared it would take a 'pro-family' position and pulp the books, thousands of Singaporeans signed an online petition calling for the books to be returned to library shelves and a 'read-in' was staged at the National Library with hundreds of parents and children reading diverse books together in a show of protest. The NLB subsequently retracted its plans, placing the books in the library's adult section instead of pulping them.

In the same year, a group of gay men stepped forward to challenge the constitutionality of Section 377A. The appellants made many arguments, but one worth noting here is their drawing on a 'born this way' discourse deployed in global LGBT justifications for marriage equality. Being criminalized for an unchangeable aspect of their identity was unconstitutional, the men argued. In rejecting the claims, however, the court, in turn, drew on the evidence of a scientific discourse still inherently conflicted on whether sexual orientation is born or bred. The constitutionality of Section 377A was ultimately upheld by the Singapore court on a narrow, if troubling, interpretation that the Constitution did not prohibit discrimination based on sexual orientation and identity. The series of contestations, intensifying over the last decade, demonstrate that the push and resistance toward same-sex equality in Singapore is very much influenced by transnational norms, values, and standards. It is unclear whether these pressures will move the government toward or against legalizing homosexuality, given the inconsistent positions between its policy agents.

Global City Aspirations and Transnational LGBT Activisms

Opening up to the world has never been a choice for Singapore. Bereft of land and population, the small nation has always been dependent on the world economy. 'Without a large domestic market and no raw materials to speak of,' said the foreign minister, Singapore would have a 'near-zero chance of survival' (Rajaratnam 1972). Thus, decades before the concept gained circulation in international urban and policy discourse, the PAP postcolonial government had already begun articulating a 'global city' vision, one where the 'world' would provide Singapore its markets and resources. The global city strategy has been pursued relentlessly, with the government ever alert and attuned to opportunities in the global marketplace. Within a short span of five decades, Singapore transformed itself from a declining British trading post to a thriving, cosmopolitan city-state.

The realization of Singapore as a global city produced cultural and material effects on the LGBT community. As the Singaporean government actively sought out and opened up global markets, it also eased into social and cultural liberalism. Consequently, Singapore has become a site of significant sexuality-related changes: the growth of creative industries supporting queer professionals and queer cultural life; vibrant gay bars and nightlife; art and film festivals spotlighting LGBT issues; more positive representations of the gay community in the media; and public disavowals of discrimination by state authorities, espousing instead rhetoric on liberalism, progress, and tolerance. Taking seriously Richard Florida's (2002) thesis that successful global cities are those that attract a creative class of technology workers, artists, musicians, and gay people drawn to open and diverse societies, the government also began addressing the role of LGBTs in Singaporean society. In 2003, Goh Chok Tong, prime minister at the time, said in an interview with *Time* magazine (2003) that his was not an inflexible government, but one that would employ openly homosexual Singaporeans to sensitive positions. 'In time,' the prime minister went on to say, 'the population will understand that some people are born that way ... we are born this way and they are born that way, but they are like you and me.' Singapore's global city aspirations thus created wide material and discursive spaces for LGBT inclusion in Singaporean society.

People Like Us (PLU), a pioneering LGBT lobby group in Singapore, which had previously tried and failed several times to register itself with the government, regrouped quickly to take the state's liberal discursive tropes at face value. It applied for a license to hold a public forum for gays and lesbians, but it was turned down. Undeterred, members wrote letters to the press appealing for greater social acceptance in light of the prime minister's acquiescence. LGBT advocacy grew strategically in and through the state's inconsistent positions, rising to assert itself through changing global and discursive contexts (Tan and Lee 2007). In recent years, LGBT politics have involved state engagement through international human rights mechanisms and institutions. Over the last several years, Sayoni, a lesbian advocacy group, has been reporting on the human rights situation for sexual minorities in Singapore at the United Nations' (UN) Convention for the Elimination of All Forms of Discrimination Against Women (CEDAW) meetings.

Local pride events have also flourished in the contemporary period of state liberalization, with LGBT groups making claims in Singaporean society. IndigNation is the annual month-long pride event, consisting of discussions, talks, photo exhibitions, art displays, literary readings, and film screenings on local and international queer issues. Pink Dot is Singapore's public gay rally. It is held each year at a park designated as Speakers' Corner, modeled after the Hyde Park in London, except in Singapore this is the only place where Singaporeans can congregate for rallies and demonstrations. Pink Dot has grown rapidly over the years. It started in 2009 with over 2000 attendees gathering to form a pink dot in the park symbolizing support for LGBT inclusiveness. In its 2016 installment, the number of participants would exceed the park's capacity, with tens of thousands in attendance. Part of Pink Dot's success is due to the involvement and support from multinational corporations (MNCs), whose entry into Singapore is one promoted by the government's global city ambitions. Companies such as Google, Bloomberg, Twitter, JP Morgan, and Goldman Sachs have generously sponsored Pink Dot, in line with MNCs' adoption of strong activist stances in countries where they have set up business, institutionalizing gay-supportive employment policies, including, for instance, same-sex spousal support. Inevitably, the success of Pink Dot, backed by big global corporations, has created anxieties among religious conservatives. Counter-campaigns have been rolled out by religious groups, most notably, a Wear White movement that saw a group of Muslims and an Evangelical Church join forces in defense of 'traditional' and 'pure' values. In a sudden twist of events, the PAP state has banned foreign companies and foreigners from supporting and participating in Pink Dot starting from 2017. In the global city of Singapore, it seems, LGBT-friendly developments on the local and transnational front have led not to progress, but to polarization and paradoxical positions.

Conclusion

The Indonesian and Singaporean stories offer exemplary cases of discursive institutionalization of gendered and sexualized subjects in contradistinction to the globalized world of LGBT identities and increasing jurisdictions where same-sex marriage has become legal. As such identities globalize and begin to be institutionalized, a series of counter-reactions has followed and subsequently produced unexpected outcomes. In the Indonesian case, the increasing visibility of LGBT identity and same-sex marriage have led to attempts of 'othering' from conservative groups and state institutions and institutionalizing it into policies and laws that further exacerbate discrimination against LGBT people. Through LGBT and same-sex marriage controversies, state and Islamic conservative groups have reasserted the nationalist imaginaries and Islamic values that were perceived to be at stake in the response to globalization.

In Singapore, the demands of being a global city have included pressures to reconcile local LGBT desires with global gay norms that hold out the promise of same-sex equality and marriage; it also has included pressures to reconcile polarizing differences over LGBT concerns in Singapore, though this is not unique to the nation but a world-wide phenomenon. In these contemporary and precarious times, same-sex marriage has become a lightning rod of contention across the world. In Singapore, the state has acknowledged that both LGBT and conservative groups are 'pressuring the government' to be responsive (Lee quoted in *Today* 2017). Among political leaders and in popular opinion, the polarization of LGBT politics in Singapore has been perceived as a 'culture war' between conservatives and progressives, one that will somehow be resolved with time as societal attitudes change. A passive 'wait and see' attitude has so far been the official position. What remains obscure in these discourses and understandings is the materiality and institutionalizations of LGBT and anti-LGBT positions, such as the economic embedding of MNCs with their pro-gay initiatives in the global city on the one hand, and the institutionalization of heteronormativity for economic developmentalist objectives on the other. The state, far from being benign, is in fact actively driving and solidifying trajectories of oppositional LGBT positions. For this moment in Singapore, same-sex marriage remains a distant reality.

For the immediate future, it seems clear that same-sex marriage has become a religious, cultural, and political fault line catalyzed by the globalization of LGBT identities in both Indonesia and Singapore. Moreover, it is likely that the advent of same-sex marriage regionally, in Taiwan and inevitability in Australia, will pose new challenges that will galvanize further institutional reaction alongside ongoing struggles for LGBT human rights across Southeast Asia.

Notes

1. The term LGBT, although it is now commonly used in Indonesia, is still highly contested. Some argue that this term is disconnected from the diverse realities and subjectivities of people with non-normative genders and sexualities. This chapter aims to unpack the sociocultural and historical contexts of the institutionalization of the term itself and reveals its political contestations.

References

Agustine, R.R. Sri. 2008. Rahasia Sunyi: Gerakan Lesbian di Indonesia. *Jurnal Perempuan* 58 (01): 59–74.
Agustine, R.R. Sri, Maesur Zaky, and Siska Dewi Noya. 2014. *Panduan Pelatihan Fasilitator Pengarusutamaan Keragaman Gender dan Seksualitas (PKGS)*. Jakarta: Rutgers WPF Indonesia.

Alicias-Garen, Maria Dolores, and Ranggoaini Jahja. 2015. Hivos Rosea: External Evaluation of LGBT Program Final Report. Unpublished.
Altman, Dennis. 2001. *Global Sex*. Chicago: University of Chicago Press.
Altman, Dennis, and Jonathan Symons. 2016. *The Queer Wars*. Cambridge: Polity Press.
Bennett, Linda Rae, and Sharyn Graham Davies, eds. 2015. *Sex and Sexualities in Contemporary Indonesia*. London: Routledge.
Blackwood, Evelyn. 2007. Regulation of Sexuality in Indonesian Discourse: Normative Gender, Criminal Law, and Shifting Strategies of Control. *Culture, Health, and Society* 9 (3): 293–307.
———. 2010. *Falling into the Lesbi World: Desire and Difference in Indonesia*. Honolulu: University of Hawai'i Press.
Boellstorff, Tom. 2005. *The Gay Archipelago*. Princeton, NJ: Princeton University Press.
———. 2007. *A Coincidence of Desires*. Durham: Duke University Press.
Broadcasting Bill Aims to Purge LGBT Content. 2017. *The Jakarta Post*, January 19.
Chua, Lynette. 2003. Saying No: Sections 377 and 377A of the Penal Code. *Singapore Journal of Legal Studies*: 209–261.
Chua, Beng Huat. 2007. Singapore in 2007: High Wage Ministers and the Management of Gays and Elderly. *Asian Survey* 48 (1): 55–61.
Chua, Lynette. 2014. *Mobilizing Gay Singapore: Rights and Resistance in An Authoritarian State*. Singapore: NUS Press.
Davies, Sharyn Graham. 2015. Surveilling Sexuality in Indonesia. In *Sex and Sexualities in Contemporary Indonesia*, ed. Linda Rae Bennett and Sharyn Graham Davies. London: Routledge.
Davies, Sharyn Graham, and Hendri Yulius. 2018. *The Unfulfilled Promise of Democracy: Lesbian and Gay Activism in Indonesia*. (Forthcoming).
Duggan, Lisa. 2002. The New Homonormativity: The Sexual Politics of Neoliberalism. In *In Materializing Democracy: Toward a Revitalized Cultural Politics*, ed. Russ Castronovo and Dana Nelson. Durham: Duke University Press.
Fassin, Didier. 2012. *Humanitarian Reason: A Moral History of the Present Times*. London: University of California Press.
Florida, Richard. 2002. *The Rise of the Creative Class: and How It's Transforming Work, Leisure, Community and Everyday Life*. New York: Basic Books.
Foucault, Michel. 1987. *The History of Sexuality: An Introduction*. New York: Penguin Books.
G. 1982. *G: Gaya Hidup Ceria*, August. Vol. 1. Solo: Lambda Indonesia.
Gopalan, Mohan. 2007. A Heftier List of s.377! *Yawning Bread*, May. Accessed 18 August 2011. http://www.yawningbread.org/guest_2007/guw-136.htm

Heng, Geraldine, and Janadas Devan. 1992. State Fatherhood: The Politics of Nationalism, Sexuality and Race in Singapore. In *Nationalisms and Sexualities*, ed. A. Parker, M. Russo, D. Sommer, and P. Yaeger. New York: Routledge.

Howard, Richard Stephen. 1996. Falling into the Gay World: Manhood, Marriage, and Family in Indonesia. Ph.D. dissertation, University of Illinois at Urbana-Champaign.

Langlois, Anthony J., Cai Wilkinson, Paula Gerber, and Baden Offord. 2017. Community, Identity, Orientation: Sexuality, Gender and Rights in ASEAN. *The Pacific Review*: 1–19.

Lee, Hsien Loong. 2007. Speech to Parliament on Reading of Penal Code (Amendment) Bill, October 22.

Leong, Wai Teng. 2005. The 'Straight' Times: News and Sexual Citizenship in Singapore. In *Journalism and Democracy in Asia*, ed. A. Romano and M. Bromley. London: Routledge.

Loh, Andrew. 2014. *FAQ on Sexuality by HPB Turns Controversial*, February. Accessed 31 May 2017. https://www.theonlinecitizen.com/2014/02/05/faq-on-sexuality-by-hpb-turns-controversial/

Murtagh, Ben. 2013. *Genders and Sexualities in Indonesian Cinema: Constructing Gay, Lesbi and Waria Identities on Screen*. London: Routledge.

New Paper. 2009. *Emotions Overflow as Women Exchange Bards*. Singapore: Singapore Press Holdings.

Nguyen, Vinh-Kim. 2010. *The Republic of Therapy*. Durham, NC: Duke University Press.

Oetomo, Dede. 2003. *Memberi Suara Pada yang Bisu*. Yogayakarta: Pustaka Marwa.

Offord, Baden. 1999. The Burden of (Homo)Sexual Identity in Singapore. *Social Semiotics* 9 (3): 301–316.

———. 2003. *Homosexual Rights as Human Rights: Activism in Indonesia, Singapore, and Australia*. Oxford: Peter Lang.

———. 2011. Singapore, Indonesia and Malaysia: Arrested Development! In *The Lesbian and Gay Movement and the State*, ed. Manon Tremblay, David Patternotte, and Carol Johnson. UK: Ashgate.

Okimoto, Jean Davies, Meilo So, and Elaine M. Aoki. 2002. *The White Swan Express*. New York: Clarion Books.

Oswin, Natalie. 2010. Sexual Tensions in Modernizing Singapore: The Postcolonial and the Intimate. *Environment and Planning D: Society and Space* 28: 128–141.

———. 2014. Queer Time in Global City Singapore: Neoliberal Futures and the 'Freedom to Love. *Sexualities* 17 (4): 412–443.

Parnell, Peter, and Justin Richardson. 2005. *And Tango Makes Three*. New York: Simon and Schuster Children's Publishing.

Perez, Hiram. 2015. *A Taste for Brown Bodies*. New York: New York University Press.

Puar, Jasbir. 2007. *Terrorist Assemblages: Homonationalism in Queer Times*. Durham: Duke University Press.

Rajaratnam, Sinnathamby. 1972. Singapore: Global City. Text of an Address to the Singapore Press Club, Ministry of Culture, Singapore, February 6.

Rappler. 2015. Cerita di balik pernikahan sesama jenis di Bali, September 17. Accessed 6 June 2017. http://www.rappler.com/indonesia/106150-pernikahan-pasangan-sesama-jenis-bali

Robinson, Kathryn. 2015. Masculinity, Sexuality, and Islam: The Gender Politics of Regime Change in Indonesia. In *Sex and Sexualities in Contemporary Indonesia*, ed. Linda Rae Bennett and Sharyn Graham Davies. London: Routledge.

Stella, Francesca, Yvette Taylor, Tracey Reynolds, and Antoine Rogers, eds. 2016. *Sexuality, Citizenship, and Belonging: Transnational and Intersectional Perspectives*. New York: Routledge.

Tan, Kenneth P., and Gary Jack Jin Lee. 2007. Imagining the Gay Community in Singapore. *Critical Asian Studies* 39 (2): 179–204.

Tang, Shawna. 2017. *Postcolonial Lesbian Identities in Singapore: Rethinking Global Sexualities*. London: Routledge.

Tempo. 2015. Setahun jumlah gay di kota depok meningkat 800 orang, November 17. Accessed 1 June 1 2017. https://m.tempo.co/read/news/2015/11/17/214719618/setahun-jumlah-gay-di-kota-depok-meningkat-800-orang

———. 2016. Jumlah Gay di Bandung Mencapai 2.000 Orang, February 23. Accessed 1 June 2017. https://nasional.tempo.co/read/news/2016/02/23/058747523/jumlah-gay-di-bandung-mencapai-2-000-orang

Time Magazine. 2003. The Lion in Winter. 30 June.

UNDP & USAID. 2014. *Being LGBT in Asia: Indonesia Country Report*. Bangkok: UNDP.

Wichelen, Sonja van. 2010. *Religion, Politics and Gender in Indonesia: Disputing the Muslim Body*. London: Routledge.

Yawning Bread. 2007. Why Section 377A Is Redundant, May. Accessed 18 August 2011. http://www.yawningbread.org/arch_2007/yax-749.htm

Yue, Audrey, and Jun Zubillaga-Pow, eds. 2012. *Queer Singapore: Illiberal Citizenship and Mediated Cultures*. Hongkong: Hongkong University Press.

Yulius, Hendri. 2015. Regulating the Bedroom: Sex in Aceh's Criminal Code. *Indonesia at Melbourne*, November. Accessed 1 June 2017. http://indonesiaatmelbourne.unimelb.edu.au/sex-in-acehs-criminal-code/

———. 2016a. Double Standards: The Defining of Homosexuality as Pornographic in Indonesia. *The Jakarta Post*, October 21. Accessed 1 June 2017. http://www.thejakartapost.com/academia/2016/10/21/double-standards-the-defining-of-homosexuality-as-pornographic-in-indonesia.html

———. 2016b. Who Constructed LGBT Identity in Indonesia?" *New Mandala*, November. Accessed 1 June 2017. http://www.newmandala.org/from-margins-to-centre/
———. 2016c. The 'Burkini', LGBT People and the Global Sex Wars. *The Jakarta Post*, August 30. Accessed 1 June 2017. http://www.thejakartapost.com/academia/2016/08/30/the-burkini-lgbt-people-and-the-global-sex-wars.html
———. 2016d. What Does the Indonesian LGBT Movement Want? *The Jakarta Post*, February 19. Accessed 1 June 2017. http://www.thejakartapost.com/news/2016/02/19/what-does-indonesian-lgbt-movement-want.html
———. 2016e. How Indonesia (Inadvertently) Promotes LGBT. *Asian Correspondent*, October. Accessed 1 June 2017. https://asiancorrespondent.com/2016/10/indonesia-inadvertently-promotes-lgbt/#j8PAyWEdraSluOEL.97
———. 2016f. Live and Let Die: A New Strategy for Criminalizing LGBTs in Indonesia. Rappeler.com, August. Accessed 6 June 2017. http://www.rappler.com/world/regions/asia-pacific/indonesia/english/144845-lgbt-discrimination-court
———. 2017a. Indonesia and 'Transparent Sex.' *New Mandala*, January. Accessed 1 June 2017. http://www.newmandala.org/indonesia-transparent-sex/
———. 2017b. Moral Panic and the Reinvention of LGBT. *Indonesia at Melbourne*, May. Accessed 1 June 2017. http://indonesiaatmelbourne.unimelb.edu.au/moral-panic-and-the-reinvention-of-lgbt/
———. 2017c. The Politics of Shaming Gay Sex in Indonesia. Magdalene.co, May. Accessed 6 June 2017. http://magdalene.co/news-1231-the-politics-of-shaming-gay-sex-in-indonesia-.html

Hendri Yulius is the author of *Coming Out* (published in Indonesian). He frequently contributes articles on gender and sexuality issues to various media outlets, including *The Jakarta Post* and *New Mandala*. He obtained a master's degree in Public Policy from the National University of Singapore and is now pursuing a master's by research in Gender and Cultural Studies at the University of Sydney, Australia.

Shawna Tang is a postdoctoral research fellow at the Sexualities and Genders Research (SaGR) group within the School of Social Sciences and Psychology, Western Sydney University, Australia. She studies the cultural and political expressions of sexuality and gender in Asia, especially Singapore. Her interest is in the convergence of feminist, queer, postcolonial, critical race, trans and disability studies in addressing sociological questions of power and inequality in society and in knowledge production. She has recently published the monograph *Postcolonial Lesbian Identities in Singapore* (2017).

Baden Offord holds the Dr Haruhisa Handa Chair of Human Rights; is Professor of Cultural Studies and Human Rights; and Director, Centre for Human Rights Education at Curtin University, Australia. An internationally recognized specialist in human rights, sexuality, culture, and education, he is part of a scholarly and activist community that works collectively to decolonize and destabilize the study of sexuality in Southeast Asia. He is a member of the international advisory board for the Palgrave Macmillan research book series Gender, Sexualities and Culture in Asia.

CHAPTER 10

Pathways to Legalizing Same-Sex Marriage in China and Taiwan: Globalization and "Chinese Values"

Elaine Jeffreys and Pan Wang

INTRODUCTION

This chapter compares the historical, political, social and discursive factors contributing to and preventing equal recognition of same-sex partnerships in the People's Republic of China (PRC) and Taiwan. The populations and cultures of China and Taiwan are generally described in homogeneous terms as "Chinese." But they have had different systems of political and social organization since 1949, when the Chinese Communist Party (CCP) won the Chinese civil war and founded the PRC, and the rival Nationalist Party fled across the Formosa Strait to the island of Taiwan where it established an authoritarian regime called the Republic of China. This situation created two "Chinas," with both political entities claiming to be the sole and legitimate representative of "China."

Despite the subsequent opening-up of both economies to globalizing forces, the PRC retains a one-party ruling system, while Taiwan became a multiparty state with a popularly elected president in 1996 and had an active lesbian, gay, bisexual and transgender (LGBT) movement by the early 2000s. In the PRC, state controls over the media and social organizations ensured that LGBT issues did not become a major feature of public

E. Jeffreys (✉) • P. Wang
University of Technology Sydney, Ultimo, NSW, Australia

© The Author(s) 2018
B. Winter et al. (eds.), *Global Perspectives on Same-Sex Marriage*, Global Queer Politics, https://doi.org/10.1007/978-3-319-62764-9_10

discourse until after the 2000s. Yet, in 2015–2016, a retired CCP official and father of a gay son petitioned the National People's Congress (the PRC's legislature) to support families by recognizing same-sex marriage, and a landmark same-sex marriage case was heard and rejected by the Chinese courts (Phillips 2016; Zhang 2015).

In Taiwan, the Constitutional Court ruled on 24 May 2017 that laws preventing same-sex marriage are unconstitutional because they violate citizen rights to equality, and instructed the Taiwan parliament to amend or enact laws within two years or the legislation will change by default ("Victory at last" 2017). Taiwan is thus set to become the first country in Asia to recognize same-sex marriage, although the exact nature of such legislation may be influenced by public protest against marriage equality on the grounds that it will undermine religious and traditional Chinese family values.

What might motivate the PRC government to recognize same-sex marriage and what has spurred Taiwan's Constitutional Court to instruct the Taiwan parliament to legalize same-sex marriage? We answer these questions via case studies of the PRC and Taiwan respectively. We explain why homosexuality was an "invisible" phenomenon in both countries until recently, and trace the emergence of advocacy for marriage equality in the context of two different and evolving political systems. We attribute Taiwan's path to becoming the first country in Asia to legalize same-sex marriage to the combination of an active LGBT movement, multiparty strategizing and government efforts to differentiate Taiwan from the PRC in international arenas. At the same time, the rise of the PRC as a global superpower, the lack of civil society opposition to same-sex marriage in that country and the current administration's emphasis on promoting "Chinese" and core socialist values may, perhaps surprisingly, enable the "peaceful" recognition of marriage equality in China by government fiat.

Case Study 1: China

What might motivate the PRC government to institutionalize same-sex marriage and endorse what is upheld in many western liberal-democratic societies as a progressive human rights policy? Writing of the 2000s, Timothy Hildebrandt (2011) provided three possible answers: (1) domestic pressure from LGBT organizations; (2) international pressure; and (3) tactical decision-making by an authoritarian government aiming to improve its international reputation. The first two answers draw on the historical experience of western social movements to obtain legal rights for LGBT people. This history involved struggles for the decriminalization of homosexuality, anti-discrimination legislation and legal recognition of same-sex partnerships respectively, and often with reference to international human rights' conventions (UNDP and USAID 2014, 23). The situation in China is different. Homosexuality is not criminalized in the PRC, but the nature of the Party-state has ensured that there is no national political discourse on LGBT matters, no protective national laws and that no specific Ministry has responsibility for issues relating to sexual orientation and gender identity (UNDP and USAID 2014, 11). Media censorship of sex-related content and controls on social organizations have further limited public advocacy on LGBT matters, and the PRC government is renowned for only talking about human rights on its own terms. Hence Hildebrandt (2011, 1313) concludes that marriage equality by government fiat is the most likely option, but "the right to marry will do little to challenge the larger social pressures that make life difficult for LGBT Chinese."

Background

From 1949 until the 1980s, homosexually was a virtually "invisible" practice in the PRC, flowing from the early CCP's adoption of centralized economic planning, and promotion of free choice, monogamous (heterosexual) marriage. Nationalization of industry and curtailment of the monetary economy meant that the Party-state provided citizen-workers with employment, housing and the necessities of everyday life, which had the corollary effect of restricting the spaces for same-sex behaviours by limiting both population mobility and the kinds of venues in which individuals could engage in anonymous or private behaviours (Jeffreys and Yu 2015, 18–21). The new Marriage Law of 1950 aimed to liberate women from a feudal Confucian-patriarchal tradition by letting them choose their own spouses and stopping concubinage and mercenary marriages. However, the promotion of free choice marriage, when combined with the importance placed in Chinese culture on marriage for procreation and the establishment of a state-controlled media, literally eliminated the space for public discussions of sexual orientation and identity until the 1990s.

The Criminal Law of the People's Republic of China, which was first issued in 1979 and then revised in 1997, does not directly criminalize homosexuality. It prohibits non-consensual sex acts such as rape, sexual assault, forced prostitution and sex with minors (Criminal Law of the People's Republic of China 1997, Articles 237–8 and 358). The age of consent for sexual activity is 14 years, with no restrictions on gender or sexual orientation. But the Law criminalizes as harmful some activities that may limit freedom of sexual expression, including the third-party organization of prostitution and orgies, and the manufacture and dissemination of pornography (Sections 8–9 and Article 301). Before 1997, homosexuals were sometimes detained by police for engaging in acts of "hooliganism" based on a 1984 ruling by the Supreme People's Court. To the extent that police targeted homosexuals, they tended to police the public spaces that men who have sex with men were known to frequent to find sexual partners and engage in sex acts, such as toilet blocks and parks (Li 2009, 86–7).

The establishment of support organizations for LGBT people was also restricted by state authorities in the 1990s, as demonstrated by the case of Wan Yanhai. In late 1992, Wan (2001, 60) organized a salon called Men's World, a health promotion group for same-sex attracted men, which held a Valentine's Day celebration in 1993. While encouraging similar gatherings in other cities, the salon was promptly closed down. The Ministry of Public Security issued a document about this decision, titled Notice on the Closure of the "Men's World" Homosexual Culture Salon (Gonganbu 1993). The Notice stated that the salon had been closed down at the request of the Ministry of Health because of public complaints. Illustrating a highly negative view of homosexuality, the Notice stated that homosexuality was a perverse form of human behaviour that violated public morality, corrupted social values, destroyed family harmony, encouraged criminality, endangered public security and contributed to the spread of AIDS. While noting that such gatherings did not comprise a form of hooliganism, it concluded that similar homosexual gatherings could be investigated and closed down as "unlawful assemblies."

Homosexuality was also defined medically in terms of sexual dysfunction and mental disorder until 2001. It was defined as a psychosexual disorder in a 1981 clinical guide for the diagnosis of mental disorders published by the Chinese Society of Psychiatry. That text was retrospectively titled the first Chinese Classification of Mental Disorders in 1989, when it was replaced by the official second Chinese Classification of Mental Disorders. The description of homosexuality in terms of mental disorder was not removed from the Chinese Classification of Mental Disorders until it was revised again in 2001 (Chinese Society of Psychiatry

2001). It is worth noting that the World Health Organization (1992) only removed homosexuality from its classification of mental and behaviour disorders at the Forty-Third World Health Assembly in 1990, with a new International Classification of Diseases coming into effect in member states in 1994. Hence, the PRC's redefinition of homosexuality followed from the eventual adoption of international standards.

While the western LGBT movement developed through struggles against the pathologization of homosexuality, state controls over the PRC's media and civil sector have ensured that there are limited venues for organized advocacy on and positive self-presentations of LGBT issues. Regulations issued by the State Administration of Press, Publication, Radio, Film and Television in 2006 banned the inclusion of content relating to pornography, licentiousness, rape, commercial sex, sexual perversion and sex organs ("Guojia guangbo dianying dianshi zongju ling" 2006, Article 14, Item 3). A 2008 notice on film and television censorship standards added homosexual sex to the list of banned sexual content. The continued potential for government censorship encourages self-censorship on the part of individuals and organizations, both to avoid regulatory repercussions and to maintain commercial viability. Hence the majority of LGBT-themed media products and publications are independently produced and not widely circulated outside of LGBT circles (Jeffreys and Yu 2015, 82–4; UNDP and USAID 2014, 44–5).

Yet some same-sex attracted people claim that the major problem faced by people in China who wish to live openly as LGBT is "not state oppression, religious fundamentalism, or job discrimination," but rather pressure from their relatives and peers (Chou 2001, 34). People of marrying age are pressured to get married to continue the family line and guarantee support for family elders. Data from the PRC's 2010 Population Census demonstrates that less than 2 per cent of men and women aged 40 years and over had never married (Jeffreys and Yu 2015, 15). The now defunct one-child-per-couple policy has ensured that some parents and grandparents are prepared to accept the non-traditional sexual and lifestyle choices of their only child/grandchild in order to retain a relationship with them, but other parents place even more pressure on an only child to marry, reproduce and otherwise lead a successful, "normal" life.

Many gays and lesbians view entering a heterosexual marriage as "the right thing to do" despite their sexual orientation, and others enter marriages of convenience to pass as straight to family members and work colleagues. In the words of one self-identified Chinese gay man who says he would consider marrying a woman to please his parents: "I am not ashamed of being gay at all. I only care about my family" (Lau 2010, see Wuhan—Robin's story). This situation has resulted in an estimated 16 million heterosexual women being married unknowingly to same-sex attracted men (Jeffreys and Yu 2015, 39). Some homosexuals avoid or delay social pressures to marry by moving away from their place of birth and family home, and practising a classical Chinese aesthetic of "don't ask, don't tell" with their families and colleagues (Jeffreys and Yu 2015, 89). Others enter a "cooperative marriage," that is, a marriage between two homosexuals of the opposite sex who present themselves to family and work circles as a heterosexual couple, while maintaining separate gay and lesbian sex lives. The social networking site ChinaGayLes.com claimed to have had more than 400,000 thousand registered users and assisted over 50,000 such marriages as of 2017 (www.chinagayles.com/).

But the space was opened for government action and domestic critique of government inaction on LGBT issues in December 2013, when the PRC government accepted recommendations at the Human Rights Council of the United Nations (UN) that it establish anti-discrimination legislation to ensure that LGBT people enjoy equal treatment (United Nations General Assembly 2013). In 2016, in an action described as the largest coordinated event in the history of China's LGBT movement, nearly 200 organizations released a publicized letter condemning violence based on sexual orientation, after a gunman killed 49 people in a gay nightclub in Orlando, Florida, in the USA in June of that year (Bai 2016). The letter added that Chinese LGBT people experience unacceptable violence and discrimination, as demonstrated by the existence of "gay conversion therapy" and schoolyard bullying of LGBT youth. This action followed media publicity on a series of landmark legal cases heard by the Chinese courts in 2015–2016, which criticized government inaction on social and workplace discrimination based on sexual orientation and gender identity, and demanded the introduction of affirmative legislation, including the legalization of same-sex marriage.

Advocacy for Same-Sex Marriage

In 2015, Sun Wenlin filed a landmark case against a civil affairs department in Changsha City, Hunan Province, for refusing to register a marriage between him and his male partner, Hu Mingliang (Phillips 2016).

The court's acceptance of the case in January 2016 attracted international publicity in the wake of the June 2015 US Supreme Court ruling, which ruled that individual states in the USA could not ban same-sex marriage without abrogating constitutional guarantees of due process and equal protection under the law. The US ruling generated widespread interest on Chinese social media, resulting in companies such as Taobao, an online shopping platform, placing the rainbow flag on their homepages. In April 2016, the Changsha court rejected Sun's claim that the PRC's Marriage Law is non-gender-specific and affirmed that marriage can only take place between a man and a woman according to extant law (Phillips 2016). However, the court's acceptance of the case is viewed as a milestone in terms of LGBT affirmative action on civil rights. It highlights the potential to alter regulations related to the legal registration of marriages in China, which are administrative rather than celebratory or religious in nature.

Activists Li Yinhe and Lin Xianzhi have advocated for legal protections for same-sex couples not through the courts, but during the annual meetings of the National People's Congress (NPC) and the Chinese People's Political Consultative Conference (CPPCC), which foreign analysts often jointly dismiss as a "rubber-stamp parliament." Li Yinhe is a famous sociologist and sexual rights' activist; her Sina.com blog alone had received more than one hundred million visitors by 2017 (http://blog.sina.com.cn/liyinhe; Jeffreys and Yu 2015, 162–8). Li unsuccessfully lobbied delegates at the CPPCC to consider a proposal on legalizing same-sex marriage on at least seven occasions between 2003 and 2016. In most instances, Li failed to find a delegate willing to present her proposal; on the few occasions when a delegate agreed to present her proposal, it failed to obtain sufficient signatures to be placed on the official agenda for discussion. In 2013 and 2014, Liang Wenhui, a male social work student, also sent Li's proposal and an open letter signed by one hundred gay parents to NPC deputies petitioning for the legalization of same-sex marriage, after two lesbians attempted to register a marriage but failed. He has since founded a Guangzhou-based organization called the Gay-Straight Alliance (http://rainrainbowcomeout.blog.163.com/).

Li Yinhe's proposal states that legalizing same-sex marriage will benefit Chinese society for six reasons (Li 2015). First, it will ensure that Chinese citizens enjoy equal rights. Second, it will reduce the spread of HIV by encouraging monogamy. Third, it will revive China's traditional cultural acceptance of same-sex eroticism. Fourth, it will build the PRC's international reputation as a promoter rather than violator of human rights. Fifth, it will reduce the number of "fake" and "cooperative" marriages. Finally, it will promote social harmony by preventing clashes between minority and mainstream groups. Despite failing to obtain formal political traction, Li's lobbying has attracted publicity and debate.

Li Yinhe obtained further news coverage in 2014–2015 when she announced on China's Twitter-like Weibo that her longstanding partner is a transman, and the *People's Daily*—the official mouthpiece of the CCP—responded to her revelations with support on its Weibo. The *People's Daily* editor stated that homosexuality and transsexuality are increasingly accepted in Chinese society and that respecting one's personal views also means respecting "the choices of the Li Yinhe's among us" (Renmingwang weiping 2014). This response constitutes a rare example of the state-controlled media encouraging respect for sexual diversity. It suggests some degree of political support for raising awareness of LGBT issues and preventing expressions of homophobia.

Lin Xianzhi, a retired government official, and member of Parents and Friends of Lesbians and Gays (PFLAG) China, petitioned representatives at the NPC in 2015 to give young gay couples legal protections, while capitalizing on his son's temporary fame as a finalist in the Valentine's Day "Rainbow Love" contest hosted by Taobao (Doland 2015; Zhang 2015). Founded in 2008, PFLAG China has subgroups across the PRC (pflag.org.cn) and is an independent version of PFLAG, an organization founded in the USA in the 1970s that now supports families and friends of LGBTIQ people. The competition featured as a rotating advertisement on the Taobao homepage through partnerships with the global marketing company China Luxury Advisors and three Chinese LGBT organizations: Danlan.org (a gay website), PFLAG China and the Beijing LGBT Centre. It offered ten same-sex Chinese couples an all-expenses paid trip to California to get married during a group wedding there, with funding from a bedding company. Taobao users voted on the finalists based on short videos of the couples telling their stories about how they met and fell in love, and why they wanted to marry. Over 400 couples competed, 1,000,000 people viewed the event page, and more than 75,000 people voted.

Lin's actions draw attention to an unfamiliar convergence of parental, activist and commercial concerns to promote marriage equality in the formal political context of the NPC. The couples who entered the Taobao-hosted competition were recruited through LGBT networks, and had the support of families and colleagues to compete, or else were unconcerned about the social consequences of having their images and love stories presented on social and broadcast media. Lin's son entered the competition as an "out" gay with a father who openly supports his son's right to live without discrimination as a member of PFLAG China. Lin petitioned the NPC as a CCP member and as a *Chinese* parent speaking for all parents who worry about the future security of their child, and especially when their child's sexual orientation affords them no legal protections vis-à-vis medical care, property purchase and inheritance (Zhang 2015). Here, Lin used traditional conceptions of family obligations to argue for improved legal protections for people in homosexual relationships.

Taobao's use of advertising featuring same-sex couples demonstrates commercial interest in the potentially huge Chinese "pink market," although Taobao representatives emphasized that the contest aimed to increase "respect and understanding for homosexuality, and support the realization of dreams" (Doland 2015). Thus, as in other parts of the world, Chinese LGBT struggles for sexual citizenship may soon become entangled with commercial interests and consumer activities. This could expand the availability of LGBT-themed venues, products and events, especially for members of younger generations. For example, Star-G Technologies is producing mobile games that target gay players ("gaymers"), with one game enabling players to select their images, clothing and accessories, and also to network with other players and participate in virtual marriages (Shan 2016). Commercial interest could also generate alternative funding for LGBT events and activism via niche and cause-related marketing.

More recently, in February 2017, Sun Wenlin and Hu Mingliang—the men who went to the Chinese courts to protest their inability to register a same-sex marriage—launched the Family Equality Network, which is styled after the Taiwan Alliance to Promote Civil Partnership Rights (TAPCPR) (Pingdengjiatingwang 2017). The TAPCPR has played a major role in bringing a same-sex marriage bill before the Taiwan parliament and prompting local governments to permit the registration of same-sex civil partnerships (see below). Although the Taiwan bill is framed in terms of meeting international conventions on human rights, Sun and Hu's website also aims to build momentum for reform within the existing legal framework of the PRC.

Sun and Hu have launched the website to raise public awareness of marriage equality and obtain 1,000,000 online signatures in support of legalizing same-sex marriage to present to the NPC. They hope that a large-scale expression of public support will oblige NPC deputies to amend the PRC's Marriage Law. They have therefore drafted and posted a gender-neutral version of that law online. This action seeks to benefit from the consultative legal approach first adopted by the PRC government in the early 2000s, when it asked for public comment on proposed amendments to the Marriage Law. It has since become common government practice to make draft laws and regulations available for public consultation before they are finalized and ratified. Sun and Hu's initiative thus represents an effort to jump-start government action on marriage equality by suggesting a similar need for public consultation.

Although Sun and Hu's efforts represent a further step towards a same-sex marriage 'movement' in the PRC, they have attracted limited public and government attention to date, and their capacity to galvanize broad support remains uncertain. Six months after the launch of the Family Equality Network, the marriage equality petition had obtained just over 7000 online signatures. It remains to be seen whether the Taiwan Constitutional Court ruling will give impetus to public debate and action on same-sex marriage in China.

Case Study 2: Taiwan

What has led the Taiwan government to go so much further down the path towards recognizing same-sex marriage? Domestic pressure from an active LGBT movement is a popular answer. Taiwan is described as "the most LGBT-friendly country in Asia" (Lee 2016, 987), with tens of thousands of people attending annual pride events (Jennings 2016). Activist Chi Chia-wei first and unsuccessfully petitioned the Constitutional Court to rule on same-sex marriage in 2001 ("Victory at last" 2017). In 2015, with legal support from the TAPCPR, Chi requested a Constitutional Court ruling on Article 972 of Taiwan's Civil Code, which states that a marriage is between a man and woman. Another request was filed that same year by the Taipei City government, "after three same-sex couples lodged an administrative lawsuit against the government when their marriage registrations were rejected" (Hunt and Tsui 2017). In May 2017, the court ruled that Article 972 violates constitutional rights to equality and gave the Taiwan parliament two years to amend or enact laws.

A second answer is party politics. The Democratic Progressive Party (DPP), which first took over government in 2000, ending 50 odd years of Nationalist Party rule, has developed a strong political identity as a party that is committed to realizing an economically prosperous, cosmopolitan, liberal and independent Taiwan. The DPP is a member of Liberal International, a founding member of the Council of Asian Liberals and Democrats, and has represented Taiwan at numerous related international forums. Its leading members are also relatively young and often overseas-trained professionals. As such, the DPP has supported lobbying by domestic gender and LGBT organizations, including demands for marriage equality.

A third and related answer is the DPP's goal of obtaining international recognition for an independent Taiwan. In 2013, the year of the PRC's second UN human rights review, the Taiwan government organized its first human rights review committees and welcomed UN experts to review its human rights reports. The committees' recommendations on LGBT issues are now considered by NGOs when monitoring law and policies (Lee 2016, 982).

Hence, the combination of an active LGBT movement and the DPP's political strategizing vis-à-vis the PRC and the Nationalist Party—the original members of which were mainland Chinese—have left Taiwan well placed to become the first country in Asia to legalize same-sex marriage. Leading DPP representatives have stated that "if Taiwan can get this [legislation] passed … it will give other Asian countries a model" (Jennings 2016). An article in *The Economist* underscores the political subtext of differentiating a democratic Taiwan from the authoritarian PRC by stating that "it would be even better if the country that hardly any others recognize became the first in Asia to recognize that gay people deserve equality" ("Taiwan debates gay marriage" 2016).

Background

In an article titled "Same sex desire and society in Taiwan, 1970–1987," Jens Damm (2005, 68) states: "Taiwanese society between the 1950s and 1960s could be described as heterosexualized in terms of discourse; 'family values' were regarded as deriving directly from a stable Confucian and Chinese tradition and public discourses of same-sex desire were almost non-existent." That tradition emphasized filial piety, respect for authority and adherence to social norms. Historically, as in China, this meant that a sexual encounter between two people of the same sex was neither immoral nor violated the Confucian ethical system so long as an individual respected familial obligations to continue the paternal family line.

During the 1970s and 1980s, the subject of homosexuality became associated with abnormality, deviancy, disease and immorality, although some activists contested such views. Same-sex desire was pathologized as a form of mental illness via the introduction of western medical discourses in the 1970s (Damm 2005, 71), as it was in the PRC during the 1980s. Although some academics argued that homosexuality was a minority rather than abnormal sexual practice, the first media reports to mention same-sex desire were about police arrests of homosexuals in parks and couched in terms of deviancy (Damm 2005, 72–3 and 75), which is also similar to the PRC experience. By the mid-1980s, when Taiwan's first case of AIDS was identified, numerous articles appeared in which AIDS was linked to "the problem of homosexuality," and AIDS was presented as a "foreign" disease associated with "western" behaviours such as sexual promiscuity (Damm 2005, 80). Again, this is not too dissimilar to events in the PRC.

However, the end of Martial Law in 1987 is generally viewed as a watershed in terms of enabling the development of a civil society in Taiwan, and subsequently active LGBT organization, although some individual activism occurred earlier. In 1983, Hsien-yung Pai published a bestselling novel, *Crystal Boys*, about the lives of socially ostracized, young gay men (Cheng et al. 2016, 321). Activist Chi Chia-wei filed an unsuccessful case with the District Court of Taipei to marry his same-sex partner that same year. Confirming the then-dominant negative views of homosexuality, the case was rejected on the grounds that homosexuality was abnormal and immoral, and therefore gay marriage should not be permitted (Cheng et al. 2016, 321).

Taiwan's first gay and lesbian organizations were established in the 1990s. The first lesbian group, Between Us, was founded in 1990; two student societies for gays and lesbians respectively were set up at National Taiwan University in the mid-1990s; and two gay-friendly religious organizations, the Tong-Kwang Light House Presbyterian Church and the Buddhist group Tong Fan Jing Sheh, were established in 1996 (Cheng et al. 2016, 321). The first formally registered gay activist group, the Taiwan Tongzhi Hotline Association, was registered in 1998; and Taiwan's first annual Pride parade was held in 2003. The Taiwan Alliance to Promote Civil Partnership Rights was founded in late 2009 by the feminist Awakening Foundation, the Taiwan Tongzhi Hotline Association and the Tong-Kwang Light House Presbyterian Church, among other organizations, and was joined by the Taiwan Adolescent Association on Sexualities in 2011 (tapcpr.org). However, as in the PRC, the cultural emphasis on social and familial harmony has ensured that many gays and lesbians prefer to stay "invisible," or "hide in the closet," rather than engage in the potentially conflictual act of "coming out" (Lee 2016, 986; Wang et al. 2009, 287).

During the administration of Chen Shui-bian (2000–2008), the first president of the Republic of China from a political party other than the Nationalist Party, "an advisory panel was established under the Presidential Office to suggest amendments to Taiwan's human rights law" (Melnik 2016, online). The DPP-led government has variously sought to obtain political support for Taiwanese independence from the international community, and to differentiate itself from China, by "ratifying" UN multilateral human rights treaties (Lee 2016, 980). In 2009, the Taiwan parliament "ratified" international covenants on civil and political rights, and on economic, social and cultural rights, and attempted unsuccessfully to deposit instruments of ratification at the UN. This attempt was unsuccessful because Taiwan is not a member of the UN; the UN recognizes the PRC as the sole and legitimate representative of China. However, in 2013, the Taiwan government organized its own first human rights review committees and welcomed UN experts to review its human rights reports. The experts' recommendations included acceptance of a 2012 report by the TAPCPR which stated that Taiwan's failure to recognize diverse families and same-sex marriage ran counter to the UN Convention on the Elimination of all Forms of Discrimination Against Women (TAPCPR 2014).

Consensual, adult same-sex sexual activity is not criminalized in Taiwan, the age of consent is 16 years irrespective of gender, and according to the Taiwan 2013 Human Rights Report the country has implemented LGBT anti-discriminatory measures. Although the Constitution does not refer to sexual orientation or gender identity, the Taiwan 2013 Human Rights Report interpreted the Constitution as prohibiting discrimination based on race, gender, disability, language, sexual orientation, gender identity and social status. Employment service laws were passed in 2007 that prohibited social and workplace discrimination based on sexual orientation or gender identity. In 2010, the Ministry of Education also announced that primary school textbooks would include topics on LGBT rights and anti-discrimination (Lee 2016, 980). The Taiwan 2013 Human Rights Report referred to marriage as being between a man and a woman in the context of bans on early and forced marriage (United States Department of State,

Bureau of Democracy, Human Rights and Labor 2013). However, arguments in favour of recognizing same-sex unions increasingly emerged as a feature of public life and debate in Taiwan from the early 2000s onwards.

Advocacy for Same-Sex Marriage

Between 2003 and 2017, a series of proposals were brought before the Taiwan parliament in support of marriage equality. A failed proposal in 2003 recommended that people have the right to marry and form families according to their free will. In 2005, a member of the DPP proposed a bill to legalize same-sex marriage, which was blocked immediately upon submission. In 2012, the TAPCPR released the Draft Revisions to the Civil Code for the Recognition of Families of Diversity, which recommended legalizing same-sex marriage by amending the Civil Code to make the sections dealing with marriage and family gender-neutral, and included new provisions for civil partnerships and multiple-person families. In 2013, DPP members proposed amending the Civil Code to make the chapter on marriage gender-neutral, thereby institutionalizing marriage equality and gay adoption. The proposal was also presented to the Judiciary Committee of the Taiwan parliament in late 2014, but was not discussed (Lee 2016, 981). By 2016, all of Taiwan's major political parties had publicized bills on same-sex marriage (Legislative Council Proceedings 2016a, b). In 2016, a bill proposed by DPP legislator Yu Mei-nu, former Chair of the Awakening Foundation, was read in parliament.

Even prior to the May 2017 Constitutional Court ruling that labelled laws preventing same-sex marriage as unconstitutional, the 2016 same-sex marriage bill was generally expected to result in legislation by mid to late 2017, with the timing subject to further cross-party negotiation. The passing of the bill in 2016 had been stalled by debate over whether opposite-sex and same-sex marriages should be differentiated in law. Instead of replacing the words "male and female parties" in the Civil Code's marriage chapter with "two parties," the amendments demanded of the bill proposed adding that "an agreement to marry shall be made by the male and female parties in their own accord," and "an agreement to marry in a same-sex marriage, shall be made by the two parties in their own accord" (Sun 2016). The amendments also guaranteed an equal application of parental rights to same-sex couples by amending Article 1079–1—the clause governing adoptions—to prohibit a court from rejecting an application to adopt on the basis of the applicants' sexual orientation. Given the significant imprimatur provided by the Constitutional Court, there are reasonable prospects that the bill will be passed in its current form. By the same token, the process of institutionalizing same-sex marriage could be slowed if additional discussion is required in the parliament to agree on the precise details of the legislation.

Alongside the growing impetus towards same-sex marriage legislation that was playing out in the national legislature, and in anticipation of eventual changes in the law, city governments contemporaneously introduced a system of same-sex partnership registration between 2015 and 2016, with the aim of respecting gender equality and human rights ("All Taiwan municipalities to recognize same-sex relationships" 2016). The city of Kaohsiung, led by Mayor Chen Chu, President of the Taiwan Association for Human Rights, became the first city to allow same-sex couples to register their partnership as part of household registration in March 2015. The household registration system records where individuals live and operates as a citizen identification system, with up-to-date registration required to obtain citizen ID cards and thus to open bank accounts and obtain passports, and so on. By March 2016, all of Taiwan's city governments had followed suit; around 75 per cent of Taiwan's population live in these jurisdictions (Melnik 2016).

In practice, the decision to allow same-sex partnerships to be registered through the household registration system established a civil precedent for legalizing same-sex marriage, prompting LGBT activist groups to urge the central government to pass legislation immediately (Chang 2016). A certificate of partnership household registration is not equivalent to a marriage certificate and offers fewer legal protections in comparison. However, it allows registered partners to sign medical contracts for each other and can be used as evidence of partnership in some legal disputes. Around 2000 same-sex couples had registered partnerships by the end of 2016 (Chou 2017).

These developments were encouraged by numerous actions organized by the TAPCPR. In late 2012, the TAPCPR launched a petition to collect 1,000,000 signatures within one year to present to the Taiwan parliament in support of LGBT rights to marry. Popstar A-Mei was the first to sign, followed by other entertainment celebrities. A-Mei and around 40 other artists also held a concert in 2016 to raise funds for the TAPCPR, named "Love is King: it makes us all equal." The 10,000 tickets were reportedly sold only one minute after they went on sale (Chang 2016). Yet the TAPCPR's year-long petition only obtained just over 100,000 rather than

1,000,000 signatures. By comparison, a petition opposing same-sex marriage launched in 2013 by the Alliance of Taiwan Religious Groups for the Protection of Family obtained close to 700,000 signatures ("Taiwan duoyuan chengjia fa'an jianjie" 2013).

The TAPCPR endorsed Tsai Ing-wen's failed bid for presidential election as the leader of the DPP in 2012 and her successful bid in 2016. Tsai's position as leader of the DPP is considered unusual because she is female, single and of aboriginal Taiwanese rather than Chinese descent. Tsai had supported arguments in favour of same-sex marriage, although not systematically. In October 2015, a year before her election as the first female president of Taiwan, she campaigned on freedom of love and expressed her support for marriage equality in a video posted on Facebook around the time of the country's LGBT pride march. Tsai (2015) declared: "I support marriage equality. Everyone has the right to pursue their own love and happiness."

A groundswell of popular support for same-sex marriage was also evident in the run-up to the December 2016 parliamentary hearing of the bill on marriage equality, following the suicide, in October, of a gay professor, Jacques Picoux, reportedly due to the absence of legal protections for same-sex couples (Kingston 2016). Picoux suffered depression after he was prevented from participating in end-of-life medical decisions regarding his partner of more than 35 years. His Taiwanese partner's family then disputed his property and inheritance rights.

Tens of thousands of people also gathered outside the Taiwan parliament to protest against marriage equality. According to media reports, the protests had a strong "Christian flavour," and involved clergy and members of groups such as the Protect the Family Alliance and the Happiness of the Next Generation Alliance, drawing upon similar arguments to those that inform North American conservative religious groups and possibly enjoying assistance from such groups (Cole 2016, 2017). The Happiness of the Next Generation Alliance encouraged around 200,000 people in the cities of Taipei, Taichung and Kaohsiung to protest against same-sex education in schools and the legalization of same-sex marriage, with some protestors reacting violently to people holding banners in support of anti-discrimination and marriage equality.

As this suggests, the legalization of same-sex marriage and adoption have proven to be potentially divisive topics in Taiwan politics and society. Although Christians comprise just over 7 per cent of Taiwan's population, many are actively opposed to marriage equality. A standard argument against same-sex marriage is that legalization will undermine traditional Chinese family values, which emphasize heterosexual marriage for the purposes of reproduction (Wang et al. 2009, 285). The Protect the Family Alliance further argues that legalization is not in the national interest because it will involve large administrative and legislative resources, cause social and political instability, undermine the rights of children, and contribute to Taiwan's already low birth rate and growing prevalence of HIV infection ("Taiwan shouhu jiating" 2016).

These shows of public support and protests prompted some Nationalist Party members to call on President Tsai Ing-wen to resign, to which the Presidential Office responded that she would meet with groups that support and oppose marriage equality (Sun 2016). Despite these overtures towards a consensus-building agenda on same-sex marriage on the part of the DPP, the marriage equality campaign now appears to have the ascendancy. Following the 2017 Constitutional Court ruling, the passing of a bill such as that proposed by Yu Mei-nu appears to be assured. However, the process of entering it into law could be protracted, depending on the extent of discussion required in the parliament to agree on the details of the legislation.

Conclusion

Taiwan looks likely to become the first country in Asia to legalize same-sex marriage, probably through acceptance of a parliamentary bill. An active LGBT movement has developed rapidly in Taiwan since the 1990s in the context of political and social liberalization, and political party strategizing for a democratic and independent Taiwan. However, Taiwanese society is split on the subject of same-sex marriage, with opponents claiming that it will undermine traditional Chinese and Christian family values. Hence, the future governmental support of LGBT couples and families may depend in part on how the major political parties strategize to win domestic votes. It may also depend on Taiwan's efforts to gain recognition in international arenas for their strong support of civil and human rights vis-à-vis the PRC.

Hildebrandt (2011) contended that a political decision on same-sex marriage in the PRC, driven by its foreign policy strategy and uninformed by activism and international pressure, represented the primary avenue for progress on the issue. Yet it can be argued that louder domestic public advocacy more recently, the formal acceptance of UN proposals to progress anti-discrimination legislation, and the striking ruling in Taiwan, combine to increase the tacit pressure on the PRC government to act on marriage equality. While the PRC government is unlikely to follow the ruling of the Taiwan Constitutional Court with a similar pronouncement of its own in short order, the ruling will undoubtedly foster public debate on same-sex marriage, rule of law and human rights in the PRC. The odds of such a debate eventually leading to regulatory or legislative changes are improved by the fact that the history of government in the PRC has removed some of the obstacles to legalizing same-sex marriage that have emerged in Taiwan, most notably oppositional political, social and religious groups, and to some extent Confucian family structures.

Although some commentators view China's Confucian tradition as a stand-in for religion in terms of discouraging homosexuality, that tradition has been transformed by the history and praxis of PRC socialism. Moreover, historically, same-sex eroticism was tolerated as long as it did not interfere with family and kinship obligations to continue the male line (Hildebrandt 2011). The nature of the "traditional Chinese family" has since been radically altered by the impact of the 1950 Marriage Law, Cultural-revolution-era injunctions for young people to attack tradition, the one-child-per-couple policy, and economic reforms and associated population mobility. The fact that the PRC government is currently promoting filial piety to meet the demands of aged care demonstrates the frail if evocative nature of that tradition. In fact, the Confucian "tradition" has been reinvented via major government advertising on citizenship and civic behaviours in recent years to promote what are described as core "Chinese" and "socialist" values such as democracy, civility, harmony, freedom, equality, justice, rule of law and friendship. All of these values could be cited in support of marriage equality and in conjunction with or even instead of the discourse of human rights.

But the fledgling nature of struggles for LGBT rights in China has meant that domestic pressure for marriage equality is a recent and restrained phenomenon. Large-scale, coordinated advocacy on LGBT issues is limited because government controls over the non-profit sector have ensured that international NGOs working in the PRC usually maintain a non-antagonistic attitude towards government authorities to continue operating (Hildebrandt 2011). Domestic non-profits need good relationships with local governments to register as a non-profit and obtain funding, and hence are wary of working with international networks, unless they are government approved. Additionally, although the number of Chinese LGBT organizations is increasing, they are small in number and weak in capacity. However, as demonstrated by the examples of Sun Wenlin, Hu Mingliang, Li Yinhe, Liang Wenhui and Lin Xianzhi, the issue of marriage equality has been raised in the Chinese courts and in the political spaces surrounding the PRC's "parliament."

As recent domestic advocacy also suggests, the PRC government could use same-sex marriage legislation strategically to improve China's international reputation, while addressing domestic issues such as improving sexual health, supporting alternative family arrangements and reducing the number of "fake" marriages, especially given the relatively low social and political risk of doing so. Legislation can be passed quickly by Party-state authorities without having to undergo prolonged parliamentary debate with different parties serving different constituencies (Hildebrandt 2011). Marriage registration in the PRC is also an administrative rather than religious affair, and religious organizations are constrained by government controls.

The PRC government could therefore meet its 2013 UN agreement to ensure that LGBT people enjoy equal treatment by recognizing same-sex marriage through government fiat. Marriage equality could improve the situation of Chinese LGBT people by sending a strong message to government officials and the general public that homosexuality is legal and acceptable, and social and institutional discrimination is unacceptable. However, the adoption of such a strategy depends on government interest, which at the minimum presupposes evident benefits in terms of international diplomacy and guaranteed domestic support, given the recent emphasis on public consultation in law formation.

Another option would be for the PRC government to follow the precedent set by Taiwan, prior to the Constitutional Court ruling, of permitting same-sex civil partnership registration through the household registration system, and then, if such a change were well received, presenting a draft law on marriage equality for public consultation. Permitting civil partnerships via the household registration system would have the advantage of increasing statistical coverage and visibility for the authorities with respect to a growing segment of the population. Such a move could hasten progress towards a "peaceful" recognition of marriage equality, presented in terms of defending China's government-endorsed "core values." Yet, as individuals are typically registered as part of an existing household by providing evidence of marriage or adoption, it is unclear how the government could allow same-sex partners to be registered without altering existing legislation or specifying new extra-legal forms of evidence. If such obstacles can be overcome, there may be hope for progress on more formal recognition of same-sex relationships in the PRC. But any proactive government action in that direction may also mean the co-option of China's nascent LGBT movement into government and Party structures in advance of an independent LGBT movement being developed.

References

All Taiwan Municipalities to Recognize Same-Sex Relationships. 2016. *The NewsLens*, March 7. Accessed 8 February 2017. https://international.thenewslens.com/article/37637

Bai, Tiantian. 2016. 190 Chinese LGBT Groups Condemn Orlando Club Shooting. *Global Times*, June 14. Accessed 8 February 2017. http://www.globaltimes.cn/content/988160.shtml

Chang, Eddy. 2016. Taipei Watcher: The Call Is Loud and Clear. *Taipei Times*, 8, August 28.

Cheng, Alice Yen-hsin, Felice Fen-chieh Wu, and Amy Adamczyk. 2016. Changing Attitudes Toward Homosexuality in Taiwan, 1995–2012. *Chinese Sociological Review* 48 (4): 317–345.

Chinese Society of Psychiatry. 2001. *Zhongguo jingshenzhang'ai fenlei yu zhenduan biaozhun disanban [Chinese Classification for Mental Disorders Version 3 (CCMD-3)]*. Jinan: Shandong Kexuejishu Chubanshe.

Chou, Wah-shan. 2001. Homosexuality and the Cultural Politics of *tongzhi* in Chinese Societies. *Journal of Homosexuality* 40 (3–4): 27–46.

Chou, Abigail. 2017. Taiwan Same-Sex Marriage Debate Heats up as Possibility Nears. *The Asahi Shimbun*, January 6. Accessed 11 February 2017. http://www.asahi.com/ajw/articles/AJ201701060024.html

Cole, J. Michael. 2016. Thousands Protest as Taiwan Inches Closer to Legalising Same-Sex Marriage. *Hong Kong Free Press*, November 18. Accessed 8 February 2017. https://www.hongkongfp.com/2016/11/18/thousands-protest-taiwan-inches-closer-legalising-sex-marriage/.

———. 2017. U.S. Hate Group MassResistance Behind Anti-LGBT Activities in Taiwan. *Taiwan Sentinel*, January 2. Accessed 30 March 2017. https://sentinel.tw/us-hate-group-anti-lgbt/

Criminal Law of the People's Republic of China. 1997. Accessed 22 January 2017. http://www.fmprc.gov.cn/ce/cgvienna/eng/dbtyw/jdwt/crimelaw/t209043.htm

Damm, Jens. 2005. Same Sex Desire and Society in Taiwan, 1970–1987. *The China Quarterly* 181: 67–81.
Doland, Angela. 2015. For Valentine's Day, Alibaba Helps Gay Chinese Couples Get Married in the U.S. *AdvertisingAge*, February 12. Accessed 8 February 2017. http://adage.com/article/global-news/alibaba-helps-chinese-gay-couples-married-u-s/297108/
Gonganbu. 1993. Guanyu qudi tongxinglian wenhua shalong 'nanren de shijie' de qingkuang tongbao [Notice on the Closure of the "Men's World" Homosexual Culture Salon], Gong tong zi [1993] 62 hao. Accessed 22 January 2017. http://www.chinaacc.com/new/63%2F71%2F2006%2F3%2Fxu6735315913360023029-0.htm
Guojia guangbo dianying dianshi zongju ling: di 52 hao [Order No. 52 of the State Administration of Radio, Film and Television]. 2006. Dianying juben (genggai) bei'an, dianying pian guanli guiding. [Regulations for the Administration of the Records of Screenplay (Outline) and Films], April 3. Accessed 22 January 2017. http://www.sarft.gov.cn/art/2006/6/22/art_1583_26305.html
Hildebrandt, Timothy. 2011. Same-Sex Marriage in China? The Strategic Promulgation of a Progressive Policy and Its Impact on LGBT Activism. *Review of International Studies* 37: 1313–1333.
Hunt, Katie, and Tsui, Karina 2017. Taiwan Is Closer to Being 1st Asian Place to Allow Same-Sex Marriage. *CNN*, May 24. Accessed 26 March 2017. http://edition.cnn.com/2017/05/24/asia/taiwan-same-sex-marriage/
Jeffreys, Elaine, and Haiqing Yu. 2015. *Sex in China*. Cambridge: Polity.
Jennings, Ralph. 2016. Taiwan Set to Legalize Same-Sex Marriages, a First in Asia. *Associated Press*, November 10. Accessed 8 February 2017. http://bigstory.ap.org/article/e9c5b9c82abe4bc987f820aa104f2893/taiwan-set-legalize-same-sex-marriages-first-asia
Kingston, Jeff. 2016. Same-Sex Marriage Sparks a 'Culture War' in Taiwan. *The Japan Times*, December 10. Accessed 13 February 2017. http://www.japantimes.co.jp/opinion/2016/12/10/commentary/sex-marriage-sparks-culture-war-taiwan/#.WKFC7Y24Zjp.
Lau, Steffi. 2010. Homosexuality in China. *US-China Today*, March 10. Accessed 8 February 2017. http://www.uschina.usc.edu/article@usct?homosexuality_in_china_14740.aspx
Lee, Po-han. 2016. LGBT Rights versus Asian Values: De/reconstructing the Universality of Human Rights. *The International Journal of Human Rights* 20 (7): 978–992.
Legislative Council Proceedings. 2016a. Meeting 1150 Proposal 19706, November 2. Accessed 13 February 2017. http://lci.ly.gov.tw/LyLCEW/agenda1/02/pdf/09/02/09/LCEWA01_090209_00020.pdf

———. 2016b. Meeting 1150 Proposal 19730, October 31. Accessed 11 February 2017. http://lci.ly.gov.tw/LyLCEW/agenda1/02/pdf/09/02/09/LCEWA01_090209_00011.pdf

Li, Yinhe. 2009. Regulating Male Same-Sex Relationships in the People's Republic of China. In *Sex and Sexuality in China*, ed. Elaine Jeffreys, 82–101. Abingdon: Routledge.

———. 2015. Zhongguo heshi pizhun tongxinghunyin [When Will China Ratify Same-Sex Marriage?], June 27. Accessed February 8, 2017. http://blog.sina.com.cn/s/blog_473d53360102vub7.html.

Melnik, Alexander. 2016. Being TONGZHI: Examining LGBT Rights in Taiwan. *Taiwan Business Topics*, October 19. Accessed 8 February 2017. http://topics.amcham.com.tw/2016/10/tongzhi-examining-lgbt-rights-taiwan/

Phillips, Tom. 2016. China Court Refuses to Allow Gay Marriage in Landmark Case. *The Guardian*, April 13. Accessed 8 February 2017. https://www.theguardian.com/world/2016/apr/13/china-court-refuse-gay-marriage-landmark-case

Pingdengjiatingwang [Family Equality Network]. 2017. Accessed 28 August 2017. http://pingjia.lgbt/zh/?tag=%E4%BA%BA%E5%A4%A7%E4%BB%A3%E8%A1%A8

Renmingwang weiping [People's Commentary]. 2014. *People.cn*, December 19. Accessed 27 May 2016. http://weibo.com/2286908003/BBAf1EJ7W?type=comment#_rnd1464314720702

Shan, Juan. 2016. 'Pink Economy' Set to Soar as Companies Target LGBT Community. *China Daily*, December 1. Accessed 11 April 2017. http://www.chinadaily.com.cn/china/2016-12/01/content_27533401.htm

Sun, Hsin Hsuan. 2016. Same-Sex Marriage Clears First Hurdle. *The China Post*, December 27. Accessed 9 February 2017. http://www.chinapost.com.tw/taiwan/national/national-news/2016/12/27/487771/Same-sex-marriage.htm

Taiwan Debates Gay Marriage. 2016. *The Economist*, December 3. Accessed 13 February2017.http://www.economist.com/news/asia/21711096-it-would-be-first-country-asia-legalise-it-taiwan-debates-gay-marriage

Taiwan duoyuan chengjia fa'an jianjie. 2013. *Hong Kong Sex Culture Society* 1: 5–6.

Taiwan shouhu jiating [Protect the Family Alliance]. 2016. Accessed 8 February 2017. https://taiwanfamily.com/related-posts/artice02

TAPCPR. 2014. Shadow Report on the Convention on the Elimination of All Forms of Discrimination Against Women. Accessed 13 February 2017. https://tapcpr.files.wordpress.com/2014/04/cedaw-shadow-report-20140430.pdf

Tsai, Ing-wen. 2015. Facebook, October 30. Accessed 8 February 2017. https://www.facebook.com/tsaiingwen/videos/10152991551061065/

UNDP and USAID. 2014. *Being LGBT in Asia: China Country Report.* Bangkok.
United Nations General Assembly. 2013. Human Rights Council Twenty-fifth Session Agenda Item 6: Universal Periodic Review, Report of the Working Group on the Universal Periodic Review, China (Including Hong Kong, China and Macao, China), December 4.
United States Department of State, Bureau of Democracy, Human Rights and Labor. 2013. Country Reports on Human Rights Practices for 2013: The Taiwan 2013 Human Rights Report. Accessed 8 February 2017. https://www.state.gov/documents/organization/220444.pdf
Victory at Last for Taiwan's Veteran Gay Rights Champion Chi Chia-wei. 2017. *The Straits Times*, May 17. Accessed 26 May 2017. http://www.straitstimes.com/asia/east-asia/victory-at-last-for-taiwans-veteran-gay-rights-champion-chi-chia-wei
Wan, Yanhai. 2001. Becoming a Gay Activist in Contemporary China. *Journal of Homosexuality* 40 (3): 47–64.
Wang, Frank, Herng-Dar Bih, and David Brennan. 2009. Have They Really Come Out: Gay Men and Their Parents in Taiwan. *Culture, Health & Sexuality* 11 (3): 285–296.
World Health Organization. 1992. *The ICD-10 Classification of Mental and Behavioural Disorders – Clinical Descriptions and Diagnostic Guidelines.* Geneva: World Health Organization.
Zhang, Yiqian. 2015. Gay Marriage Advocates Ask Legislators to Present Their Proposals at the Two Sessions. *Global Times*, March 16. Accessed 22 January 2017. http://www.globaltimes.cn/content/912260.shtml

Elaine Jeffreys is a professor in the School of International Studies, Faculty of Arts and Social Sciences, University of Technology Sydney, Australia. Her recent books include *New Mentalities of Government in China* (2016), *Sex in China* (2015), *Celebrity Philanthropy* (2015), and *Celebrity in China* (2010).

Pan Wang is a lecturer in the School of International Studies, Faculty of Arts and Social Sciences, University of Technology Sydney. She is the author of *Love and Marriage in Globalizing China* (2015). Her recent publications also include "Inventing traditions: television dating shows in the People's Republic of China," *Media, Culture and Society*, 2016, 39(4): 504–19; and "Media presentations of cross-strait marriage in contemporary China," *China Media Research*, 2015, 11(1): 46–57.

CHAPTER 11

Conclusion

Bronwyn Winter

Same-sex marriage fascinates, whether as a key social and political cause of our century affecting an increasingly visible and vocal global minority, as a barometer of a nation's human rights and social justice credentials—themselves a barometer of the strength of national democracy, as a sign of the continued preponderance of masculinist and heteronormative conceptions of society and challenges thereto, or as a test of the boundaries of national, international and supranational law, especially in their regulation of intimate relations and the family. Framed as a global lesbian, gay, bisexual, transgender, intersex and queer/questioning (LGBTIQ) rights issue, and even—rightly or wrongly—as an endpoint objective of LGBTIQ rights claims, same-sex marriage has inevitably become imbricated within broader debates over national politics, and national or regional cultural and religious values, versus (or within) the impacts of globalization. Indeed, same-sex marriage, as a sub-theme of gender and sexuality issues more generally, lies at the heart of contemporary battles over the meaning of the nation, and the role of the state and its laws in shaping and reshaping that meaning.

Throughout the huge diversity represented by the contributions to this book, these factors remain a constant thread. In our supposedly postnational or post-Westphalian world, the values of the nation and the

B. Winter (✉)
University of Sydney, Sydney, NSW, Australia

apparatus of the state are routinely mobilized in national and transnational debates over sexuality and the family—and they are mobilized by both advocates and opponents of same-sex marriage. Hence the value of neo-institutionalist analyses of such mobilizations, as they show how national institutions and their representative discourses may be built, shaped, reinforced, challenged or changed. Although all chapters show the importance of national path dependencies in shaping the ways in which the issue is brought onto the national agenda, they also show how specific political opportunities created by both endogenous factors (such as a national election or a key court decision) and exogenous ones (such as possibilities for policy transfer or the effect of institutional isomorphism in a regional or supranational context—notably within the EU or Latin America—or transnational support or opposition) are used by both civil society and political actors to institutionalize same-sex marriage or, on the contrary, to institutionally reinforce the heterosexual bases of marriage.

Most particularly, these analyses show us that—path dependencies notwithstanding—the march of history is not a linear one, and as many of us have observed time and again, no social change is irrevocable. Moreover, the most vulnerable of rights, the most fragile of gains, are almost always those that involve gender, sexuality and control over one's own body and intimate relations. Questioning of gender roles and identifications by both feminist and LGBTIQ movements over the last half-century has resulted in some significant practical gains and fundamentally shifted much of our thinking about sex and gender, but has also met with a ferocious backlash as traditional notions of masculinity and femininity, and the appropriate place of the family in society and of women in the family, reassert themselves through the actions of powerful religious and conservative lobbies. We are indeed very, very far from a society, anywhere in the world, where gender might cease to be a marker of social distinction.

The analyses in this book also show us how debates over these hard-won rights open up many paradoxes. For example, received wisdom would indicate that progress on women's sexual, marital and reproductive rights is more often than not a litmus test of how likely a country is to legalize same-sex marriage. Yet, one does not always follow the other, and the reasons for legalizing abortion may not always play in women's favour, as the infamous one-child policy in China shows. This policy was introduced in 1979, and began to be formally phased out from 2015, although various relaxations or exceptions to the policy had been introduced many years earlier. In two of the other countries covered in this book, Ireland

and Argentina, women's rights to abortion remain severely limited. In Ireland, the proposed amendment to the Constitution to allow same-sex marriage was overwhelmingly approved in the 2015 referendum, but women are still battling to have the Eighth Amendment, which outlaws abortion, repealed. A similar situation holds in Argentina.

Conversely, most Central and Eastern European Countries (CEECs) have relatively liberal abortion laws, and have had them for longer than many Western nations; yet as we saw in Chap. 7 of this book, that liberal approach has not transferred to law and policy on same-sex marriage. Even though challenges to the abortion laws, driven by religious lobbies or demographic anxieties on the part of politicians, have emerged in the post-Communist era, those challenges have met with huge public opposition and have as a result mostly not been successful (with the notable exception of Poland, where protest nonetheless continues). Faced with this failure, the religious right—and others suffering from demographic angst or concern over the preservation of ethno-national values—have found a new cause in their opposition to LGBTIQ rights in general and to same-sex marriage in particular. There, such movements have had greater success, as we saw in Chap. 7, notably in the case of the successful Slovenian referendum blocking same-sex marriage in 2015. Although voter turnout in that referendum was very low, which means that the anti-gay marriage vote was a minority of the total *possible* vote, one can infer at the very least from this low turnout that those who did not vote simply did not care enough about the issue, on either side of the debate. Contrasted with the huge public outcry in the face of attempts to restrict abortion rights (such as that proposed in 2006 by the then Slovenian Minister for Labour, Family and Social Affairs, Janez Drobnič, who was forced to resign over the issue), this apparent apathy concerning LGBTIQ rights is striking.

So, although gender equality and same-sex rights often do go in tandem—for both supporters and opponents, as we saw in the case of France in Chap. 6—they just as often seem not to. Advances in women's sexual, marital and reproductive rights are no guarantee of advances in LGBTIQ rights, and vice versa. Part of the explanation of these paradoxes may lie in the reasons for liberalizing rights for women in the first place, which have often had nationalist rather than egalitarian political justifications—either to control the birth rate, as in the case of China, or to "free up" women to join the productive (rather than reproductive) labour force, as in much of CEE. As concerns the restrictions to women's reproductive rights in countries that have embraced same-sex marriage, one might be led to conclude that Catholic countries that have embraced neoliberalism are more easily accommodating of same-sex marriage, which in the end does not fundamentally undermine the marriage institution to the extent that opponents of same-sex marriage claim, than they are of women's reproductive autonomy, which *does* fundamentally alter women's role in the family and, by extension, the national reproductive labour force, and significantly undermines men's ability to control women in these areas.

Same-sex marriage and gender equality/women's bodily and reproductive autonomy thus cannot be assumed to be straightforward litmus tests of each other—nor indeed of a nation's progressive values more generally. In this last respect, the institutional structure of the country in question plays a significant role, and perhaps the most glaring example of the coexistence of progression and regression that is enabled by specific institutional structures is the United States. The 2015 Supreme Court decision in *Obergefell vs. Hodges* extended same-sex marriage rights to all within a federal structure where such rights had already been enjoyed for some years by residents of many US states. Yet a little over a year later, the US population—or rather, its Electoral College—elected its most right-wing and most controversial president in a country that has seen its share of such figures in recent decades. The strength of federalism and the independence of the courts (notwithstanding the fact that Supreme Court justices are appointed by the president, albeit with significant vetting during the Senate confirmation process), together with the peculiarities of the presidential voting system (with a decisive role played by the Electoral College in the 2016 election), combined to produce this national paradox—doubtless one among many. The role of federalism in both enabling and blocking same-sex marriage has also been observed in a number of other countries discussed in this book, such as Mexico and Brazil, discussed in Chaps. 2 and 3.

Interacting with these various national peculiarities, we have seen that globalizing influences can act for both better and worse, whether it is through the assertion of national cultural values in the face of a globalized "homosexual threat" such as in the case of Malawi, discussed in Chap. 5, or through the political and financial contribution of transnational religious lobbies, either conservative Christian or Middle-Eastern Islamic, to anti-same-sex marriage campaigns, such as in the Taiwanese and Indonesian cases, discussed in Chaps. 10 and 9 respectively. At the same time, religious lobbies can also support pro-same-sex marriage movements, as in the case of transatlantic Catholic support for the "yes" campaign in the Irish referendum, discussed in Chap. 8.

Another global trend—and paradox—that I touched upon in my own contribution to this book (Chap. 8) is that just as the LGBTIQ movement has made same-sex marriage one of its core issues, heterosexuals are losing interest in the institution. For example, in 2017 EU statistics showed that in the three decades between 1985 and 2015, the marriage rate across the EU had halved while the divorce rate had doubled (Europa website).[1] The EU's report pointed to the generalization of other types of cohabitation, such as registered partnerships (including among couples having children), as partially explaining this trend—yet global and national LGBTIQ movements, which have access to registered partnerships in many more countries than those where they can legally marry, are saying the existence of such partnerships is not enough.

Moreover, the growing success rate of same-sex marriage campaigns, even in hitherto unlikely places such as Ireland or Taiwan, rather begs the question of whether some institutional actors are agreeing to same-sex marriage as a way of preserving the institution (at the very least). It also begs the question of how national regimes may evolve in coming years, notably as concerns their welfare and fiscal regimes, broadly considered, given that most states embed into their laws distinctions—often significant ones—between married and unmarried couples, and between married-parent families and unmarried- or sole-parent families. What advantages are gay and heterosexual couples seeking—or constraints eschewing—in their (apparently somewhat divergent) choices of couple-registration? How might states reconfigure those advantages and constraints in the light of evolving demographics?

The trend is also being exhibited elsewhere; in 2015 the Organization for Economic Co-operation and Development (OECD) reported a significant decline in marriage rates in almost all member countries since 1970. The trend in divorce rates is more patchy (partly because of its illegality, until relatively recently, in some countries such as Ireland or Chile), but has followed the EU trend in rising overall. The Chinese are the most likely among the OECD countries to marry (but only middlingly likely to remain so), which could lead to some rather fanciful speculation about what might happen in the area of same-sex marriage once Chinese heterosexuals start shunning the institution in greater numbers.

These demographic trends warrant exploration in further detail as same-sex marriage becomes institutionalized in an increasing number and variety of countries. Most especially, the question must be asked: is there a correlation between increasing demand for, and legalization of, same-sex marriage and the decline in heterosexual marriage? Or is the institutionalization of same-sex marriage at the same time as heterosexual marriage appears to be moving towards de-institutionalization a mere coincidence? The relative consistency of the figures, however, considerably weakens the "coincidence" hypothesis and leads one to ask what symbolic, institutional and/or sociocultural role same-sex marriage is being mobilized to play in the twenty-first century nation. Is same-sex marriage a new weave in the national fabric, changing perhaps its colours but not its overall design?

Finally, what can be said of same-sex marriage, as a microcosm (or for some, an apex-point) of progress on LGBTIQ rights more generally, concerning its status as an indicator of the strength or weakness of liberal democracies? In our post-Cold War and post-dictatorship period of democratization, the now-democratic world is further polarized into liberal and illiberal democracies—or in other words, strong or weak ones. One could even suggest a three-way split, as many liberal regimes are now becoming neoliberal ones, with relatively strong credentials on social justice issues having minimal economic implications, particularly those favoured by the middle classes (such as same-sex marriage), but increasingly weak credentials on socioeconomic justice issues (such as workplace and welfare regulation). This development has clear implications for the evolution of the welfare and fiscal regimes I referred to above. It further raises questions concerning what forms the passage from illiberal democracy to liberal democracy might take in the foreseeable future, in many parts of the world: will neoliberalism on one level start to combine with illiberalism on another? Has that process already started, as former Communist countries, such as Poland—the largest economy in the CEE part of the EU and the sixth largest in the EU overall—or still ostensibly Communist ones, such as China, embrace globalized capitalism with fervour, all the while remaining illiberal on many domestic fronts? How does the evolution of marriage—decline in heterosexual marriage concurrently with increased legalizations of, or campaigns for, same-sex marriage—fit into these shifting and overlapping patterns?

Hopefully, the comparative study of the interaction between national, regional and global factors in shaping the institutionalization of same-sex marriage that we have offered in this book will act as a springboard for exploring these and other new questions. For it is certain that same-sex marriage will continue to be an object of political, civil society and scholarly fascination in the years to come, and will continue to generate new questions about which institutions count, how they are (re)constructed and how they impact, not only on the lives of individuals and social groups, but also on the types of political conversations we (are able to) have.

Notes

1. http://ec.europa.eu/eurostat/statistics-explained/index.php/Marriage_ and_divorce_statistics#Fewer_marriages.2C_more_divorces. Accessed 4 July 2017.

Bronwyn Winter is Deputy Director of the European Studies Program at the University of Sydney, Australia. Her research addresses a range of global theoretical and political issues that lie at the intersections of gender, sexuality, ethnicity, religion, globalization, militarization and the state. Her publications include *Hijab and the Republic: Uncovering the French Headscarf Debate* (2008) and *Women, Insecurity and Violence in a Post-9/11 World* (2017). She is currently working on a monograph on the political economy of same-sex marriage. She holds the French title of *Chevalier dans l'Ordre des Palmes Académiques*.

Erratum to: Global Perspectives on Same-Sex Marriage

Bronwyn Winter
Maxime Forest
Réjane Sénac
Editors

© The Editor(s) (if applicable) and The Author(s) 2018

B. Winter et al. (eds.), *Global Perspectives on Same-Sex Marriage*, Global Queer Politics, https://doi.org/10.1007/978-3-319-62764-9_1

DOI 10.1007/978-3-319-62764-9_12

The book was inadvertently published with an incorrect affiliation for Book Editor "Maxime Forest and Réjane Sénac". The correct affiliation is given below:

Maxime Forest
Sciences Po - OFCE
Center for Political Research CEVIPOF
Paris, France

Réjane Sénac
Sciences Po - CNRS
Center for Political Research CEVIPOF
Paris, France

The updated original online version of this book can be found at
DOI 10.1007/978-3-319-62764-9

© The Author(s) 2018
B. Winter et al. (eds.), *Global Perspectives on Same-Sex Marriage*,
Global Queer Politics, https://doi.org/10.1007/978-3-319-62764-9_12

Index[1]

A

Abbott, Tony, 165, 166
Abortion
   health subsidies, 110
   laws, 107, 110, 130, 223
   legality, legal, 107, 110, 222
   legalization, 110
   prohibition of, 158
   protests against, 92, 223
   recriminalization of, 110
   re-legalization, 131
   rights, 128, 223
Activism, activists
   gay and lesbian, LGBTIQ, 6, 7, 24, 26
   judicial, 50, 51, 56
Adoptions, 11, 21, 26–28, 32, 33, 39, 44, 53, 56, 82, 83, 92, 95, 99, 106, 109, 111, 119, 136–143, 150, 152, 159, 176, 190, 199, 201, 210, 212, 215, 216
sme-sex couples, 210
See also Same-sex, parenting
Advocacy, 3, 145, 159, 189, 198, 199, 201–206, 210–214
   coalitions, 6
See also Same-sex marriage, advocates of
Affirmative action, 203
Africa, 41, 100
Age of consent, age of sexual majority, 109, 131, 132, 200, 209
   equalization of, 131, 136, 137
Agencies, 5, 25, 63, 64, 77, 83, 99, 152, 173, 184
Agents of change, 119
Althusser, Louis, 174
Americas, the, 3, 100
Amparos (legal injunctions), 20, 30, 34
Amsterdam Treaty, 139
Anglican Church, 86
Anti-colonialism, 94

---

[1] Note: Page number followed by 'n' denotes note.

Anti-discrimination policies, laws, measures, provisions, 26, 44, 54, 69, 116, 128, 129, 134, 135, 144, 145
Anti-LGBT, *see* Resistance; Homophobia
Anti-miscegenation laws, 74
Apartheid, 84
Argentina, 9, 11, 19, 43, 152, 223
Arrests of gay men, LGBTIQ individuals, 182
Asia, 10, 183, 198, 206, 207
Australia, 9, 10, 12, 13, 67, 72, 149, 173, 191
Australian Capital Territory (ACT) Marriage Equality (Same-Sex) Act, 165
Authoritarianism, authoritarian, 22, 24, 42, 86, 108, 176, 178, 197, 198, 207
Autocratic regime, 92
Autonomous, 22, 26, 53, 131, 135, 152, 179, 224

B
Bachelet, Michelle, 47–49, 55, 56
Backlash, *see Resistance*
Baehr v. Lewin, 68, 70
Baltic States, 144
Banda, Joyce, 90, 91
Belgium, 105, 107
Birth rate, *see* Demographics
Bisexual, *see* LGBTIQ
Black Lives Matter, 74
Blairism, 157
Born this way discourse, 188
Bowers v. Hardwick, 70
Brazil, 11, 21, 115, 224
British Columbia, 9, 71, 155
Brown, Bob, 165
Brown, Gordon, 156

Brunei, 172, 183
Bulgaria, 131, 132
Burwell v. Hobby, 74
Bush, George W., 164

C
Cameron, David, 156–158, 160, 166
Canada, 9, 11, 20, 22, 33, 61, 152
Capitalism, capitalist, 63, 65, 150, 164, 226
Carlist, 107
Castañeda, Lol Kin, 29, 31
Catholicism, Catholic, 141
  Church, 12, 24, 27, 31, 45, 46, 49, 106, 113, 119, 121n2, 132, 134, 139–141, 143, 144, 160, 161
  and gay/LGBTIQ rights, 13, 158, 159
  inclusiveness, 161
  movements, 106, 224
  opposition to same-sex marriage, 106, 158, 161
  support for same-sex marriage, 160, 161
  values (*see* Traditional values, Catholic)
  and women's rights, 158, 159
Central Europe, Central and Eastern European Countries (CEECs), 4, 8, 127–145, 223
Centralism, centralization, 12, 42, 61, 67, 75, 105, 152, 199
Children
  care of children, 151
  child rights, 92
Chile, 11, 225
Chimbalanga, Tiwonge, 88, 89
China, People's Republic of (PRC), 9, 10, 13, 197–216, 222, 223, 226
Christianity, Christian, 94, 173

counter-movement, 186
evangelists (*see* Evangelical Church)
LGBTIQ community, 94
See also Anglican Church;
    Catholicism; Protestantism
Cisgender, 82, 88, 92
Citizenship
  demands, 85
  intimate, 109, 128, 130, 135, 143, 144
  sexual, 113, 151, 172, 175, 176, 205
Civic principles, 118
Civil law
  marriage, 96, 136
  reforms, 136
  system, 34
Civil partnership/civil union
  heterosexual, 6
  legislation, 7
  recognition of, 7, 8, 96, 154–156
  rights, 157
  same-sex, 6, 7, 23, 26, 28, 39, 41, 44, 47, 53, 54, 93, 129, 154, 167, 205
Civil rights, 43, 51, 65, 66, 75, 76, 109, 203
  racialized backlash against, 75
Civil society, 5, 8, 13, 43, 86, 87, 115, 116, 131, 132, 143, 150, 172, 173, 176, 180, 181, 198, 208, 222, 226
  activism, lobbying, 44, 116, 153, 154, 159
Clinton, Bill, 67, 68
Cohabitation, 111, 120, 145n1, 225
  unregistered, 136, 145n1
Collective action, 24, 135
Collective apprehension, 11, 82
Colonialism, colonial, 12, 83, 84, 161, 183–185
  british colonialism, 173, 183–186
  legacy, 183–185
  See also Post-Communist; Sodomy laws
Common law relationships, 71, 73, 86
Commonwealth, 10, 152
Communism, Communist, 144, 226
  See also Post-Communist
Confucianism
  confucian traditions, family structures, 13, 214
Conscience clause, 20, 118
Conservatism, conservative, 13, 50
  counter-attacks on LGBTIQ rights as reactionary responses, 177, 178
  opposition to same-sex marriage (*see* Same-sex marriage, opposition)
  social forces, 20
  values, 13, 74, 156, 157, 166 (*see also* Traditional values)
  voting blocs, 40, 46
Constitutional
  amendments, 70, 143, 158
  courts, 7, 10, 14, 54, 82, 87, 92, 107, 133, 136, 138, 139, 198, 206, 210, 211, 213–215
  law, 66
  monarchy, 12, 105
  reforms, 19, 22, 26, 35, 88
  rights, 11, 66, 69, 206
Constitutionality, 70, 71, 139, 188
  of same-sex marriage, 34, 36
Constitutionalizing gay marriage, 11
Convention for the Elimination of All Forms of Discrimination Against Women (CEDAW), 189
Convergence, 128, 150, 154, 156–158, 204
Corrective rapes, 10, 98
Council of Europe, 150, 151
Couple-registration, 225

Court system, courts, 50
  impact on same-sex marriage, 50
  independence of, 224
  judicial activism (*see* Activism)
  role of, 11, 61, 62, 66, 69
  See also Judicial
Criminalization, vii, 90, 173, 181, 188, 199, 209
  of homosexuality, of LGBTIQ subjects, 173, 181
  See also Sodomy laws
Croatia, 8, 10, 127
Customary law, 96
  marriage (*see* Marriage)
Czech Republic, 129, 133, 141
Czechoslovakia, 110, 131–133

D
Da Silva, Lula, 46, 47
Decentralization, decentralized, 10, 178
  decision-making, 62
Decriminalization
  of abortion, 29
  of homosexuality, sodomy, 10, 82, 87, 110, 144, 199
Democracy, democratic
  delegative, 22
  discourses, 24, 92, 93, 99, 108
  institutions, 22, 65
  transition, 43, 94, 130, 131, 144, 145
Democratization
  in Central and Eastern Europe (CEE), 127
  in Latin America, 21
  in Spain, 109
Demographics
  anxiety, 223
  birth rate, fertility rates, 131, 140, 186, 213, 223
  trends, 140, 225
Dictatorship, 12, 24, 43, 110, 112
Discourse, discourses
  feminist, 97
  homophobic, 84
  queer, 97
  of religion, 94
  of rights, 93, 94, 96
  of sexuality, 175
  racially encoded, 74
  role of, 82
Discrimination
  on the basis of sexual orientation and gender identity, 68, 75
  discriminatory treatment, 51
  job, in the workplace, 109, 201, 202, 209
Discursive
  anxiety, 11, 12, 81, 82, 84–92, 94, 99
  commitments to human rights, 94
  constructions of same-sex relations, 92
  frames, framings, 2, 10, 99, 136, 139
  institutionalism (*see* Institutionalism)
  institutionalization (*see* Institutionalization)
  resources, 6, 62
Diversity, vii, 2, 8, 134, 135, 143, 161, 179, 210, 221
Divorce
  legalization of, 158
  rate, 167, 225
Domestic violence, *see* Violence

E
Eastern Europe, 12, 130
  See also Central and Eastern European Countries (CEECs)

Education
  to eradicate stigma on homosexuality, 176
  gender equality, 111
  sex education, 212
  transmission of values and morality, 118
Egalitarianism, egalitarian, 117, 121, 162, 223
Elections, 7, 26, 27, 29, 32, 35, 46, 47, 56, 68, 72, 105, 111, 117, 138, 139, 156, 157, 212, 222, 224
Endogenous variables/ discursive factors, 13, 76, 133, 150, 197
Enfranchisement, 3, 185
Equal marriage, *see* Marriage equality
Equality, 5
  gender (*see* Gender equality)
  laws, 106
  principles of, 108, 114, 119
Ethnic homogeneity, 138
European Commission, 143
European Convention of Human Rights, 155, 159, 160
European Court of Justice (ECJ), 135, 139
European Economic Community, 108, 112
European Union (EU)
  accession, 12, 129, 130, 133, 135, 141
  conditionality of enlargement, 3, 128
  legal provisions on gender equality and non-discrimination, 128
  membership, 10, 141
  transpositions of EU law, 10
  values, 135, 142, 143
Europeanization, 4, 6, 12, 116, 128, 129, 134, 135, 140–143, 145, 159

Evangelical Church, Evangelists, *see* Christian Evangelists
  LGBTIQ opposition, 45, 46
Exogenous variables/discursive factors, 8, 76, 150, 197

F
Family, 10
  alternative family arrangements, 215
  definition of, 88, 130
  law, 21, 36, 118, 140
  rights, 3, 110, 112, 117
  roles, 76, 151, 167, 224
  traditional, 106, 117, 118, 128, 143
  values (*see* Traditional values)
Federalism, 12, 61, 62, 66, 76, 116, 224
  competitive federalism, 115, 116
Feminism, feminist
  activism, movement, 159
  backlash against, 159
  scholarship, 5, 6
  state feminism, 109, 113
Fernández de Kirchner, Cristina, 20, 30, 31
Flannery, Tony, 160
Foucault, Michel, 84, 174
Fraisse, Geneviève, 112, 117
France, 9, 12, 105–121, 152, 154, 161, 223
  French Revolution, 109, 110 (*see also* Secularism)
Franco, Francisco, 12, 108, 110, 112
Francophone, 9
Freedom
  of choice, 119
  of religion, 62, 154
Fundamentalism, fundamentalist, 173
  Christian, 95
  discourses, 95

G

Gay
  conversion therapy, 202
  culture, 162, 173
  pride, 133
  See also LGBTIQ
Gay marriage, *see* Same-sex marriage
Gay rights, *see* LGBTIQ rights
Gender
  diversity, 55
  equality, inequality, 5, 106,
    110–112, 115, 116, 119, 128,
    134, 211, 223, 224
  identity, 54, 68, 75, 171, 172, 176,
    177, 199, 202, 209
  pay gap, 111
  policies, 23, 112, 113
  regimes, vi, 118, 130, 143
  roles, 75, 106, 222
  and sexuality, 8, 173, 182, 184,
    185, 221
  and sexual politics, 86
  theory, 112, 118, 119
Gender-based violence, *see* Violence
Germany, 7, 154
Gillard, Julia, 164
Global city strategy, 188
Global North, 22, 63
Global South, 42
Globalization
  globalized homosexual "threat,",
    224
  of LGBTIQ identity, of sexual
    identities, vii, 171
  of LGBTIQ rights discourse, 171
Goh Chok Tong, 189

H

Harper, Stephen, 33
Hate crimes, 98
  See also Violence
Hawai'i's, 70

Health policy, 44
Heteronormativity, heteronormative
  definitions of marriage, 29
  as foundational to the state, 181
  framing of sexual and family rights,
    112
  gender roles, 97
  nationalism, 140
  privileging of, 140, 184
Heterosexism
  racialized, 118
Heterosexuality, heterosexual
  disinterest in marriage, 225
  marriage, 12, 116, 140, 142, 144,
    161, 167, 173, 199, 201, 213,
    222, 226 (*see also* Marriage,
    heterosexual character of)
  nuclear family, 161, 184, 185
HIV/AIDS
  crisis, epidemic, 24
  prevention programs, 41
Hollande, François, 111, 118
Homonationalism, homonationalist,
  62, 73, 117
Homophobia
  antigay/homophobic discourse,
    vitriol, 12, 82, 84, 99
  homosexual "threat,", 224
  judicial protection against, 131
  political, 83–86, 88–91, 172
Homosexuality, 10, 173
  "is un-African" discourse, 82, 94
  as foreign or Western import, 142
  as invisible, 198, 199, 209
  criminalization of (*see*
    Criminalization)
  decriminalization of (*see*
    Decriminalization)
  legal recognition of, 6, 12, 67, 87,
    117, 130, 132, 133, 140, 143,
    199
  pathologization of, as abnormal/a
    disease, 201

repression of, 25, 43
social acceptance, 110
stigma associated with, 24, 175, 178
Howard, John, 153, 163–165
Human rights, fundamental rights, 3
  Charter, 6, 75, 76, 152
  discourse, 82, 92–99, 176
  legislation, 70, 75
  treaties, 151, 209
  See also Children, child rights; LGBTIQ rights; women's rights
Hungary, 8, 10, 12, 127

I
Ideational
  approach, 64
  factors, 11, 66, 72
  power, 5, 62, 64, 65
  resources, 62, 72, 75
Illiberalism, illiberal, 226
  democracies, 12, 226
Immigration, immigrants, 66, 98, 162, 184
Incrementalism, incrementalist
  legal, 6–8, 154–158
Indigenous peoples, 64
Indonesia, 10, 13, 171–191
Institutionalism, institutionalist, neo-institutionalism
  discursive, 4, 11, 12, 62, 64, 76, 77, 81, 83, 84
  historical, 4, 11–13, 40, 52–54, 61–77, 182
  institutionalist theory, 83
  rational choice, 5, 83
  sociological, 4–6, 8, 11, 13, 83, 182
Institutionalization
  contributing factors, 2, 128
  discursive, 173, 174, 179, 180, 190
  informal, 21
  of gender norms, 185
  of LGBTIQ movements, 13
  of same-sex marriage, 2, 9, 21, 23, 74, 149, 158, 171, 172, 182, 225, 226
  of sexuality, 173
  paths of, processes of, 6, 8, 11
Institutions, institutional
  designs, 11, 21, 36, 40, 50
  isomorphism, 6, 222
  pathways, 9, 62
  variables, 40, 134
Interdependency, 162
Intersectionality, 120
Intimate citizenship, *see* Citizenship
Iotti, Paulo, 55
Ireland, Republic of, 149
Islam
  Islamic values, 13, 178, 190 (*see also* Traditional values)
  Islamicist, Islamism, 10
  Islamophobic agenda, 117
  political Islam, 179

J
Judiciary, judicial, 28
  autonomy, 93
  empowerment, 61, 75
  judicialization of LGBTIQ rights, 40, 52
  power, 62, 67–72
  See also Court system
Jurisdiction over marriage, 61, 62, 70
  jurisdictional conflict, disputes, 33
Justices, 2, 33, 92, 93, 98, 118, 150, 151, 214, 221, 224, 226

K
Ki-moon, Ban, 89

L

Latin America, 11, 21–25, 27, 31, 41, 42, 46, 47, 54, 127, 158, 222
Latin Americanization, 6
Latvia, 132
Lawrence v. Texas, 70
Legal
  equality, 72
  formalism, 36
  pluralism, 66
Legal incrementalism, *see* Incrementalism
Legalization, *see* Same-sex marriage, legalization
Legal norms, *see* Norms
LGBTIQ
  bisexual, 184
  discrimination, repression, 43
  gay, 1, 3, 8–13, 20, 22, 24–26, 29, 31, 33, 40–43, 51, 52, 55, 63, 65, 67, 72, 73, 75, 86, 87, 89–94, 113, 118, 120, 131–133, 136, 141, 144, 151, 154, 157, 159, 161, 162, 164, 165, 167, 174–176, 179–186, 188–190, 198, 201–205, 207–210, 212, 225
  identities, vii, 13
  intersex, 177
  lesbians, 1, 3, 10, 20, 22, 24, 26, 31, 40, 43, 52, 65, 67, 75, 85, 91–94, 98, 99, 113, 120, 128, 131, 132, 138, 141, 155, 157, 161, 162, 164, 165, 167, 174, 175, 179, 185, 187, 189, 201–203, 208, 209
  liberation movements, 65
  queer, vii, 65, 74, 76, 82, 97, 98, 100, 188, 189
  stereotypes, 120
  transgender, 88, 92, 113, 174, 176, 180
LGBTIQ rights
  advocacy, 9, 134
  discrimination against, 190
  as human rights, 221
  movement, 7, 9, 13, 222, 225
  opposition to/opponents of, 223
  politics of, 3
Li Yinhe, 203, 204, 215
Liberalism, 119, 163, 189
liberal (market) democracy, 12, 130
Loving case, 66

M

Malawi, 9–11, 81–100, 224
Malaysia, 165, 172, 183
Marriage
  civil law, 96
  customary law, customary, 96
  definitions of, 34
  free choice, 199
  heterosexual, 10, 12, 96, 139, 140, 142, 144, 161, 167, 173, 199, 201, 226
  heterosexual character of, heterosexualized marriage, 2
  interracial, 66
  marital rights, 222
  married-parent families, 225
  minimum age, 92
  rate, 167, 225
  religious connotations of, 7
Marriage equality, 31
  arguments based on, 64
  backlash against, counter-reactions to, 76
  ideational strength, 72
  See also Same-sex marriage

Martin, Paul, 71
Masculinist, 163, 221
Massachusetts, 66
McAleese, Mary, 160
Media, 27, 32, 82, 90, 99, 107, 115, 140, 165, 167, 174, 178, 180, 181, 184, 188, 197, 199, 201–205, 208, 212
  opinion-shaping role of, 5
Mexico, 11, 19–36, 43, 224
Middle East, 143
Minority rights, 46, 91, 113, 159
Mobilization, *see* Social mobilization
Modernization, 12, 120, 186
Monjeza, Steven, 88, 89
Moral panics, 172, 180, 181
Muslim, *see* Islam
Mutharika, Bingu wa, 86, 89, 90

N
Nassah, Idriss Ali, 87
National
  agenda, 28, 222
  institutions, 222
  laws, 151, 155, 199
  regimes, 225
Nationalism, nationalist, 12, 13, 62, 72, 75, 76, 88, 117, 140, 142, 143, 171, 190, 223
Natural Law, 140
Neo-institutionalism, *see* Institutionalism
Neoliberalism, 224, 226
  economic, 154, 160, 164
Netherlands, the, 1, 7, 105, 115, 149, 164
New Zealand, 173, 182
Non-imbrication, 10
Norms
  legal, 6

  social, societal, 4, 9, 29, 115, 207
Northern Ireland, 152

O
Obama, Barack, 68, 76
Obergefell *vs.* Hodges, 61, 66, 71, 224
One-child policy, 222
Ontario, 9, 71, 155
Opposition, 223
  to LGBTIQ rights (*see* LGBTIQ rights opposition)
  to same-sex marriage (*see* Same-sex marriage, opposition)
Orban, Viktor, 137
Organization for Economic Co-operation and Development (OECD), 225

P
Pai, Hsien-yung, 208
Parliamentarism, parliamentary
  democratic systems, 12
  politics, 2, 9
Party politics, 11, 13, 137, 139, 152, 206
Paternalism, 112, 156, 207
Path dependencies, vii, 12, 108, 110, 112, 120, 149, 222
Patriarchy, patriarchal traditions, 27, 29, 199
Peña Nieto, Enrique, 19, 20, 35
People of color, 64, 74
People with disabilities, 64, 179
Philippines, the, 172
Piñera, Sebastian, 44, 49, 55
Pinochet dictatorship, 42, 43
Poland, 130–132, 223, 226

Policy, policies
  change, 23, 61, 62, 64, 67, 69, 76, 129
  discourses, 2, 5, 9, 73, 188
  frames, 129
  legacies, 11, 53, 62, 63, 65, 66, 72–76, 135
  paradigms, 9
  stasis, 50
  transfer, 2, 3, 6, 10, 128, 139, 154, 222, 223
Political, 178
  elite, 40, 52, 55, 56, 81, 82, 84–88, 91
  homophobia (*see* Homophobia)
  Islam (*see* Islam)
  will, 5, 64, 68, 72, 150, 163
Politicization
  of reproductive rights, 127
  of sexuality, 84
Populism, 100
Pornography, 200, 201
Postapartheid, 10, 81, 82, 93, 94
Post-authoritarian, 176
Postcolonialism, postcolonial, 84, 182–186, 188
  recycling of legal provisions, 13
  See also Colonialism
Post-Communist, 138, 223
Post-socialism, post-socialist, 10, 127, 128, 143, 145
Post-structuralism
  post-structuralist discourse theory, 5
Protestantism, Protestant Church, 161, 165
Public opinions, 7, 14, 64, 77, 110, 157, 166, 186

Q
Quality in Gender + Equality Policy (QUING), 108
Quebec, 9, 62, 71, 75, 76

R
Race, racial
  complementarity, 118
  politics of racial backlash, 76
  racialization of marriage debates, 73
  racialized inequality, 98
  racism, 117
Rape, *see* Corrective rape
Referendums, 9, 10, 12, 139, 141, 143, 144, 152–154, 157, 158, 160, 161, 166, 223
  Irish referendum, 7, 161, 166, 224
Refugees
  anti-refugee discourse, 164
  refugee crisis, 137
Regionalism
  competitive regionalism, 115, 116
Registered partnerships, 116, 136, 139, 141, 211, 225
Religion
  and same-sex marriage, 94, 160
  religious lobbies, 154, 223, 224
  See also Marriage, religious connotations of
Reproductive
  autonomy, 224
  labor force, 75
  rights, 30, 75, 109, 128, 130, 131, 177, 222, 223
Resistance to LGBTIQ rights
  backlash against LGBTIQ communities, 180
  counter-movement to LGBTIQ rights, 42, 45–47, 50, 173, 186
Resistance to same-sex marriage, 63
  anti-same-sex marriage campaigns, 224
  anti-same-sex marriage discourse, 92
  political, 7
  religious, 191
  societal, 133
  See also Same-sex marriage, opposition

Rights, *see* Children, child rights; Civil rights; Human rights; LGBTIQ rights; Minority rights; Social rights; Women's rights
Right-wing, 49, 99, 107, 112, 118, 119, 136, 138, 141, 143, 224
Robinson, Mary, 151, 159, 160
Romania, 131, 132
Roudy, Yvette, 109
Rouseff, Dilma, 47, 50, 51
Rousseau, Jean-Jacques, 112
Royal, Ségolène, 105, 111
Rudd, Kevin, 162
Russia, Russian Federation, 110, 134

S

Same-sex
cultural acceptance of, 203
eroticism in traditional cultures, 203
parenting, 106
rights, 3, 6, 7, 12, 14, 24, 32, 39, 50, 61, 62, 65, 75, 82, 86, 87, 107, 117, 119, 138, 153, 155, 166, 172, 183, 211, 223
Same-sex marriage, 2
advocates of, advocacy, 69, 75, 76, 151, 154, 166, 215, 222
backlash against, 75, 76, 129, 144
birth rate fears, 213
business case for, 166
campaigns, 3, 47, 50, 70, 81, 85, 86, 96, 160, 213, 224, 225
family arguments for, 128, 155, 166, 186
international norms, 2
legal prohibition of, 6
legalization of, 2, 3, 6, 7, 10, 11, 14, 44, 54, 66, 67, 85, 87, 91, 109, 111, 121, 152, 162, 167, 178, 180, 202, 203, 212, 225, 226
legislation, 6, 21, 67, 69, 71, 92, 94, 152, 182, 198, 211, 215
movement, movements, 3, 7, 12, 85, 94, 97, 99, 113, 198, 206, 225
opposition to/opponents of, 2, 10, 62, 64, 68–70, 75, 92, 112, 116, 119, 120, 151, 165, 173, 198, 222–224 (*see also* Resistance to same-sex marriage)
popular support for, 9, 161, 212
by popular vote, 158
recognition of, 8, 9, 11, 14, 65–67, 71, 75, 154
refusal on religious grounds, 33 (*see also* Conscience clause)
rights, 3, 7, 24, 32, 39, 50, 61, 62, 65, 82, 86, 107, 117, 166, 172, 223
role of active LGBTIQ movements, 7, 13, 225
role of domestic factors, 2, 10, 206
role of transnational factors, 62, 150
Scandinavian equality model, 106
Schulz, Martin, 7
Secularism, secularization, secular, 9, 12, 105, 108, 114, 115, 120, 132, 154
Separate but equal discourse, 96
Separation of powers, 11, 23, 61, 62, 66, 68, 69
Sexism, 112, 117, 120
Sexual, 3
and reproductive health, 110
citizenship (*see* Citizenship)
complementarity, 111, 115–118
differentiation, 112, 116, 118
diversity, 55, 84, 85, 204
minorities, 4, 55, 56, 87–90, 131, 132, 136, 137, 143, 144, 183, 189
orientation, 19, 54, 87, 91, 93, 105, 110, 111, 114, 115, 118–120, 129–135, 137–139, 142, 172, 177, 180, 188, 199–202, 205, 209–211

Sexual (cont.)
  politics, 22, 36
  rights, 4, 36, 46, 109–113, 116, 203
  subjectivities, 97, 177
Sexualities, 6, 8, 25, 29, 62, 63, 81–86, 88–90, 94, 98, 99, 113, 131, 171–182, 184, 187, 188, 191n1, 208, 221, 222
Shui-bian, Chen, 209
Singapore, 13, 171
Slovakia, 10, 127
Slovenia, 9, 10, 127
Social change, 222
Social conservatism, see Conservatism
  relationship with economic neoliberalism, 154
Social justice, 98, 154, 221
Social mobilization, 14, 22, 24, 25, 40, 43, 132, 145
  gay and lesbian/LGBTIQ mobilization, 40, 43, 132
Social movements, 3, 4, 6, 12, 25, 39, 40, 52–54, 62, 65, 74–77, 85, 86, 89, 113, 150, 156, 199
  lobbying, 3, 40
Social movements, 40–44
Social norms, see Norms
Social rights, 93
  common property, 140
  inheritance rights, 138
  mutual support, 140
  pension rights, 138, 141
  shared medical insurance, 138
  See also Children, child rights; Civil rights; Human rights; LGBT rights; Minority rights; Women's rights
Socialism, socialist, 4, 10, 12, 13, 48, 49, 105, 106, 108, 111, 113, 114, 120, 128, 130–133, 136, 144, 145, 172, 198, 214

state socialism, 4, 10, 12, 128, 130, 144, 145
Sodomy laws, antisodomy laws, 70, 91, 183
  See also Criminalization
Soeharto, Muhammad, 176, 178
Sole-parent families, 225
  See also Unmarried couples/families
South Africa, 9–11, 81, 115
Southeast Asia, 172, 186, 191
South-Eastern Europe, 144
Soviet Union (USSR), 130, 131
  former Soviet Republics, 130
Sovietization, 12, 130
Spain, 3, 9, 12, 26, 105
State, 109
  feminism (see Feminism)
  harassment, oppression, 25, 43, 201
  role of, 74, 108, 118, 120, 221
  socialism, 4, 10, 12, 128, 130, 144, 145
Subjectivities, 174, 177, 191n1
  gay and lesbian, LGBTIQ (see Sexual, subjectivities)
Switzerland, 110

T
Taiwan, 9, 10, 13, 14, 173, 182, 191, 197, 225
Tasi Ing-Wen, 212
Tasmania, 162
Teichman, Judith, 22
Terrorist attacks, 106
Thailand, 172
Tong Fan Jing Sheh, 208
Tong-Kwang Light House Presbyterian Church, 208
Traditional values, 142, 160, 203
  African values, 84
  Asian values, 198, 213

Chinese values, 198, 203, 207, 213, 214
cultural values, 84, 94, 99, 108, 142
European values, 142
family values, 117, 118, 128, 143, 174, 178, 198, 213, 214, 222
Islamic values, 224
nationalist values, 94
religious values, 85, 94, 190, 222
socialist values, 4, 27, 76, 106, 214
See also Conservative, values
Transgender
transexuality, 107
transphobia (*see* Homophobia)
See also LGBTIQ
Transnational
constants, 6
debates on sexuality, marriage and/or the family, 3, 12, 20, 83, 155, 177, 187, 222
impact of the institutionalization of same-sex marriage, 6, 150, 171
Trump, Donald, 68, 76, 164
Tsai Ing-wen, 213
Tudjmam, Franjo, 140
Turnbull, Malcolm, 166

U
Unions, 6, 8, 26–29, 39, 44, 47, 49, 51, 53, 88, 116, 138, 142, 159, 164, 210
Unitary state, 11, 53, 56
United Kingdom (UK), 10, 12, 13, 115, 149–167
United Nations (UN), 89, 134, 150, 159, 189, 202, 207, 209, 214, 215
United States (U.S.), 4, 7, 11, 21, 22, 24, 61, 87, 110, 150, 152, 160–164, 173, 178, 209, 224
missionaries, 45
Universal Church, 45

Universalism, universalist, 151
Unmarried couples, 73, 225
See also Sole-parent families
Uranga, Enoé, 26, 29, 31

V
Venezuela, 21
Vietnam, 172, 173
Violence, 90, 98, 99, 106, 176, 202
Violence, gender-based violence, 10
against LGBTIQ individuals/lesbians/gay men, 10
against women, 106
bullying of LGBTIQ youth, 202 (*see also* Hate crimes)
domestic, 73

W
Waria (transgender woman, Indonesia), 174, 175, 179, 180
Welfare state, welfare regimes, 63, 65, 72, 75, 76
Western Europe, 150
Westminster system, 71, 151
Windows of opportunity, 13, 55, 131
Women's rights, 43, 223
Wong, Penny, 165
World Bank, 41, 42
World Health Organization, 109, 201
list of mental illnesses, 109
World War II, 12, 130, 157

Y
Yogyakarta Principles, 3, 176
Yugoslavia, 131

Z
Zapatero, José Luis Rodríguez, 121